RESILIENCE AND OPPORTUNITY

Best Wishes,

Robert R. Collins

JAMES A. JOHNSON METRO SERIES

**JAMES A. JOHNSON
METRO SERIES**

The Metropolitan Policy Program at the Brookings Institution is integrating research and practical experience into a policy agenda for cities and metropolitan areas. By bringing fresh analyses and policy ideas to the public debate, the program hopes to inform key decisionmakers and civic leaders in ways that will spur meaningful change in our nation's communities.

As part of this effort, the James A. Johnson Metro Series aims to introduce new perspectives and policy thinking on current issues and attempts to lay the foundation for longer-term policy reforms. The series examines traditional urban issues, such as neighborhood assets and central city competitiveness, as well as larger metropolitan concerns, such as regional growth, development, and employment patterns. The James A. Johnson Metro Series consists of concise studies and collections of essays designed to appeal to a broad audience. While these studies are formally reviewed, some will not be verified like other research publications. As with all publications, the judgments, conclusions, and recommendations presented in the studies are solely those of the authors and should not be attributed to the trustees, officers, or other staff members of the Institution.

On growth and development

Boomburbs: The Rise of America's Accidental Cities
Robert E. Lang and Jennifer B. LeFurgy

Edgeless Cities: Exploring the Elusive Metropolis
Robert E. Lang

Growth and Convergence in Metropolitan America
Janet Rothenberg Pack

Growth Management and Affordable Housing
Anthony Downs, editor

Laws of the Landscape: How Policies Shape Cities in Europe and America
Pietro S. Nivola

Reflections on Regionalism
Bruce J. Katz, editor

Revisiting Rental Housing: Policies, Programs, and Priorities
Nicolas P. Restinas and Eric S. Belsky, editors

Sunbelt/Frostbelt: Public Policies and Market Forces in Metropolitan Development
Janet Rothenberg Pack, editor

On transportation

Still Stuck in Traffic: Coping with Peak-Hour Traffic Congestion
Anthony Downs

Taking the High Road: A Metropolitan Agenda for Transportation Reform
Bruce Katz and Robert Puentes, editors

On trends

Redefining Urban and Suburban America: Evidence from Census 2000, vol. 1
Bruce Katz and Robert E. Lang, editors

Redefining Urban and Suburban America: Evidence from Census 2000, vol. 2
Alan Berube, Bruce Katz, and Robert E. Lang, editors

On wealth creation

Building Assets, Building Credit: Creating Wealth in Low-Income Communities
Nicolas P. Retsinas and Eric S. Belsky, editors

The Geography of Opportunity: Race and Housing Choice in Metropolitan America
Xavier de Souza Briggs, editor

Low-Income Homeownership: Examining the Unexamined Goal
Nicolas P. Retsinas and Eric S. Belsky, editors

Savings for the Poor: The Hidden Benefits of Electronic Banking
Michael A. Stegman

On other metro issues

Borrowing to Live: Consumer and Mortgage Credit Revisited
Nicolas P. Retsinas and Eric S. Belsky, editors

Moving Forward: The Future of Consumer Credit and Mortgage Finance
Nicolas P. Retsinas and Eric S. Belsky, editors

RESILIENCE AND OPPORTUNITY

Lessons from the U.S. Gulf Coast after Katrina and Rita

AMY LIU
ROLAND V. ANGLIN
RICHARD M. MIZELLE JR.
ALLISON PLYER
editors

BROOKINGS INSTITUTION PRESS
Washington, D.C.

Library of Congress Cataloging-in-Publication data

Resilience and opportunity : lessons from the U.S. Gulf Coast after Katrina and Rita /
Amy Liu . . . [et al.], editors.
   p. cm.
   Includes bibliographical references and index.
   Summary: "Examines the roles of community grassroots and charitable organizations
as well as national, state, and local governments in post-disaster recovery and reform in
the education, health care, legal, and political systems and in land use planning. Focuses
on rebuilding to achieve more resilient, prosperous, and equitable communities"—
Provided by publisher.
   ISBN 978-0-8157-2149-9 (pbk. : alk. paper)
   1. Hurricane Katrina, 2005. 2. Hurricane Rita, 2005. 3. Social problems—Gulf Coast
(U.S.) 4. Disaster relief—Gulf Coast (U.S.) 5. Emergency management—Gulf Coast (U.S.)
6. Emergency management—United States—Planning. I. Liu, Amy.
   HV6362005.G85 R47 2011
   363.34'9220976—dc23   2011022960

9 8 7 6 5 4 3 2 1

Printed on acid-free paper

Typeset in Sabon and Strayhorn

Composition by Cynthia Stock
Silver Spring, Maryland

Printed by R. R. Donnelley
Harrisonburg, Virginia

Contents

Acknowledgments

The editors would like to thank the Community Revitalization Fund of the Greater New Orleans Foundation, Ford Foundation, Foundation for Louisiana (formerly Louisiana Disaster Relief Fund), Foundation for the Mid South, Foundation to Promote Open Society, Henry J. Kaiser Family Foundation, Surdna Foundation, and W. K. Kellogg Foundation for their support of this book and related research. The Metropolitan Policy Program at Brookings and the Greater New Orleans Community Data Center also greatly appreciate the support from the Bill and Melinda Gates Foundation, Living Cities, Inc., and the Rockefeller Foundation for enabling us to conduct foundational research and policy work in greater New Orleans and the Gulf Coast immediately following the 2005 storms.

The Brookings Metro Program is also grateful to the John D. and Catherine T. MacArthur Foundation, the Heinz Endowments, the George Gund Foundation, and the F. B. Heron Foundation, which provide general support for the program's research and policy efforts. Finally, the program wishes to give special thanks to the Metropolitan Leadership Council, a bipartisan network of individual, corporate, and philanthropic investors that provide financial support but, more important, are true intellectual and strategic partners. While many of these leaders act globally, they maintain a commitment to the vitality of local and regional communities, a rare blend that makes their engagement even more valuable.

Nonprofit Knowledge Works would like to thank Baptist Community Ministries and United Way for the Greater New Orleans Area for their foundational and ongoing support of the Greater New Orleans Community Data Center.

Finally, the editors are indebted to Allison Harris, Mariela Martinez, and Willa Speiser for their high-quality organization, coordination, and editorial assistance. This volume is much improved because of their hard work and commitment.

1

Introduction

Amy Liu, Roland V. Anglin, Richard M. Mizelle Jr., and Allison Plyer

Policy analysts, historians, and social commentators will analyze the impact of the 2005 storms on the Gulf region for years
to come. It is important that they do, because the 2005 catastrophe
will not be a unique event in human history. Since 2005 the United
States has felt the wrath of more than one natural disaster, including massive wildfires in southern California in 2007, hurricanes
Ike and Gustav in 2008, and the multiple tornadoes that struck
in spring 2011. In 2010 Haiti was devastated by a 7.0 magnitude
earthquake. And in March 2011, Japan suffered a catastrophic
triple punch: earthquake, tsunami, and nuclear disaster.

As for future risk, the United Nations has concluded that large
concentrations of people across the world live at risk of natural disasters such as earthquakes, hurricanes, and flooding or of
manmade disasters such as industrial contamination or terrorist
attacks.[1] In the United States, West Coast residents may be well
aware of the earthquake risks that they face, but East Coast residents, particularly in the North, may be less prepared for a natural
disaster in the form of a catastrophic storm surge. By 2100, Boston, for example, could well experience such a surge, worsened by
the combined effects of natural subsidence over the century, a sea
level rise of fifteen inches due to climate change, and a high tide,
which could inundate downtown Boston and Cambridge, with
coastal flooding from Rockport to Duxbury.[2]

The nation would do well to learn from catastrophic events like Katrina and Rita. Such disruptive forces not only expose the breakdown in government responses but often reset the social, economic, and political forces in the areas that they impact. The hurricanes and their disastrous aftermath shed light on issues unresolved in American life, such as race, poverty, and the ability, or inability, to tame nature for our economic and personal use.

For instance, Katrina and Rita revived national attention concerning the failure of levees in a way that echoed concerns raised during the Great Mississippi River Flood of 1927.[3] By the late nineteenth and early twentieth centuries, the Army Corps of Engineers had largely adopted the highly contested "levees only" policy that gave precedence to constructing levees on the Mississippi River and its tributaries over adopting diversified control mechanisms such as spillways, outlets, and reservoirs. The 1927 flood shattered the "levees only" policy and led to passage of the 1928 Flood Control Act, which pushed the federal government to become much more active in the nation's river and water protection systems. The system of levees that existed during the 1927 flood was considered inadequate. Despite post-1927 changes, the levee system remained inadequate seventy-eight years later.[4]

Many books written in the aftermath of the Gulf Coast storms focus on a forensic analysis of what went wrong, the inadequacy of the levees, and the perceived incompetence of government. Such analysis is critical to understanding how to improve safety and systems to prepare for future disasters. This book, in contrast, occupies a different and more cautiously hopeful niche: it examines the progress that Gulf Coast communities are making to bounce back after a major disaster to rebuild a stronger and more prosperous region for the long term.

This book assesses changes in core areas of policy, planning, and civil society through the prism of resilience and opportunity. Resilience is in part a function of the extent to which leaders intentionally strengthen economic characteristics and civic capacities (including by retooling policies) that help a community rebound and become less vulnerable to future crises. That adaptive ability is especially critical because catastrophes can come often and in different forms. In the past six years alone, the Gulf Coast has been grappling with an ongoing series of crises—the 2005 hurricanes, the 2007 recession, and the 2010 Gulf of Mexico oil spill. All three events have caused leaders to readjust their long-term rebuilding strategies.

Resilience is also defined by improving opportunities through adaptation. Are leaders implementing strategies that will lead to better outcomes than before the storm, such as stronger economic growth and reduced income inequality? Or are the billions of private, philanthropic, and government dollars pouring into the Gulf region simply rebuilding the status quo? This is of particular concern if the status quo generated poor social, economic, and environmental outcomes prior to the disaster.

The chapters in this volume examine the five- to six-year progress in the Gulf Coast in terms of achieving the dual goals of resilience and opportunity. They are not all encompassing; rather, they constitute a sample of community issues central to developing resilience and opportunity in the devastated areas of the Gulf Coast. We reach beyond the common focus on New Orleans and Louisiana to include the experience of leaders and families in the devastated areas of Mississippi. While other neighboring states were located in the horrible path of the first devastating storm, Katrina, their communities faced different challenges due to the breadth and magnitude of its destructive force. We do not, for example, include a chapter on Alabama. This is not a slight. Many organizations worked to help local communities recover in the aftermath of the storm, but improving larger systems of governance and increasing equity did not rise to the level of prominence in Alabama that they did in Louisiana and to a lesser extent Mississippi.

Even after six years, efforts to recover are still in development and will remain so, especially after the explosion of the *Deepwater Horizon* oil platform spilled tons of oil into the Gulf of Mexico. Our goal is to use this midway point in the region's long-term transformation to step back, offer lessons and cautions, and highlight the remaining challenges for the Gulf Coast and indeed the nation.

The Dimensions of Destruction

Prior to Hurricane Katrina the Gulf Coast was beset with high poverty along with racial and ethnic exclusion in communities that were both economically and physically vulnerable. Table 1-1 shows that in 2004, the three states where Katrina had the most impact were among the poorest in the nation. As the Center for Budget and Policy Priorities pointed out, "Of the 5.8 million individuals in these states who lived in the areas struck hardest by the hurricane, more than one million lived in poverty prior to the hurricane's onset."[5]

TABLE 1-1. Poverty and Income in States Hit Hardest by Hurricane Katrina

Location	Poverty (percent)	Rank	Median household income (dollars)	Rank
Alabama	16.1	8th worst	36,709	9th lowest
Louisiana	19.4	2nd worst	35,110	5th lowest
Mississippi	21.6	Worst	31,642	2nd lowest
United States	13.1		44,684	

Source: U.S. Census Bureau, American Community Survey (ACS), 2004. Compiled by the Center for Budget and Policy Priorities (www.cbpp.org/9-19-05pov.htm).

In August 2005 Hurricane Katrina hit the Gulf Coast, tearing up more than 93,000 square miles in its path.[6] More than 1 million people were displaced.[7] Some people returned home within days, but up to 600,000 households remained displaced a month later.[8] The storm damaged over 1 million housing units, about half of which were located in Louisiana.[9] Figure 1-1 indicates that housing damage in Louisiana was more severe than in neighboring states, although the extent of damage in Mississippi also was severe. In New Orleans, arguably the epicenter of the disaster, 134,000 housing units—70 percent of all occupied units—suffered damage when the levees protecting the city failed.[10] The Federal Emergency Management Agency (FEMA) and the U.S. Department of Housing and Urban Development (HUD) estimate that 78,810 of these units in New Orleans were severely damaged or destroyed.[11] The total picture is one of a region that required a massive housing rebuilding effort.

In response to the widespread devastation, the federal government authorized a total of $142.6 billion in spending and tax relief by 2009 to help the Gulf states respond to the impacts of hurricanes Katrina, Rita, and Wilma. Of that amount, merely $36 billion in discretionary spending was directed at measures to promote long-term recovery, such as by building nonemergency housing, repairing levees, restoring wetlands, improving infrastructure, and other community development needs.[12]

Defining Resilience

The dictionary defines *resilience* as "an ability to recover from or adjust easily to misfortune or change." However, assessing whether a region has that ability and measuring whether it has been exercised is challenging.

FIGURE 1-1. Number of Homes Damaged by the 2005 Hurricanes in Louisiana, Mississippi, and Alabama[a]

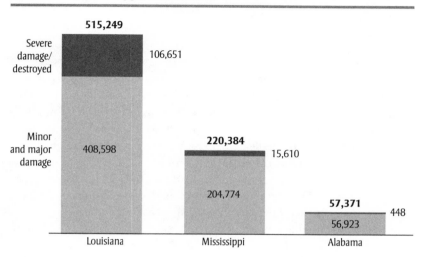

Source: FEMA and HUD, "Current Housing Unit Damage Estimates: Hurricanes Katrina, Rita, and Wilma," February 12, 2006 (www.dhs.gov/xlibrary/assets/GulfCoast_HousingDamageEstimates_021206.pdf).

a. Louisiana had far more homes severely damaged or destroyed by Katrina than neighboring states: 7 times the number in Mississippi and 238 times the number in Alabama. Over 21 percent of Louisiana's damaged properties are estimated to be severely damaged or destroyed.

Kathryn Foster contributes greatly to our understanding of regional resilience in her chapter, "Professing Regional Resilience." She points out that resilience represents both the capacity to respond to a shock and the performance of the region once a shock has occurred.

A region's capacity to be resilient after a disruption depends on the extent to which it has the resources, skills, infrastructure, processes, attitudes, and other factors necessary to anticipate, mitigate, and cope with any potential crisis. Those factors include hazard mitigation, of course, but also economic strengths and intangible attributes such as social networks. A review of the literature suggests a set of characteristics besides hazard mitigation that may enhance regional resilience:[13]

—a strong and diverse regional economy with a relatively small gap between the incomes of high- and low-income residents

—large numbers of skilled and educated workers with the capacity to adapt to changing needs

—wealth, whether government, private, philanthropic, or individual, to invest in rebuilding as well as reforms and resilience capacity

—strong social capital, including high levels of civic participation and social cohesion between and across groups.

Imagining Opportunity

Opportunity is a critical component of post-disaster recovery. It is defined by the extent to which a community uses a disaster as an occasion not simply to return to normal but also to achieve a new and better standard of living. It means retaining assets and correcting flaws while rebuilding. By all accounts, the Gulf Coast had many flaws prior to the onslaught of Katrina and Rita, not the least of which were poor and unequal educational and employment opportunities and unsustainable growth patterns.[14] Why did we not see significant efforts to address these issues before the storms? The inescapable answer is that we should not expect change from entrenched interests that see no reason for change.

Mancur Olson makes the point that the significant economic growth rates seen in Japan and Europe after World War II resulted from the disruption of entrenched economic and political interests, which allowed new and emerging economic and institutional arrangements to innovate and bring about growth.[15] This is the essence of creating post-disaster opportunity: being able to suspend, or at least keep in abeyance, the existing forces of self-interest, which would normally challenge innovation and change.

If Olson is right, leaders, residents, and institutions in the Gulf Coast should be taking the "opportunity" presented by the 2005 disasters to create a new and brighter future, one that will differ from the region's historic course. Greater New Orleans and coastal Mississippi are currently works in progress. Though enormous challenges and unmet needs remain on the region's long road to recovery, there are promising signs of reinvention and increased capacity to withstand future crises. Meanwhile, the forces of the status quo are hard to resist, especially as urgency fades and new priorities surface.

Many of the authors in this volume remain cautiously optimistic, however, and urge that collective efforts continue to remake the systems, policies, and social and cultural dynamics that can put this region on a sustained path to greater opportunities. These writers, many of whom are from the Gulf region, bring expertise in specific policy arenas but also their unique perspective as residents and civic participants in the recovery. While there is no chapter dedicated to the federal government response, most of the authors touch on the role that the federal and state governments played in serving as partners (or sometimes barriers) to reform. We hope that scholars, politicians, analysts, the media, and the public will take notice of their research and experience. The following is an overview of the chapters included in this book.

New Policies and Plans to Build Greater Resilience and Opportunity

A series of reforms in the key areas of city services, housing, and planning are demonstrating that New Orleanians have the capacity to work together to begin undoing the policies and habits that have contributed to the region's long-standing social, economic, and environmental problems. John Renne (chapter 8) describes how the city of New Orleans, Jefferson Parish, and the state of Louisiana have developed a new emergency evacuation plan that takes into account the needs of carless households, the elderly, and other vulnerable populations. The new plan was put to the test during Hurricane Gustav in 2008 and proved so successful (as evidenced by the uneventful media coverage) that the evacuation plan could serve as a model for other cities and states. This is precisely the kind of preparedness needed to increase the disaster resilience of New Orleans in a way that is more socially inclusive.

Beyond emergency preparedness, New Orleanians have organized themselves to advocate for the overhaul of the public services that failed citizens and taxpayers in the past and to collaborate with many government, business, and nonprofit partners to achieve that goal. Andre Perry and Michael Schwam-Baird (chapter 3) carefully document how the post–Hurricane Katrina environment created an opening for the state of Louisiana to undertake one of the nation's boldest charter school experiments to fix the city's failing public school system. To date, school reform has led to some encouraging improvements in student academic performance and in school facilities. Karen DeSalvo (chapter 4) describes how the region is moving toward improved delivery of quality, affordable, and accessible health care to all populations, including low-income and minority patients, through the creation of a new, region-wide network of community health clinics. Nadiene Van Dyke, Jon Wool, and Luceia LeDoux (chapter 5) explain that leaders are making progress in reinventing key aspects of the city's criminal justice system to convert the historically corrupt, abusive, inefficient, and ineffective system to one that will improve fairness, accountability, and public safety outcomes. And David

Marcello (chapter 6) documents the adoption of ethics reform in New Orleans city government that not only will lay the foundation for greater transparency, trust, and integrity in public spending and decisionmaking but also will help improve the city's ability to respond and adapt to future crises.

All such efforts to deliver good schools, safe streets, quality health care, and reliable government are critical to attracting and maintaining families and businesses in the community in the near and longer term. But as disaster coverage and subsequent research have shown, Hurricane Katrina was fundamentally a housing disaster. Rebuilding homes and neighborhoods, especially for renters and low-income families, has been challenging. Still, promising developments in housing and land use planning exist.

In New Orleans, enormous attention has been paid to the Lower Ninth Ward as a barometer of neighborhood progress. Kalima Rose (chapter 7) tells us that in the Lower Ninth as well as many other neighborhoods, residents have organized themselves to ensure a future for their families and communities. The result is the emergence of a sophisticated network of neighborhood organizations and nonprofit developers aiming to rebuild more opportunity-rich neighborhoods for returning and existing residents. State leaders endeavored to foster the creation of more economically integrated housing and neighborhoods, while federal leaders reformed the long-troubled public housing authority and helped families in trailers and other vulnerable households find permanent housing. Robert Collins (chapter 11) describes how New Orleans finally developed a citywide master plan, despite many missteps. The new master plan, also codifies an inclusive community participation process, promotes livability, economic opportunity, and ways to "live with water." With the comprehensive plan in place, the city will likely be more resilient, recovering from future disasters in faster, fairer, and more cost-effective ways.

Housing recovery and planning in coastal Mississippi faced a different set of political and policy challenges, with uneven results for social equity. Unlike Louisiana, where Hurricane Katrina hit primarily one major urban center, Mississippi coped with the impacts on approximately one dozen smaller communities spread across three coastal counties (for example, Bay St. Louis, Waveland, Biloxi, Moss Point, and Gulfport). Governor Haley Barbour stepped into the recovery by taking a strong leadership role and establishing the Governor's Commission on Recovery, Rebuilding, and Renewal within two weeks of the storm. But the state's housing recovery plan did not place a premium on serving low-income homeowners or renters. Instead, the state diverted federal housing and community development funds to finance economic development projects such as the expansion of the state port at Gulfport.

Within that context, Mukesh Kumar (chapter 10) and Reilly Morse (chapter 9) describe how some communities and organizations succeeded in pursuing equitable and sustainable development outcomes during recovery. For instance, some saw the Governor's Commission and its partnership with the Congress for New Urbanism as an opportunity to address some of the development challenges that many coastal communities faced prior to Katrina, such as urban sprawl, inadequate affordable housing, and weak downtown centers. On the positive side, Kumar notes that some local communities adopted the new goals for the region along with new urbanist design recommendations, resulting in a greater variety of urban forms in coastal Mississippi. However, it appears that most communities are reverting to the familiarity of pre-Katrina local growth and development patterns. On housing, Morse carefully describes how a new coalition of housing advocates developed a set of data-driven, media-oriented reports and strategies that effectively pushed the state to eventually respond to and address key affordable housing needs.

Finally, the failure of the levee system in greater New Orleans served as a wake-up call to southern Louisianans about the limitations of manmade infrastructure and the need to strengthen the region's natural protections to mitigate the effects of future hurricanes. Mark Davis (chapter 12) reviews coastal Louisiana's history of living with water and notes the decided shift in public attitudes and public policies in support of wetland restoration and a new framework for coastal restoration in the wake of both Hurricane Katrina and the subsequent Gulf oil spill. Yet a meaningful commitment to investments, laws, and policies to secure the long-term economic health and sustainability of the region remains out of reach.

Increased Civic Capacity to Build Resilience and Opportunity

The chapters described above show that a spirit of reform has permeated the civic culture in New Orleans and other parts of the Gulf Coast, a phenomenon that many of the authors note did not exist before the storm. The new capacity to engage in civic affairs, build cross-sector partnerships, and solve problems as a community are critical signs of resilience and adaptation.

The remaining chapters present additional ideas about how to expand the region's capacity to respond to crises and the need to accommodate post-Katrina's new demographic realities. Frederick Weil (chapter 14) documents and confirms the unprecedented rise in community engagement in New Orleans after the storm. His surveys of approximately 6,000 residents, accompanied by extensive ethnographic research, found an increase in the number of New Orleanians participating in public meetings and processes, greater organizational capability among grassroots organizations, and dozens of newly formed umbrella groups.The Greater New Orleans Community Data Center (GNOCDC) is one of the nonprofits that has adapted nimbly and innovatively since Katrina. But the data center itself has also contributed to the effectiveness of citizen leaders, government, and other nonprofits through its deployment of timely, accurate, and accessible demographic, economic, housing, and other rebuilding data to inform decisionmaking. In chapter 13, Allison Plyer and Elaine Ortiz explain how philanthropy and public policies can help empower such data intermediaries in the wake of a disaster.

Critical to community self-reliance is the presence of strong social networks. Ann Carpenter and Nancy Montoya (chapter 15) add an important dimension to existing work on social networks in their case study of Bay St. Louis in Hancock County, Mississippi, and of the Broadmoor neighborhood in New Orleans. They find that physical gathering places such as restaurants, schools, and places of worship are critical to facilitating social networks and civic engagement, while the loss of such establishments can hamper the development of community ties. Such places helped fuel communication during the days right after Katrina and enabled residents to organize to rebuild in the months and years that followed.

Behind every collective action or transformational change is a leader. James Joseph, Lance Buhl, Richard McCline, and Leslie Williams (chapter 17) offer lessons on how to strengthen the culture of leadership in Louisiana so that an enduring supply of leaders is available to work to advance justice and opportunity for all citizens. Improving the capacity to rebuild better for all populations must also incorporate the new demographic realities of the region. Jasmine Waddell, Silas Lee, and Breonne DeDecker (chapter 16) directly address the issue of race and class by arguing that the recent influx of Hispanics to New Orleans and their shared experience with African Americans in facing poor labor and living conditions provides an opportunity to build interracial alliances to advance common causes.

Finally, fueling much of the increased capacity in the Gulf region's community and social infrastructure is the vast power of national and local philanthropic organizations to provide advice and funds for investment and to convene interested parties to work toward rebuilding the area. Ivye Allen, Linetta Gilbert, and Alandra Washington (chapter 18) examine the important role of philanthropy in driving systems change after the storms and call for continued investment in the development and capacity of local and regional philanthropic groups in the Gulf Coast. As national philanthropies recede, local foundations must further the goals of social and economic equity and prepare to respond to future crises.

In addition to chronicling the shift toward resilience and opportunity in the Gulf region, the chapters in this volume raise concerns about the factors that threaten the Gulf region's six-year effort to make progress and offer lessons or propose next steps to further social and economic transformation. How will we know whether a new and better course is indeed being crafted? At the hurricane's five-year anniversary, Brookings and GNOCDC published *The New Orleans Index at Five,* in part to begin measuring the key outcomes of the region's rebuilding strategies. While it is still too early to tell, there are some indications that greater New Orleans is bouncing back better than before.[16] In the future, additional efforts must be made to further examine the region's economic development strategies and to measure the region's overall performance in working to attain the following goals of prosperity:

—economic growth that boosts productivity, spurs innovation and entrepreneurship, and generates quality jobs and rising incomes

—inclusive growth that expands educational and employment opportunities, reduces poverty, and fosters a strong and diverse middle class

—sustainable growth that conserves natural resources, maintains environmental quality, mitigates risk, and increases the overall safety of the area

—a high quality of life for residents and businesses, which often includes a package of strong amenities and public services, like good schools and safe streets.

Only then will we know whether the reforms documented in this book, along with other efforts, are truly putting New Orleans and the Gulf region on a brighter course.

Conclusion

Since the 2005 hurricanes, other communities, like those in Haiti and the coastal towns of Japan, have been decimated by the brute force of nature. Those catastrophes have prompted an outpouring of support, but they also raise questions about the prospects of future recovery. Six years into rebuilding efforts, the Gulf Coast has much to teach these and other communities about the nature of renewal after such ruin. Catastrophes hit communities that have varying historical, economic, social, cultural, and political contexts. Yet history is replete with examples of communities that ultimately find ways to rebuild.[17]

This book offers the first comprehensive glimpse into how communities in the Gulf Coast may be emerging as models of post-disaster makeovers that go beyond achieving a speedy recovery to rebounding as more prosperous and resilient communities than they were before. They have been able to do so because many leaders and citizens have intentionally used the unprecedented opportunity presented by the 2005 storms to overhaul critical areas of policy and planning that were badly broken prior to the storm. However, the region remains in the early stages of a long reconstruction process. The path to transformation is fragile. Reinventing an economy to offer more diverse, richer opportunities takes time. Our hope is that regional leaders, with their state, federal, private sector, and national nonprofit partners, will heed the sound advice from the authors in this book to help the Gulf Coast achieve its promise of becoming a sustainable, prosperous region.

Notes

1. United Nations Development Program, "Reducing Disaster Risk: A Challenge for Development," 2004 (www.undp.org/cpr/whats_new/rdr_english.pdf).
2. The Boston Indicators Project, "Global Warming"(www.bostonindicators.org/Indicators2006/SummaryReport.aspx?id=4536).
3. John Barry, *Rising Tide: The Great Mississippi Flood of 1927 and How It Changed America* (New York: Simon and Schuster, 1997).
4. Ibid.
5. Center for Budget and Policy Priorities, "Essential Facts about the Victims of Hurricane Katrina," 2005 (www.cbpp.org/cms/?fa=view&id=658).
6. Frances Townsend, "The Federal Response to Hurricane Katrina: Lessons Learned" (White House, 2006) (http://georgewbush-whitehouse.archives.gov/reports/katrina-lessons-learned/index.html).
7. Blaine Harden and Shankar Vedantam, "Many Displaced by Katrina Turn to Relatives for Shelter," *Washington Post,* September 8, 2000 (www.washingtonpost.com/wp-dyn/content/article/2005/09/07/AR2005090702415.html).

8. Statement of Robert David Paulison, acting director of the Federal Emergency Management Agency, *Hurricane Katrina: How Is FEMA Performing Its Mission at This Stage of Recovery? Hearings before the Senate Committee on Homeland Security and Governmental Affairs*, 109 Cong., October 6, 2005 (http://hsgac.senate.gov/public/index.cfm?FuseAction=Files.View&FileStore_id=dd0bdb70-d821-4a1e-b7d4-c5c1a570a06c).

9. Office of Policy Development and Research, *Current Housing Unit Damage Estimates: Hurricanes Katrina, Rita, and Wilma* (Department of Housing and Urban Development, 2006) (http://gnocdc.s3.amazonaws.com/reports/Katrina_Rita_Wilma_Damage_2_12_06___revised.pdf).

10. Ibid.

11. Ibid.

12. Department of Homeland Security and Office of Management and Budget, "Katrina/Rita Financial Assistance," unpublished PowerPoint slide on file with Amy Liu, 2009.

13. Edward Hill and others, "Economic Shocks and Regional Economic Resilience," working paper (Building Resilient Regions, Institute of Governmental Studies, University of California at Berkeley, 2011); Kathryn A. Foster, "In Search of Regional Resilience," in *Building Regional Resilience: Urban and Regional Policy and Its Effects,* vol. 4, edited by Margaret Weir, Howard Wial, and Harold Wolman (Brookings, forthcoming 2011); Kathleen Sherrieb, Fran H. Norris, and Sandro Galea, "Measuring Capacities for Community Resilience," *Social Indicators Research* 99, no. 2 (2010), pp. 227–47; and Edward L. Glaeser and Albert Saiz, "The Rise of the Skilled City" (Cambridge: Harvard Institute of Economic Research, 2003).

14. "New Orleans after the Storm: Lessons from the Past, a Plan for the Future" (Brookings, 2005) (www.brookings.edu/reports/2005/10metropolitanpolicy.aspx)

15. Mancur Olson, *The Rise and Decline of Nations: Economic Growth, Stagflation, and Social Rigidities* (Yale University Press, 1982).

16. Amy Liu and Allison Plyer, "An Overview of Greater New Orleans: From Recovery to Transformation," in *The New Orleans Index at Five* (Washington: Brookings Institution and Greater New Orleans Community Data Center, 2010)

17. Lawrence J. Vale and Thomas J. Campanella, "Conclusion: Axioms of Resilience," in *The Resilient City: How Modern Cities Recover from Disaster,* edited by Lawrence J. Vale and Thomas J. Campanella (Oxford University Press, 2005), p. 336.

PART 1

Defining Resilience

2

Professing Regional Resilience

Kathryn A. Foster

In marking the fifth anniversary of Hurricane Katrina, leaders often credited recovery to one key attribute—resilience.

Speaking at Xavier University, President Barack Obama said of New Orleans, "This city has become a symbol of resilience and of community and of the fundamental responsibility that we have to one another."[1] Governor Haley Barbour of Mississippi credited progress on the Gulf Coast to "the resilient, hard-working people of Mississippi [who] took a tremendous body blow during the worst natural disaster in our nation's history, and then we got up, hitched up our britches and went to work."[2] Senator Thad Cochran (R-Miss.) joined the chorus: "Our recovery has been made possible by the resilience and hard work of the people who live on or near the coast."[3] Noting that in August 2010 the region was recovering from not one but three disasters—Hurricane Katrina, the Great Recession, and the Gulf of Mexico oil spill— the Brookings Institution's *New Orleans Index at Five* invoked resilience to frame regional progress: "It has been often said that New Orleanians are resilient. They have to be."[4] As *Wall Street Journal* writer Larry Blumenfeld summed up the sentiment a few days later, "Nearly everywhere, the word 'resilience' popped up."[5]

Yet beyond the assertions, how would we really know if this region, or any region for that matter, was resilient? What is resilience? How does the concept guide practice in regions seeking to better prepare for and recover from traumas?

This chapter, fashioned as the transcript of a conversation between a professor and a student, draws from a growing literature on regional resilience to provide a foundation for this volume's assessments of resilience and opportunity on the Gulf Coast. The discussion reinforces both the promise of resilience and its challenges as an intellectual and practical guide for regional recovery.

Office Hours on Regional Resilience

Consider Antoine, a new graduate student relocated to the Gulf region to study issues of resilience. Antoine knows challenges well, having recently experienced the trauma of lost employment and relocation far from his hometown support network in Cleveland. To speed his settlement into his new grad program and region, Antoine stops by the office of Professor Lorna Bartlett, an expert on resilience and the bounce-back potential of people and communities under stress. What follows is an excerpt of their conversation.

Antoine: Friends have called me resilient, but maybe just for surviving the move here. What does resilience mean?

Bartlett: In short, resilience is the ability of a person or place to bounce back from a blow. Most people and places are routinely resilient, recovering to the state that they were in before the shock. That said, there is no single accepted definition of the term. A study by the Community and Regional Resilience Institute (CARRI) amassed forty-five different definitions in contemporary research, suggesting great fluidity in the interpretation of resilience.[6] Different fields use the term differently.

Antoine: Could you give some examples?

Bartlett: Among others, psychology, business, ecology, planning, disaster studies, anthropology, and engineering employ the concept of resilience, using it to inform issues as varied as a widower's quality of life, the strength of commodity supply chains, post-fire forest recharge, and the rapidity of repairing a collapsed bridge. I ran a Google News search in late November 2010, which identified 6,200 news citations for "resilience," including op-eds, feature articles on ecological science, and sports coverage using resilience to mean comebacks, season turnarounds, and playing while injured.[7] Resilience is trendy, and it gets a lot of play.

Antoine: So is resilience an attribute to help you cope with a stress? Or an outcome you exhibit when you recover from a stress?

Bartlett: Both. As you suggest, resilience supports two different meanings, capacity and performance. Resilience capacity, which is measured "pre-stress," captures the attributes of a person or place that enable it to withstand a future unknown stress. This meaning was evident in President Obama's August 27, 2010, proclamation for National Preparedness Month: "I encourage all Americans to recognize the importance of preparedness and [to work] together to enhance our national security, resilience, and readiness."[8] Enhancing resilience capacity means amassing the resources, skills, infrastructure, processes, attitudes, and other factors that help you anticipate, mitigate, and cope with the next crisis, whatever it may be.

In contrast, resilience performance, which is measured "post-stress," captures how well a person or place responds to and recovers from trauma. When the *New Orleans Index at Five* measures Greater New Orleans' post-Katrina progress on twenty indicators, such as wages, median household income, and access to better schools, it has resilience performance in mind.

While some separate the two aspects of resilience, the meanings often come together for those in the field.[9] Capacity reveals which areas of intervention offer the greatest potential for increasing regional readiness. Performance reveals the degree to which a community has effectively used its capacity to achieve resilient outcomes. Because both meanings matter, I usually combine them into a single definition of regional resilience: the ability of a region to anticipate, prepare for, respond to, and recover from a disturbance.

Antoine: Okay. But surely there is a difference between coping with a surprise shock—which, like the Gulf oil spill, hits in an instant—and a long-standing strain, such as the prolonged economic decline affecting my hometown of Cleveland. Do resilience experts make that distinction?

Bartlett: They sure do, and you're right about the two basic types. An acute stress is instantaneous, as occurs with an earthquake, overnight plant closing, or terrorist attack. A chronic stress plays out over time, as evidenced in the slow burn of climate change, regional growth, or long-standing cross-border disputes.

It's interesting, though, to note that determining whether a stress is acute or chronic is not always easy. Between 2005 and 2010, did the Gulf Coast experience a series of distinct acute stresses—hurricane, levee breaks, rapid population loss, oil spill—or did Katrina simply reveal a region beset by chronic social, economic, political, and environmental stresses, conditions that were merely exacerbated by the storm and its aftermath?

It's hard to say. What we do know is that it's easier to assess resilience to acute stresses than to chronic ones, in part because acute shocks have relatively clear pre-stress, stress, and post-stress stages and in part because the large number of factors shaping a chronic stress makes it difficult to isolate any one factor as most significant.[10] Acute stresses also get more attention. I will get dozens of media calls on a catastrophic hundred-year flood, but hardly any on, say, incremental changes in climate. Chronic stresses lose out in other ways, too. Contrast the outpouring of concern and financial largesse for the post-Katrina Gulf Coast with the relative dearth of support for areas suffering similar economic, physical, and psychological devastation occurring over decades rather than days.[11] Detroit must wish that its decline had happened overnight.

Antoine: Does resilience differ then for acute and chronic stresses?

Bartlett: It's not clear. Certain attributes, such as educational attainment, health, and social support networks, are presumed useful to people no matter what the kind of stress. Similarly, places with good governance, strong external networks, relative affluence, and a diversified economy are presumably better positioned to withstand stress than are places without those characteristics.

What we can observe is that resilience performance may vary for acute and chronic stresses, as when the Buffalo region capably responds to a major snowstorm but is knocked back by chronic economic challenges.[12] A key research question is whether resilience capacity and resilience performance move in lockstep—that is, whether low-capacity regions have low performance while high-capacity regions have high performance. If so, practitioners could concentrate on boosting capacity, confident that performance would follow. Unfortunately, it's not clear in practice. People who are strong and capable may falter under stress, while those with scant capacity perform above expectations in a crisis. There is some evidence that places may exhibit similarly unexpected responses.[13]

Antoine: I'm so glad you mentioned expectations. Are there "norms" for the timing and degree of recovery that earn the label "resilient"?

Bartlett: That's a tough one. Fields such as medicine and engineering have ample data from which they derive norms of recovery. The norm for recovery from a broken leg, for example, might be eight weeks. But note that norms are typically qualified. The recovery norm for a broken leg might be twelve weeks for an elderly woman but six weeks for a healthy teen. Medical history also comes into play; norms are adjusted if the break is a repeat break or if there is a family history of bone brittleness.

So, too, for regions. Because stresses vary by degree of physical, economic, or ecological disruption, we would expect different time periods for recovery. A bridge could be rebuilt in a year, yet environmental systems could take generations to repair.[14] Starting conditions also vary by place, as does the prevalence of the stress. It might take Denver, for example, only two days to plow roads and dig out from a three-foot snowfall, but the same amount of snow in Baltimore could set it back for a week. So is Denver more resilient than Baltimore? At first blush, yes— it recovered three times faster from an equivalent snowfall. Yet given Denver's experience with storms and its consequently greater capacity for responding, perhaps it should have recovered in one day, not two. And perhaps, given the rarity of snow in Baltimore and hence the lack of equipment and capacity to address it, the city's one-week recovery signals greater resilience than does Denver's two-day recovery. The point is that establishing resilience norms is complicated.

Now add the challenge of insufficient data for deriving norms in the first place. Unlike a medical office with thousands of broken-leg profiles, the regional universe offers too few examples of similar stresses hitting places at similar times under roughly similar circumstances to compute norms or averages. It's difficult for acute stresses and nearly impossible for chronic ones. How do we measure recovery while the strain persists?

Antoine: But wouldn't emergency responders have time-based protocols for responding to a disaster, at least an acute one?

Bartlett: Yes, emergency response and planning more generally are in the business of thwarting crises or lessening their effects. One assessment of vulnerability and resilience in New Orleans before, during, and after Katrina offered a useful time-based framework, identifying specific actions by time period for demonstrating resilience in the areas of emergency response, health and safety, utilities, building systems, environmental resources, and the economy.[15] For building systems, for example, immediate action (within seventy-two hours) involves removing debris, followed by emergency action (within three to seven days) to provide shelter for the homeless, short-run action (within one to six months) to provide temporary housing and business sites, and long-run action (over more than one year) focused on rebuilding and mitigation. Planners are especially focused on mitigation: what people and places can be doing now to best position them in the event of the next crisis.[16]

Antoine: Are there post-disaster insights?

Bartlett: Yes, reinforcing several themes. Creating community resilience takes a long time and brings surprises. Short-term warning systems are essential, but so are continually updated long-term emergency plans. Long-term resilience requires sound environmental and economic systems able to mitigate forces of disaster and rapidly marshal financial and other resources. Indeed, resilience depends in the long run on hazard mitigation and wise choices about development regulations and regional form. "Soft" preparation, including open communications, social trust, and a culture of intergovernmental cooperation, is likewise important. Finally, practice makes perfect—if you aren't holding workshops and running drills, then you're simply hoping for the best, rather than preparing for and ensuring it.

Still, despite planning, outcomes often are uneven. One fifth anniversary account of conditions on and near Jourdan Avenue in New Orleans told of "streets where refurbished homes sit next to ones with boarded windows and shin-high grass."[17] At the individual level, "some people have been inspired to rebuild or even move to New Orleans for the first time, while others are still trying to get back to where they were."[18] And for all the inspiration, energy, and even confidence generated by a big challenge—"We're a bunch of bad-ass, strong, committed people," said New Orleanian Nilima Mwendo about her four grown children and neighbors, who are rebuilding their Holy Cross neighborhood[19]—discouragement is not far behind. Commenting on the still-closed hospital that once served her New Orleans East neighborhood, Loretta Harrison said, "We didn't realize it would take so long."[20]

Antoine: Okay. But are there particular factors that improve the odds of being resilient in the face of a challenge?

Bartlett: Long lists of factors actually, typically divided by category— social, economic, institutional, community, and infrastructure.[21] General capacities include person-centered characteristics (for example, median income, poverty level, language ability, educational attainment) and place-centered considerations (for example, economic diversity, degree of income inequality, place attachment, civic involvement). The logic is that places do better when their people are armed for success with sufficient financial and other resources and operate in an environment of ample socioeconomic capacity. Specific resilience capacities would matter for particular shocks. For example, resilience capacity for an acute environmental disaster might include the number of hospital beds per

10,000 population (to accommodate mass population medical needs), the percentage of dwelling units that are not mobile (to measure housing stability), and the number of hotels and motels per square mile (to accommodate displaced persons and emergency personnel).

The research challenge is to discern the degree to which one factor or another matters more, for what stresses, at what times, and in which places. As one group put it, "some factors that promote resilience to potentially traumatic events may be maladaptive in other contexts."[22] And to complicate matters more, new research suggests that resilience may vary not only by the nature of the stress but by also by its origins. Apparently, people and systems respond differently to "natural" shocks and "man-made" ones, with the former generating the positive energy and camaraderie of a shared crisis and the latter more often yielding malaise, depression, and distrust. The contrast between the post-disaster recovery experiences of those affected by the *Exxon Valdez* disaster and the Gulf of Mexico oil spill, each of which happened because of human actions, and the experiences of those affected by tidal waves, earthquakes, or other natural events offers an example.[23]

Antoine: Can a region really call itself resilient if some of its parts or population groups are still suffering?

Bartlett: Your question raises a real conundrum. Can a region be resilient even while some residents or businesses or organizations fall short in the face of a stress? Regions are complex, encompassing individuals, households, social groups, neighborhoods, businesses, civic organizations, governments, and myriad other actors and actor types, each with options and considerable autonomy in making choices. We should expect some individuals, households, social groups and so forth to have ample resilience capacity, but others will not, finding themselves unprepared for challenges and faltering in the wake of a crisis.

Assessing resilience at the regional level will therefore inevitably obscure uneven or incomplete recovery for particular communities, neighborhoods, or households. Just as regional measures of poverty, educational attainment, and other individual characteristics mask a potentially wide range of outcomes, so will a regional resilience score—calculated, say, as an index of capacity and performance in a region's pre- and post-stress stages—mask the different fortunes of the area's individuals, households, and communities.

A promising line of inquiry reframes resilience to recognize varied scales, specifically identifying three nested levels of analysis.[24] The first scale focuses on the individual, assessing resilience as a function of personal attributes such as physical disability, old age, and poverty status that make a person more vulnerable to challenges. The second scale focuses on a larger household, dwelling unit, or firm within which individuals operate. In the case of a dwelling unit, for example, the precariousness of housing conditions—living in substandard housing, say, or on blocks with significant vacancy—renders occupants and the region generally less resilient to challenges. The third scale considers the broader environment: how its turbulence—its status as drought- or earthquake-prone, for example—makes the region and its people more vulnerable when stresses come. The utility of this model is its implication that regional actors can influence a region's resilience by addressing any of the three levels of vulnerability. That awareness opens the way to policies, programs, and processes that directly mitigate risks at those levels, thus enhancing regional resilience.

Antoine: But isn't it possible that making an individual more resilient could make a region less so?

Bartlett: Antoine, you've identified an uncomfortable truth of resilience. A household could indeed enhance its resilience by escaping a region, which in turn diminishes the region's human and fiscal resources. The massive outmigration from New Orleans and the Gulf Coast in the wake of Hurricane Katrina is an example. Trade-offs also are evident when firms decide to move operations offshore and lay off local workers. Those actions presumably make the firm more resilient to global economic conditions, enabling it to survive and perhaps thrive into the future. But the firm's choices reduce the resilience of the firm's workers (who lose their jobs), suppliers (who lose business), area governments (whose tax revenues fall), and the region more generally (by loss or downsizing of a major employer). You could also theorize, uncomfortably, that assisting laid-off workers might erode regional resilience. Extending unemployment benefits and social supports in hard times could be hard for business owners, state and federal governments, and other organizations that are made less well off in the short term by offering such benefits. Resilience choices are often value laden.

Antoine: But is the region better off in the long run because of these adjustments? Why bounce back to "normal" if it means perpetuating lousy conditions?

Bartlett: Good questions. When we have a fever we want our body temperature to return to 98.6 degrees because that's a healthy norm. But if a place norm is undesirable, disaster can create opportunity for a different future. In hindsight, one of the best things to happen to downtown San Francisco was the 1989 Loma Prieta earthquake, which badly damaged the two-story Embarcadero Freeway paralleling—and cutting off—the city's bayside waterfront. The original proposal was to express the city's resilience by rebuilding the freeway and returning to "normal." Others saw the opportunity for a no-freeway transformation, a view that ultimately prevailed. Places disadvantaged before a storm could be wise to leverage the crisis to achieve a new norm. Governor Haley Barbour certainly took that view when he declared in his fifth anniversary remarks, "The Coast is coming back bigger and better."[25] That, however, begs the value question: bigger and better for whom?

Antoine: That's thought provoking. Anything else I should ponder before next office hours?

Bartlett: Only to add that humans and places may be resilient to some aspects of a crisis but not to others. I can remember coping well with the professional transition in my first job, but my belongings were in boxes for months and I took a long time to settle in outside of work. Was I resilient? Yes and no, I suppose. A big part of resilience is adapting to change, finding ways to be flexible in the moment, ready for and open to whatever comes your way. That ultimately worked for me, and maybe for you and places, too.

Antoine: I feel better already about the cartons still stacked in my living room. Thank you, Professor, I'm feeling more resilient than ever.

Notes

1. Barack Obama, "Transcript of President Barack Obama's Katrina Anniversary Speech at Xavier University," *Times-Picayune*, August 29, 2010 (www.nola.com/ katrina/index.ssf/2010/08/transcript_of_president_barack.html).

2. Office of Governor Haley Barbour, *Five Years after Katrina: Progress Report on Recovery, Rebuilding, and Renewal* (Jackson, Miss.: August 29, 2010), p. 2.

3. Quoted in Roland Weeks, "With Strong People and Effective Leadership, We Will Endure," *Sun Herald* (Biloxi-Gulfport and South Mississippi), August 26, 2010 (http://sunherald.com/2010/08/26).

4. Amy Liu and Allison Plyer, "An Overview of Greater New Orleans: From Recovery to Transformation," *New Orleans Index at Five* (Brookings Institution and Greater New Orleans Data Center, 2010), p. 1 (https://gnocdc.s3.amazonaws.com/NOIat5/ Overview.pdf).

5. Larry Blumenfeld, "New Orleans, 5 Years On," *Wall Street Journal*, September 2, 2010 (http://online.wsj.com/article/SB10001424052748703882304575465460710 758270.html?KEYWORDS=larry+blumenfeld+new+orleans).

6. John M. Plodinec, *Definitions of Resilience: An Analysis* (Oak Ridge, Tenn.: Community and Regional Resilience Institute, 2009).

7. See David Ignatius, "Thankful for Resilience," *Washington Post,* August 25, 2010 (www.washingtonpost.com); and Maywa Montenegro, "Urban Resilience," February 16, 2010 (http://seedmagazine.com/content/article/urban_resilience/).

8. President Barack Obama, "Presidential Proclamation: National Preparedness Month, 2010," August 27, 2010 (www.whitehouse.gov/the-press-office/2010/08/27/presidential-proclamation-national-preparedness-month-2010).

9. Cathy Grace and Elizabeth F. Shores, *Preparing for Disaster: What Every Early Childhood Director Needs to Know* (Silver Spring, Md.: Gryphon House, 2010); Cathy Grace and Elizabeth F. Shores, *After the Crisis: Using Storybooks to Help Children Cope* (Silver Spring, Md.: Gryphon House, 2010).

10. This is evidenced by the empirical literature assessing acute stress, which is more voluminous than that assessing chronic stress. The acute crisis of Hurricane Katrina alone generated a sizable body of work, including Eugenie L. Birch and Susan M. Wachter, *Rebuilding Urban Places after Disaster: Lessons from Hurricane Katrina* (University of Pennsylvania Press, 2006); Thomas J. Campanella, "Urban Resilience and the Recovery of New Orleans," *Journal of the American Planning Association* 72 no. 2 (2006): 141–46; Craig E. Colton, Robert Kates, and Shirley Laska, *Community Resilience: Lessons from New Orleans and Hurricane Katrina* (Oak Ridge, Tenn.: Community and Regional Resilience Initiative, 2008); and Robert B. Olshansky and Laurie A. Johnson, *Clear as Mud: Planning for the Rebuilding of New Orleans* (Chicago: APA Planners Press, 2010).

11. Megan Willis, "Detroit: Our Latest Katrina," *Albany Times Union* (Albany, New York), November 17, 2010 (http://blog.timesunion.com/davenport/detroit-our-latest-katrina/440/).

12. Kathryn A. Foster, "A Case Study Approach to Regional Resilience," working paper (MacArthur Foundation Research Network on Building Resilient Regions, 2007) (http://brr.berkeley.edu).

13. Kathryn A. Foster, "Regional Capital," in *Urban-Suburban Interdependencies,* edited by Rosalind Greenstein and Wim Wieviel (Cambridge, Mass.: Lincoln Institute of Land Policy, 2000), pp. 83–118.

14. Michael Grunwald, "Katrina: A Man-Made Disaster," *Time,* December 6, 2010, pp. 70–74.

15. Colten, Kates, and Laska, "Lessons from New Orleans."

16. See, for example, Stephen Flynn and Sean Burke, *Before the Next Katrina: Urgent Recommendations for the President and Congress on Gulf Coast Resilience* (Washington: Center for National Policy, 2010).

17. Jennifer Levitz and Mike Esterl, "On One Block, Resilience and Despair," *Wall Street Journal,* August 28, 2010 (http://online.wsj.com/article/SB10001424052748704913704575454500722704746.html?mod=WSJ_topics_obama#printMode).

18. Ibid.

19. Quoted in Levitz and Esterl, "On One Block."

20. Ibid.

21. For useful compilations and empirical tests on factors of resilience, see Kathleen Sherrieb, Fran H. Norris, and Sandro Galea, "Measuring Capacities for Community Resilience, *Social Indicators Research* 99, no. 2 (2010): 227–47; and Susan L. Cutter, Christopher G. Burton, and Christopher T. Emrich, "Disaster Resilience Indicators

for Benchmarking Baseline Conditions," *Journal of Homeland Security and Environmental Management* 7, no. 1 (2010): 1–22. For an issue-specific list of capacity factors, in this case for climate protection, see Sammy Zahren and others, "Risk, Stress, and Capacity: Explaining Metropolitan Commitment to Climate Protection," *Urban Affairs Review* 43, no. 4 (2008): 447–74. For factors relevant to Mississippi Gulf Coast communities, see Tom Lansford and others, *Fostering Community Resilience: Homeland Security and Hurricane Katrina* (Surrey, U.K.: Ashgate, 2010).

22. George A. Bonanno and Anthony D. Mancini, "The Human Capacity to Thrive in the Face of Potential Trauma," *Pediatrics* 121, no. 2 (2008): 369.

23. Debbie Elliott and Marisa Peñaloza, "BP Spill Psychological Scars Similar to Exxon Valdez," *National Public Radio,* December 1, 2010 (www.npr.org/2010/12/01/131694848/bp-spill-psychological-scars-similar-to-exxon-valdez).

24. Rolf Pendall, Brett Theodos, and Kaitlin Franks, "Vulnerable People, Precarious Housing, and Regional Resilience: An Exploratory Analysis," paper presented at the 51st Annual Conference of the Association of Collegiate Schools of Planning, Minneapolis, Minnesota, October 7, 2010.

25. Quoted in Ross Dellenger, "Memory Will Never Die," *Clarion Ledger* (Jackson, Mississippi), August 30, 2010 (www.clarionledger.com/article).

PART 2

Building Resilience and Opportunity through Policy and Planning

3

School by School:
The Transformation of
New Orleans Public Education

Andre Perry and Michael Schwam-Baird

Education reform in New Orleans is often cited as one of the brighter spots in the city's uneven post–Hurricane Katrina recovery. New Orleans is an interesting case because of the speed and scope of the changes in its public education system, including the following:

—*State takeover of low-performing schools.* In other district takeovers, states typically take control of the entire school district apparatus, including the central office. In New Orleans, the state of Louisiana took over individual schools based on their performance while leaving the local school board and its central office intact, albeit with far fewer schools to oversee.

—*Charter schools.* While charter schools in other districts usually educate a small minority of students, the majority of public school students in New Orleans now attend charter schools.

—*School choice.* Most school districts assign students to schools on the basis of where they live, with only a few exceptions. By

The authors draw heavily on their previous research. In particular, this chapter draws from a recent chapter by Henry M. Levin, Joseph Daschbach, and Andre Perry in *Between Public and Private: Politics, Governance, and the New Portfolio Models for Urban School Reform*, edited by K. E. Bulkley, J. R. Henig, and H. M. Levin (Harvard Education Press, 2010). In addition, research conducted by the Cowen Institute for Public Education Initiatives at Tulane University is featured throughout.

contrast, nearly all public school attendance zones in New Orleans were eliminated after Hurricane Katrina.

—*School staff.* Most school districts around the country have collective bargaining agreements with a local teachers' union that govern hiring, promotion, pay, work rules, and other conditions of employment. In addition, state laws often codify school staff tenure and seniority protections. Following the state takeover of most public schools in New Orleans, the financially insolvent Orleans Parish School Board (OPSB) fired nearly all of its teachers and school staff. As of the 2010–11 school year, no district or charter school in New Orleans has a collective bargaining agreement. In addition, schools run by the Recovery School District (RSD) and all of the charter schools in New Orleans have significant flexibility under state law to set hiring, promotion, salary, and work rules.

Due to these rapid-fire changes, New Orleans public education has become a major focus of local and national audiences. In this chapter we examine the history of New Orleans public schooling in the years before Hurricane Katrina and how public education in the city evolved in the storm's wake. We discuss both the advantages of the new system and the political and operational problems that it has created. Finally, we highlight key areas of concern for education policy in the coming years.

New Orleans Public Education before Katrina

Since legal school segregation ended in the early 1970s, public schools in New Orleans have witnessed many of the same trends as other large, urban school districts: white and middle-class flight to suburban and private schools, a student population of predominantly high-needs students, and a decreasing student population overall. During the 1970s, white enrollment in New Orleans public schools fell by over half and fell again by half in the following decade (figure 3-1). In the same period, black enrollment was roughly stable.[1] In the 2004–05 school year, when the population of New Orleans was 68 percent African American, the public school population was 94 percent African American. The school population was also disproportionately poor: 73 percent of New Orleans public school students qualified for the free lunch program (indicating that their family income was less than 130 percent of the income defined as the poverty line).[2]

In addition to serving an increasingly high-needs population, the school system faced a number of governance and management problems. Over the decade preceding Hurricane Katrina, the OPSB and the district

FIGURE 3-1. New Orleans Public School Enrollment, by Race, 1900–2000

Number of students

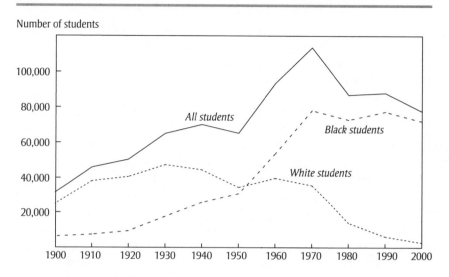

Source: Louisiana Department of Education, *Annual Financial and Statistical Reports*, various years.

administration engaged in ineffective—and sometimes illegal—practices while governing and operating the school system. These ongoing problems prevented the school board and the school system administration from addressing the educational requirements of an overwhelmingly high-needs population of students.

A Troubled School District

The OPSB often was a source of political strife and controversy in the years before Hurricane Katrina. The school board was frequently criticized for awarding contracts that hurt the district financially and resulted in provision of low-quality services.[3] The OPSB and the district central office were considered sufficiently corrupt that in 2004 a special Federal Bureau of Investigation task force was assigned to investigate the school system.[4] In 2008, a former school board president pled guilty to accepting $140,000 in bribes.[5]

Board members also engaged in public spats among themselves and with other government entities, community groups, and parents.[6] In one extreme example, board members filed lawsuits against one another after an attempt to fire the superintendent split the board.[7] In addition, school board members were often over-involved in the details of administering the school district and were frequently accused of micromanaging super-intendents.[8] At least one member of the board, in concert with a strong local political machine, influenced the hiring of principals.[9]

In addition to the board's political and governance troubles, the district administration faced a host of management and financial problems in the years preceding Hurricane Katrina. In the decade before Katrina hit, a total of eight (three permanent and five interim) superintendents ran the school system.[10] Between February 1999 and March 2005, five different chief financial officers were named in OPSB audits, with some gaps in which it is unclear whether anyone filled the position.[11]

The high turnover of top management and the school board's governance problems may have contributed to the mismanagement and fraud in the New Orleans school system's central office that came to light in the years before Hurricane Katrina. A 2004 state audit report revealed high management turnover, poor controls in the payroll and finance departments, and overpayments of millions of dollars to terminated employees.[12] In 2004, the FBI indicted eleven employees for criminal financial offenses against the OPSB.[13]

Financial problems finally pushed the school system to the brink of bankruptcy in the school year before Hurricane Katrina. In March 2005, auditors reported that the school system was out of money, having spent down its reserves over a number of years, a finding that led the state to demand that an outside firm take over the district's finances.[14] In July 2005, having just fired its last permanent superintendent before the storm, the OPSB handed its finances over to a private consulting firm.[15]

Student Achievement

In 2005, Orleans Parish ranked sixty-seventh of sixty-eight Louisiana parishes in student achievement. With the exception of a few high-performing, selective admissions schools where white and middle-class students were concentrated, most public schools in the decade before Katrina were low-performing schools.[16] In the 2004–05 school year, 64 percent of public schools in New Orleans were deemed "academically unacceptable" by Louisiana accountability standards; the figure was 8 percent for public schools in Louisiana overall (table 3-1) . In the same year, the city's public schools had a twelfth-grade dropout rate of 16.8 percent while the statewide rate was 7.6 percent.[17]

TABLE 3-1. New Orleans Public Schools' SPS Levels,
by Number and Percentage of Schools at Each Level, 2005

School performance score (SPS) level	Number of schools	Percentage of 2005 schools
Academically unacceptable (below 60.0 percent)	73	64.0
One star (60.0–79.9)	23	20.2
Two stars (80.0–99.9)	7	6.1
Three stars (100.0–119.9)	7	6.1
Four stars (120.0–139.9)	2	1.8
Five stars (140 and above)	2	1.8

Source: Louisiana Department of Education, "2004–05 District Accountability Report."

Low student achievement along with ongoing governance and man-agement problems made the public schools in New Orleans an opportune target for state intervention. Indeed, a number of attempts were made by the legislature to change the structure and governance of the school system in the decade before the storm. Ultimately, however, Hurricane Katrina and its terrible aftermath would determine the method and scope of the state's intervention in New Orleans public education.

The Evolution of Post-Katrina Public Education in New Orleans

Hurricane Katrina provided the incentive for a series of political, legisla-tive, and fiscal events that expedited education reform in New Orleans. The race to open schools for students returning to the city was as big an impetus for New Orleans' noted restructuring as any intentional reform strategy. Indeed, many of the enacted policies had existed in some form before the storm. At the same time, the absence of the evacu-ated stakeholders changed the political dynamics that held the previous system together. The school board's financial problems, the need to open schools immediately, and the destruction of school facilities precipitated many of the subsequent reforms. The rapid expansion of the Recov-ery School District, the removal of school attendance zones, and the rise of charter schools were arguably convenient solutions to the acute needs that arose after the storm. In this regard, New Orleans education recovery can be interpreted as a series of reactions to unfolding events that built on preexisting policies rather than as a process based on pre-established goals.

Governance and the Expansion of Charter Schools

Contrary to what the name now suggests, the Recovery School District existed before Hurricane Katrina as a mechanism to allow the state to take over failing public schools, which were defined as those that did not make adequate yearly progress over a number of years. Chartering is one of the RSD's primary interventions for school improvement. In 2004, Pierre A. Capdau Elementary School became Louisiana's first "takeover" charter school. In return for a five-year charter to run the school, the University of New Orleans committed to increasing the school's performance.[18] Just before Hurricane Katrina, four other New Orleans schools were taken over the by the RSD and turned over to charter school managers.[19]

Hurricane Katrina hit the Gulf Coast on August 29, 2005, only a week into the new school year. Because of the levee failures and the city's evacuation, many of the usual education stakeholders (including parents, teachers, and local community and political organizations) were not present in the subsequent debate about rebuilding the public education system in New Orleans. In their absence, the Louisiana state legislature in November 2005 passed Act 35, which dramatically expanded the RSD. Under Act 35 the legislature changed the state's definition of an academically unacceptable school, making individual schools eligible for placement in the RSD if their School Performance Score (SPS) was below the state average instead of below 60, as in the previous law. The new definition applied only to schools in districts that were considered by the law to be in "academic crisis," meaning that the district operated more than thirty academically unacceptable schools or had more than 50 percent of its students in such schools.[20] By setting the cut-off for transfer to the RSD at the state average, policymakers tailored Act 35 to take over the vast majority of schools in New Orleans, the only district in the state that was in academic crisis according to the law. In addition to management rights, the legislature also granted the RSD authority over the land and buildings occupied by the schools that it took over. Act 35 set in motion the rapid restructuring of the city's public schools.

In the effort to open more schools after the storm, the OPSB exercised its rights as a charter school authorizer to charter numerous schools that were not placed in the RSD. Some of the schools that the OPSB chartered were selective magnet schools before the storm. Both the OPSB and the RSD also opened district-run schools as families returned to the city. However, school capacity was initially less than required by the returning families. In

FIGURE 3-2. Public School Enrollment in New Orleans, Traditional and Charter Schools, 2006–11

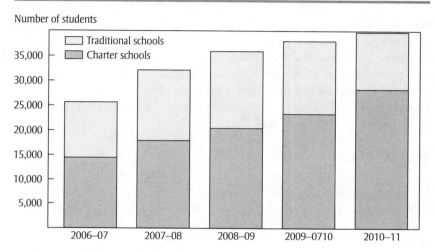

Source: Louisiana Department of Education, "Student Data: Multiple Statistics, 2006–11."

January 2007, the RSD placed more than 300 children on waiting lists as the state-run school system rushed to open additional schools.[21]

From three charter schools in 2004 to sixty-one in the 2010–11 school year, the number of charter schools in New Orleans has expanded dramatically (figure 3-2). In 2010–11, 71 percent of all public school students in New Orleans attend charter schools, the highest rate of charter attendance in the country. Ninety-five percent of New Orleans public school students are minority, and 84 percent are eligible for free and reduced-price lunches. In total, public school attendance is down from its pre-Katrina numbers of 65,000 to approximately 40,000. However, the number of enrollees has climbed steadily from 2006, when 25,600 students enrolled in public schools.[22]

Under state law, the RSD has five years to operate schools before the state Board of Elementary and Secondary Education (BESE) can decide whether to return schools to local control. In September 2010, state superintendent Paul Pastorek presented a draft plan that would extend every school's stay in the RSD by two years and give better-performing schools the choice to stay in the RSD or to return to local control. Under the initial recommendation, the RSD would keep low-performing schools in order to close them or convert them to charter schools.[23] While many RSD charter school supporters did not want to return to the OPSB, members of the OPSB and supporters of local control saw Pastorek's recommendation as an attack on local democratic control of schools. A well-attended October 2010 BESE meeting highlighted this division.[24] Pastorek amended his recommendation in December 2010 to allow low-performing RSD schools to leave the RSD if qualified groups come forward to run them. Local school districts can also apply to take over low-performing RSD schools under the plan.[25] BESE adopted the revised recommendation in December 2010.[26]

School Choice

Before Katrina, most public schools in New Orleans had attendance zones that determined whether a student could attend those particular schools, but the limited availability of schools immediately after the storm led to the abandonment of the zones. In addition, most charter schools were required by state law to take any student in the city. As schools reopened, the RSD and OPSB retained school choice, particularly in light of the RSD's intent to charter most of its schools. Education leaders also wanted parents to have a choice in the new decentralized environment. As a result, nearly every public school in New Orleans accepts students regardless of where they live.

Choice has the potential to empower parents and students to select higher-quality schools if their local school is low performing. On the other hand, the process of choosing a school can be daunting. In New Orleans, different application processes have created confusion for some parents when enrolling their children. In order to address some of the concerns, the RSD and its charter schools developed common application procedures to streamline the process.[27] School choice can also undermine the connections between neighborhoods and schools, since living near a school no longer gives a student guaranteed access. Finally, some school leaders have stated that transportation costs are a major challenge because many students attend schools in other neighborhoods.[28]

Human Capital

As explained above, the OPSB was effectively broke in the months before Hurricane Katrina. With unpredictable tax revenues and an unknown number of students returning, the OPSB concluded that it could not afford to rehire its former employees immediately. In September 2005, the board placed all school employees on disaster leave, meaning that they would receive no pay or benefits until the schools reopened.[29]

In December 2005, the OPSB officially terminated 7,500 school district employees.[30] The terminations had a large impact on the city's black middle class: in the 2004–05 school year, 81 percent of school employees and 73 percent of teachers were African American.[31] The United Teachers of New Orleans (UTNO), the local teachers' union, fought vigorously against the terminations. However, in June 2006, the UTNO collective bargaining agreement with the district expired, and the school board did not renew the contract.[32] With a significant reduction in membership and no collective bargaining agreement, the union saw its influence diminish.[33]

The expansion of the RSD and charter schools in the post-Katrina years created new schools with more flexibility regarding whom they could hire. That opened the door for alternative teacher and school leader training programs to take root in New Orleans. Organizations like Teach for America, the New Teacher Project, and New Leaders for New Schools established or expanded existing branches in New Orleans. As a result of their growth, these local education providers and the national philanthropic groups that fund them have gained significant influence in the region.

School Facilities

Before the storm, New Orleans schools were housed in some of the oldest and most fragile facilities in the state.[34] In 2007, state superintendent Paul Pastorek and RSD superintendent Paul Vallas developed a plan to build five new schools with existing Federal Emergency Management Agency (FEMA) settlement dollars. Factors that education leaders took into consideration for the five "quick start" schools included their geographic alignment with the city's recovery plans.[35] The quick start schools helped create the framework for a larger initiative to rebuild the city's school facility infrastructure. After an extensive public planning process, the OPSB and the RSD adopted a comprehensive plan to renovate, rebuild, or land bank existing buildings in 2008. The plan will cost approximately $2 billion dollars. After extensive negotiations, in August 2010 federal officials announced that FEMA would provide $1.8 billion to renovate and rebuild flooded schools in New Orleans.[36]

School Finances

One of the more dramatic differences between the pre-Katrina and post-Katrina public schools lies in the resources available to schools (tables

TABLE 3-2. Public School Spending, Pre-Katrina

U.S. dollars

Year	New Orleans current expenditures per pupil	Louisiana current expenditures per pupil
2002–03	6,571	6,906
2003–04	7,296	7,248
2004–05	7,893	7,630

Source: Louisiana Department of Education, "Resource Allocation (Revenue/Expenditure Data), 2002–05."

TABLE 3-3. Public School Spending, Post-Katrina

U.S. dollars

Year	New Orleans current expenditures per pupil	Louisiana current expenditures per pupil
2006–07	14,122	8,881
2007–08	15,557	9,966
2008–09	13,070	10,510

Source: Louisiana Department of Education, "Resource Allocation (Revenue/Expenditure Data), 2006–09."

3-2 and 3-3). In the three years before Hurricane Katrina, the OPSB spent between $6,500 and $7,900 per pupil in total current expenditures. Current expenditures capture the amount spent on operating schools while excluding major construction and debt costs.[37] Between 2002 and 2005, OPSB spending was largely in line with the Louisiana average.

Following Hurricane Katrina, the federal government committed $196 million in federal "restart" grants to reopen schools in New Orleans.[38] The federal government also provided funds to help start new charter schools in New Orleans, and many private foundations and individuals made donations to schools. As a result, in the years following Katrina, schools in New Orleans spent much more per pupil than the state average.

Though buoyed by a one-time influx of federal money, school spending in New Orleans is beginning to return to a level closer to the Louisiana average. As a result, certain programs that supported improvements in public schools may need to be curtailed. Indeed, without more recurring funding or significant operational savings, public schools in New Orleans may soon face financial problems.

T A B L E   3 - 4 . Pre- and Post-Katrina New Orleans Public Schools' SPS Levels, by Number and Percentage of Schools at Each Level

School performance score (SPS) level	Number of 2005 schools	Percentage of 2005 schools	Number of 2009 schools	Percentage of 2009 schools
Academically unacceptable (below 60.0 percent)	73	64.0	31	41.9
One star (60.0–79.9)	23	20.2	22	29.7
Two stars (80.0–99.9)	7	6.1	12	16.2
Three stars (100.0–119.9)	7	6.1	6	8.1
Four stars (120.0–139.9)	2	1.8	2	2.7
Five stars (140 and above)	2	1.8	1	1.4

Source: Louisiana Department of Education, "District Accountability Reports, 2004–05 and 2008–09."

Academic Performance

Public schools in New Orleans have demonstrated sustained academic growth since Hurricane Katrina (table 3-4). When comparing pre-Katrina with post-Katrina performance, analyses of grade-level test scores indicate that New Orleans public schools are generally, though not in every case, improving at a faster rate than before the storm.[39] In addition, the proportion of academically unacceptable schools has fallen while more schools are scoring at the one-, two-, three-, and four-star levels than did before Katrina. Finally, the percentage of students attending academically unacceptable schools has also fallen considerably since Katrina (table 3-5).

Academic performance has been promising since the storm. However, a large proportion of schools, especially high schools, remain very low performing. In addition, there is no simple explanation for why school performance has improved since Hurricane Katrina. All of the major reforms described above were implemented at once, making it difficult to evaluate their individual effects. Changing demographics in the city, the tremendous diversity of school types, student mobility between schools, and the academic growth of students who relocated to other states also make it difficult to make definitive claims about causation.[40] Finally, schools have had more money to spend on student instruction since Hurricane Katrina, potentially confounding any direct comparisons. As promising as student achievement results are to date, until a more robust study that incorporates multi-level data analysis can be undertaken, it is

TABLE 3-5. New Orleans Public Schools' SPS Levels, by Percentage of Students at Each Level

School performance score (SPS) level	Fall 2003	Fall 2004	Fall 2008	Fall 2009
Academically satisfactory (60.0 percent and above)	28	30	44	59
Academically unsatisfactory (below 60.0)	69	67	30	34
No score assigned to school	3	3	26	7

Source: Louisiana Department of Education, "District Accountability Reports, 2003–09"; Louisiana Department of Education, "Student Data: Multiple Statistics, 2003–09."

hard to make any concrete claims about the main drivers of public school performance since Hurricane Katrina.

Conclusion

In the first five years after Hurricane Katrina, public school reformers in New Orleans expanded on preexisting structures, like the RSD and charter schools, to transform the city's public education landscape. Their efforts were facilitated by a chaotic physical and political environment and unfolded in the absence of many of the usual education stakeholders. Even so, there was general public support for radical reform in the wake of the storm. Families, political leaders, business leaders, and others collectively wanted to improve public schools as a part of the city's recovery.

Changes to the public education system in New Orleans have produced some encouraging results. Student achievement has improved, schools are being rebuilt better than before, and students now have a range of schools from which to choose. At the same time, the system faces a host of challenges. These include a final decision on the system's long-term governance, the school system's reliance on a one-time grant of federal funds, provision for special education students, and a process to ensure that school choice is fair and sustainable. These are not small challenges, and both citizens and public officials are divided on many of the potential solutions. The next five years will test the structures created by post-Katrina reformers as local officials and stakeholders argue for returning schools to local control, limiting some aspects of school choice, and slowing the process of chartering schools. In many ways, the future of New Orleans will be determined by its transition to normalcy and by how much the city's "new normal" will be able to overcome the deep problems of the old.

Notes

1. Louisiana Department of Education, *Annual Financial and Statistical Reports: 1960–1980* (www.louisianaschools.net/lde/pair/1607.html).

2. Louisiana Department of Education, *Annual Financial and Statistical Report: 2004–2005* (www.louisianaschools.net/lde/pair/1607.html).

3. Rhonda Nabonne, "Firm Faces Scrutiny as Board Members Fume," *Times-Picayune,* September 9, 1997; Anand Vaishnav, "School Board Feels Somewhat Mowed Over," *Times-Picayune,* May 18, 1999; Brian Thevenot, "Final Antics of School Board Laid Bare," *Times-Picayune,* August 23, 2009.

4. Brian Thevenot, "New Probe of N.O. Schools Is Launched," *Times-Picayune,* April 20, 2004.

5. Gordon Russell, "Role in School Bribes Admitted," *Times-Picayune,* January 25, 2008.

6. Leslie Williams, "School Board Watchdog Curbed, Citizen Panel to Lose Clout," *Times-Picayune,* September 25, 1996; Brian Thevenot and Aesha Rasheed, "School Board President Ousted," *Times-Picayune,* January 27, 2004; Brian Thevenot, "School Board OKs Outside Managers," *Times-Picayune,* April 12, 2005.

7. Aesha Rasheed and Brian Thevenot, "Move May Be Afoot to Fire Amato," *Times-Picayune,* June 4, 2004; Janet McConnaughey, "Board Barred from Vote on School Chief," *The Advocate* (Baton Rouge), June 5, 2004, 11A; Brian Thevenot, "Officials Balk at Amato's New Deal," *Times-Picayune,* July 9, 2004.

8. "School Board Split on Reforms," *Times-Picayune,* February 11, 2001; Brian Thevenot, "School Board Searches Soul for $30,000," *Times-Picayune,* September 3, 2000; Aesha Rasheed and Brian Thevenot, "Hopefuls for School Chief ID'd," *Times-Picayune,* December 11, 2002; Brian Thevenot, "'It's Time': Schools Chief Davis to Leave," *Times-Picayune,* June 14, 2002; Thevenot, "Final Antics of School Board Laid Bare."

9. Thevenot, "Final Antics of School Board Laid Bare."

10. Legislative Auditor, *Orleans Parish School Board Audit Reports: 1995–2005* (http://app1.lla.state.la.us/PublicReports.nsf).

11. Louisiana Legislative Auditor, *Orleans Parish School Board Audit Reports: 1999–2005* (http://app1.lla.state.la.us/PublicReports.nsf).

12. Louisiana Legislative Auditor, *Orleans Parish School Board Audit Reports: 2004* (http://app1.lla.state.la.us/PublicReports.nsf).

13. Brian Thevenot, "Schools Sweep Indicts 11 More," *Times-Picayune,* December 17, 2004.

14. "Auditor: Orleans Schools Fall in the Red," *The Advocate* (Baton Rouge), March 31, 2005.

15. Brian Thevenot, "Schools Financial Manager Approved; Watson Survives Attempt to Oust Her," *Times-Picayune,* July 15, 2005.

16. Louisiana Department of Education, 2004–05 District Accountability Report (www.louisianaschools.net/lde/pair/2228pa.asp).

17. Louisiana Department of Education, 2004–05 District Accountability Report (www.louisianaschools.net/lde/pair/2228pa.asp).

18. University of New Orleans, "History of UNO Charter Network" (www.unocharternetwork.net/?page=32).

19. Emily Brown, "Four Seized Schools Retain 79 Percent of Former Pupils," *Times-Picayune,* June 25, 2005.

20. Louisiana State Legislature, "Act No. 35 of the First Extraordinary Session, 2005" (www.legis.state.la.us/billdata/streamdocument.asp?did=329650).

21. Steve Ritea, "300 Students Turned Away by N.O. Schools; Buildings, Teachers Are in Short Supply," *Times-Picayune*, January 24, 2007.

22. Louisiana Department of Education, *Student Data: Multiple Statistics: 2006–2010* (www.louisianaschools.net/lde/pair/1489.html).

23. Cindy Chang, "Pastorek Reveals Plan for N.O. Schools," *Times-Picayune*, September 15, 2010.

24. John Pope, "Meeting on N.O. Schools Draws Passionate Crowd," *Times-Picayune*, October 15, 2010.

25. Cindy Chang, "Pastorek Revises Plan for N.O. Schools' Future," *Times-Picayune*, December 7, 2010.

26. Cindy Chang, "Landry Alumni Confront BESE," *Times-Picayune*, December 9, 2010.

27. Darran Simon, "School Sign-Up Simplified in New Orleans, but Kinks Stand Out in New Unified Process," *Times-Picayune*, April 21, 2008.

28. Cowen Institute at Tulane University, *The State of Public Education in New Orleans: 2010 Report*, p. 23.

29. Susan Finch, "Orleans School Board Approves Lusher Charter Application; Unity Dissipates Quickly at First Post-Storm Meeting," *Times-Picayune*, September 16, 2005.

30. "About 7,500 Orleans School Workers Face Loss of Jobs," *The Advocate* (Baton Rouge), December 2, 2005.

31. Louisiana Department of Education, *Annual Financial and Statistical Report: 2004–2005*.

32. Steve Ritea, "Teachers Union Left without Contract; School Board Lets Pact Expire, Era Ends," *Times-Picayune*, July 1, 2006.

33. The detailed perspective of the teachers' union is best presented in United Teachers of New Orleans, *"National Model" or Flawed Approach? The Post-Katrina New Orleans Public Schools* (2006) (http://education.tulane.edu/NationalModelFlawedApproach.htm).

34. Recovery School District, *School Facilities Master Plan for Orleans Parish: 2008* (www.rsdla.net/InfoGlance/Rebuilding_schools/SFMPOP.aspx).

35. Darran Simon, "Hopes for Schools Put to Test in N.O.; 'Quick Start' Picks Are Expected Today," *Times-Picayune*, September 12, 2007.

36. Cindy Chang, "$1.8 Billion Approved for N.O. Schools; Accord with FEMA Called Historic," *Times-Picayune*, August 26, 2010.

37. Louisiana Department of Education, *Resource Allocation (Revenue/Expenditure Data): 2009* (www.louisianaschools.net/lde/finance/1793.html).

38. Louisiana Department of Education, *Third Allocation of HERA: Immediate Aid to Restart Schools, Public Schools, 2009* (www.louisianaschools.net/lde/uploads/11248.pdf).

39. Michael Schwam-Baird and Laura Mogg, "Is Education Reform in New Orleans Working? A Few Facts Swimming in a Sea of Unknowns," *Loyola University Journal of Public Interest Law* (May 2010).

40. Texas Education Agency, *An Analysis of Academic Performance of Students Affected by Hurricane Katrina* (March 2010) (http://ritter.tea.state.tx.us/student.assessment/resources/studies/KatrinaAnalysis2010.pdf).

4

Delivering High-Quality, Accessible Health Care: The Rise of Community Centers

Karen DeSalvo

In August 2005, Hurricane Katrina unleashed a series of catastrophic levee breaks that resulted in widespread, devastating flooding in the greater New Orleans area. The city was under a mandatory evacuation order for thirty days, and the water inundated the infrastructure to such an extent that the health sector was completely disrupted across the continuum of care, from basic 911 services to specialty care to hospital services.[1] Hospital and ambulatory facilities in the city were severely damaged, some beyond repair, and many remained closed for months. For weeks, only three of sixteen hospitals remained in even limited operation, and they were in the suburbs adjacent to New Orleans. Complicating matters, the disaster impacted a significantly disadvantaged population burdened by chronic illness, a high rate of uninsurance, and poverty.[2] The public hospital was unable to open for fourteen months, leaving hundreds of thousands without access to their principal source of care, including both those who had successfully evacuated and those left behind. Though horrific in scope and impact, the widespread devastation of the health care infrastructure gave the New Orleans region an unprecedented opportunity to redesign a major American health sector from the ground up.[3]

As local providers and organizations of all types responded to the acute health crises and urgent primary care needs of the city's population, the community began to consider a policy framework that would support the vision of a more patient-centered and effective health sector than the one decimated by Katrina. Broad reform was discussed, but inevitably attention was focused on the needs of the safety net to serve the low-income population, given that more than half of the population's health care was supported through some sort of public program.[4] The efforts at rebuilding and redesign began early and in earnest, with stakeholders working simultaneously to restore services and to develop a policy framework that would guide and support the new vision and infrastructure. The redesigned health system that was envisioned was to be a high-quality, cost-effective system founded on a distributed network of community health sites that used health information technology to improve the safety and efficacy of care. An important point was that the newly designed health system would need to be supported by a sustainable, flexible financing model that would provide for community-based primary care and give even the most vulnerable better access and choice.[5]

The community moved forward quickly and successfully. Five years after Hurricane Katrina, the city was able to boast an innovative, modernized community health network providing neighborhood-based access to quality care for everyone, including the most vulnerable populations in the region. This chapter provides an overview of the series of deliberate policy actions and grassroots activities that worked to build access to a high-quality health care system in the New Orleans area. In addition, the chapter provides insight into the lessons learned in establishing this network—including those related to the significant local, state, and federal barriers to developing quality, sustainable primary care in the United States, particularly for low-income populations—and discusses the challenges that this innovative system faces in spite of its success and broad support.

The State of Pre-Katrina Health Care

The rationale for redesigning the health care system of the New Orleans region following Hurricane Katrina arose from the system's longstanding poor performance and the poor health outcomes of the population. United Health Foundation consistently placed Louisiana at the very bottom of its ranking of quality of health care by state for the decade leading up to the storm. Health system rankings by the Commonwealth Fund for overall performance with respect to quality, access, and effectiveness demonstrated recurring poor performance, irrespective of payer. The quality of care for the Medicare population in Louisiana was the lowest in the nation and the cost of care was the highest.[6] Though specific data for the New Orleans region were scarce when planning commenced, the region represented approximately 25 percent of the state's population at the time of Hurricane Katrina; given similarities in population and system structure, planners extrapolated state statistics to cover the region.

The root causes of the region's poor performance and poor outcomes were thought to be related to the health system's infrastructure, including the low density of primary care physicians per population, high density of specialty care physicians, and higher number of hospital beds per capita than the national average.[7] Access to primary care was an issue for low-income uninsured populations in particular. The population served, which had high rates of chronic illness, a high percentage of minorities, and low socioeconomic status, was at high risk for poor health.[8] As in most places in the United States in 2005, technology was minimally deployed and providers relied largely on paper medical records.

Weak and Centralized Delivery Model

The greater New Orleans area, like the rest of the state, had relied on a centralized safety-net model for care of low-income, uninsured, and largely minority populations. At the center of the greater New Orleans health system for the past 275 years was the state-run public hospital, locally known as Charity Hospital.[9] In the year before the storm, the hospital had 264,800 visits to one of its seventy downtown hospital-based clinics, but most were to the emergency department.[10] Most of the clinics offered specialty services supporting graduate medical education for health professional programs in the region. Access to care, particularly primary care, was limited because of the hospital's central location, and years of chronic underfunding led to the closure of clinics and a reduction in service hours. Metrics of quality were generally positive for those patients who entered the system.[11] However, many patients reported experiencing fragmented care delivered in clinics located downtown, whose operating hours generally were more convenient for physicians and trainees than for patients.[12]

Limited and Mismatched Financing

The means of financing care for the uninsured in Louisiana had become increasingly dependent on the federal Medicaid program called the Disproportionate Share Hospital (DSH) Program, funds for which were used as an alternative to traditional Medicaid funds to finance the public hospital system as a source of care for the uninsured.[13] That originally was an advantageous approach because Louisiana was able to access a significant amount of DSH funding due to the high burden of uninsured residents in the state. In addition, because of the state's low per capita income, the federal government funded the vast majority of the program after a state match. Federal rules for DSH funding require it to be used only to support hospital care, not primary care. In Louisiana, the state had preferentially applied these funds to support care in the statewide public hospital system.

Because of the reliance on DSH revenue to support the care of low-income populations, Louisiana did not develop programs to expand additional safety-net financing options, such as Medicaid. The Medicaid program in Louisiana has maintained strict eligibility criteria for adults, requiring an adult to be a parent or to be disabled and to have an income of less than $1,656 a year for a family of two (parent/caregiver and child)—criteria that mean that many working poor are uninsured.[14] Their income is too high to meet Medicaid standards, yet most are employed by small businesses, most of which cannot afford to offer health insurance to their employees.

Shortage of Community Health Centers

Because the state relied on DSH and the public hospital system for care of uninsured and low-income people, it had failed to develop policies and programs to support primary care in community health centers, resulting in a lack of primary care infrastructure, a critical element in low-cost, high-quality health systems. Nationally, such community health centers, formally known as Federally Qualified Health Centers (FQHCs), are funded through the federal "330" grant funding program, which is administered by the Health Resources and Services Administration (HRSA). These centers receive enhanced reimbursement from public payers, a core grant to aid with supportive services, and other advantages that support them in providing health care for low-income populations. Nationally, such centers are a major source of safety-net primary care, serving 17 million people.[15] Louisiana has fewer sites per capita than other markets of similar size. Not only does that limit accessible neighborhood-based primary care, but it also means that the state is not availing itself of all available federal funding to support primary care.

High-Risk Population

The city's population was disadvantaged on a number of fronts. At the time of Hurricane Katrina, 44 percent of the New Orleans population lived on an income below 200 percent of the federal poverty level, or $37,000 for a family of four.[16] Rates of chronic illness such as obesity, diabetes, heart disease, and asthma were among the highest in the nation, and mortality from chronic disease also exceeded the national average. The area was also noted for its wide health disparities by race and socioeconomic status. Louisiana was ranked by the United Health Foundation in the bottom three states in the nation each year from 1990 to 2005 in terms of the overall health of the population.

Consensus on a Patient-Centered, Prevention-Oriented, Community-Based Health Care System

Health policy planning for a redesigned health sector began as early as October 2005, when a broad group of stakeholders came together under the leadership of the U.S. Public Health Service. A series of other planning entities carried the concepts forward, further elucidating key elements and taking into consideration the needed changes in financing to support a redesign of the health sector. Their vision and goals were based on strong evidence and focused on the need to move away from a hospital-centered safety-net model to a distributed primary care system. Communities served by systems anchored by primary care provision have better health outcomes, reduced disparities in health, better efficiency, and lower cost.[17] The major recommendations from the final blueprint of the Louisiana Health Care Redesign Collaborative included the following:

—Redesign health care delivery to create "medical homes" as its foundation.

—Adopt interoperable, standards-based technology to support practices aimed at reducing waste and improving safety and quality.

—Create the Louisiana Health Care Quality Forum to convene payers, providers, consumers, and businesses with the goal of implementing strategies to improve health care quality.

—Ensure meaningful choice by expanding insurance coverage through increased public and private funding.

Community Engagement and Funding to Build Community Health Capacity

Progress in realizing this vision of community-based infrastructure for community health care has been dramatic, and its success rests largely in the grassroots efforts that started just after Katrina in the very early days of rescue and recovery. A series of makeshift care sites cropped up across the greater New Orleans region, established by volunteers to meet the needs of those who were not evacuated, those who returned quickly, and first responders. The volunteers began with meager resources, practicing basic urgent care wherever they were needed, in tents, mobile vans, and borrowed buildings—wherever they could find space. They worked without power, potable water, or sewerage.[18] Over time, some of the sites evolved into permanent facilities that were independently operated by a broad range of academic, government, and faith-based organizations, and some became federally qualified health centers and free clinics. This volunteer disaster response created the foundation for a new community health care network that is now an important source of care for a population that historically had relied on the public hospital and emergency rooms for primary care.

Initially, the operations of the community health care sites were largely supported by volunteers and private philanthropy. The sites received their first significant support from an emergency social service block grant to Louisiana from the U.S. Department of Health and Human Services Administration for Children and Families, which contributed $21.7 million of the $220 million received by the state for providing primary care and mental health services to the greater New Orleans region.[19] That financial infusion was enough to maintain necessary care for the population for a year while the policy efforts continued and the design of a more sustainable financing system could be completed. Immediately following issuance of the Louisiana Health Care Redesign Collaborative report, the state of Louisiana requested a waiver to allow flexibility in the use of Medicaid disproportionate share funds to support expansion of coverage as well as gap coverage for the community health network. Negotiations between the state and federal government on the proposed changes then fell apart.[20]

Volunteers from the Tulane School of Medicine faculty and house staff provide care at a makeshift clinic in September 2005.

When the state government's plans for health care financing were unsuccessful, the community of providers worked collaboratively to secure other sources of funding while long-term financing could be structured. Community health providers jointly testified at a hearing of the House Oversight and Investigations Subcommittee of the Energy and Commerce Committee of Congress in March 2007.[21] During that hearing, providers requested the allocation of $100 million to support community health care for the uninsured in the greater New Orleans area. Providers also asked for workforce development support and a partnership with the federal government to ensure responsible use of the funds and to work toward sustainability.

In May 2007, following the hearing, the U.S. Department of Health and Human Services (HHS) established a special grant program to allocate $100 million to support the community health network and allow continued expansion to meet the population's needs. That primary care access and stabilization grant (PCASG) was awarded to the Louisiana Department of Health and Hospitals to support the development and operation of a community-based care network providing primary care

The entrance to one of the new primary care sites, the Tulane Community Health Center at Covenant House.

and behavioral health services.[22] The Louisiana Public Health Institute served as the local administrator and worked with the community and providers to create an innovative model of delivery supported by a new payment method that enabled the rapid development of a high-quality, affordable, patient-centered network. All providers who shared a common mission to maintain an open door policy, offering access to services for patients regardless of their ability to pay, were eligible to participate, thus establishing an inclusive approach to the development of the primary care network.

The PCASG funding was intended to act as bridge financing until coverage expansion could be enacted in Louisiana. However, in spite of aggressive activity to achieve that goal, an expansion program was never implemented. With funding for the network of community clinics ending, the federal and state governments acted to protect the important new infrastructure not only because it was considered an innovative model but because its capacity would be needed when coverage was expanded under the Affordable Care Act. To protect the community health infrastructure, in the fall of 2010, the state and federal governments, with significant input from local government and community leaders, negotiated a solution to allow traditional hospital financing to be redirected to support the care of the uninsured in the new community health care sites. The financing provides a bridge until 2014, when health care coverage will be increased through expansion of Medicaid or the private insurance exchange.

Concurrent with the $100 million grant for primary care, HHS also provided $35 million in funding to expand and retain the primary care and mental health workforce to support the community health care sites. The resulting organization, called the Greater New Orleans Health Services Corps, was given an additional boost by a $35 million professional workforce supply grant. This program allowed organizations to provide incentives to recruit health workers back to the area. It built on a $15 million professional workforce grant program funded in March 2006 to bolster the numbers of the health care workforce, which was reduced by the storm. These programs have successfully recruited and retained hundreds of primary care and mental health clinicians, and they have been critical to the successful development of the community health network.

Innovations in the Community Health Care Model

The New Orleans community health centers are remarkable, and not only for the speed with which they were developed following the catastrophe of Katrina and the intense community involvement in their development. They are considered innovative by national thought leaders because of their implementation of key health care delivery elements, including the patient-centered medical home model; integration of primary care and mental health services; a balance of competition and cooperation between providers; and a flexible payment method.

The successful implementation and continuation of this model can be attributed largely to the flexible payment method. Since its inception, providers have been paid a prospective, multi-month lump sum that was risk adjusted for patient age and gender and type of service (primary care or mental health) provided for the entire population of patients linked to the clinic. That allowed for stable budgets and allowed the providers to develop cost-effective models focused on serving their population as a whole rather than the individual patient who presented at the clinic. The limited risk-adjustment method used in the program encouraged network providers to take on those with higher risk. Also, the payment structure supported team-based care, allowing providers to include social workers and provide legal assistance and other enabling services, such as health education and support for patients referred for services outside of the primary care medical home (PCMH), to assist the population served in achieving better health outcomes.

On the basis of lessons learned from this model, the state Medicaid program is moving ahead with supplemental payments for medical home status through its traditional and newly emerging managed Medicaid programs. In addition, the major commercial player in Louisiana, Blue Cross/Blue Shield (BCBSLA), stepped forward in autumn of 2010 to recognize the network's innovative service delivery system and began providing incentive payments to providers who achieve recognition as patient-centered medical homes, including the newly developed community health sites. All of these payment methods and incentive programs are moving away from volume-based models to support instead the quality of care and the medical home model implemented by community health providers. This broadening of the new payment system will mean sustainability for the local community health centers.

Evaluation and Outcomes: Quality, Accessible Care for Low-Income Patients

The newly developed community health network has been regarded as a success at both the local and national levels and by external evaluation.[23] Early assessments—which include reviews of access to care, quality of care, patient experience, and cost-effectiveness—show promising results.

FIGURE 4-1. Greater New Orleans Community Health Centers after Hurricane Katrina[a]

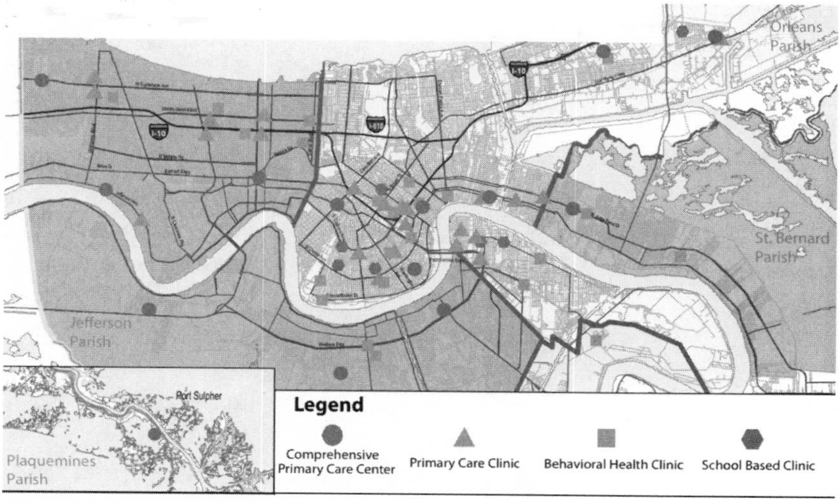

a. Dental clinics not included.

Access

The network has met the goal of increasing access to care. Since data collection began in September 2007 until September 2010, there was a dramatic increase in community health providers' capacity to provide care for the population, with a 25 percent increase in the number of sites available. At its peak, the network included ninety-three care sites in the four-parish area of greater New Orleans (see figure 4-1). The sites vary in the comprehensiveness of the care offered, the services available on site, and staffing and structure. Together, they represent an innovative approach to filling geographic and other gaps in care using techniques such as mobile medical units, school health centers, and faith-based programs for mental health.[24]

The number of patients seen at the sites also has grown steadily since the program began. According to data from the Louisiana Public Health Institute, between September 2007 and September 2010, more than 329,320 individuals have sought care at one of the sites.[25] An important point is that this newly emerged community health network is serving the minority, low-income, and uninsured population most likely to lack

TABLE 4-1.   **Characteristics of Population Served by the Greater New Orleans Community Health Providers[a]**

Characteristic	Number (percent)
Total population	329,320 (100)[b]
Age	
0–18 years	113,681 (34.5)
19–64 years	204,197 (62.0)
65 years and older	10,953 (3.3)
Gender	
Female	178,659 (54.3)
Male	150,294 (45.6)
Transgender	23 (0.0)
Race	
Black	140,118 (42.5)
White	68,600 (20.8)
Asian	3,950 (1.2)
Native American	226 (0.1)
Other	12,033 (3.7)
Ethnicity	
Non-Hispanic	183,159 (55.6)
Hispanic	21,257 (6.5)
Unknown	124,904 (37.9)
Insurance status	
Uninsured	149,376 (45.4)
Medicaid	79,778 (24.2)
Medicare	9,557 (2.9)
Commercial	49,493 (15.3)
More than one insurer	37,008 (11.2)

Source: Maria Ludwick, Louisiana Public Health Institute, internal data, on file with author. Adapted with permission.
a. September 21, 2007, to September 20, 2010.
b. Totals may not all add up to 329,320 or 100 percent due to missing information.

adequate health care and to have health problems (see table 4-1). This is a critical success for the community health clinics because they were designed to serve as a safety net to provide care for the most vulnerable and for those who received care through the public hospital system before Hurricane Katrina.[26] The respondents to the Commonwealth Fund Evaluation survey had a higher burden of medical illness than the average

American,[27] but less than one-third of survey respondents reported that they went without needed health care because of cost. The national figure, in contrast, was 41 percent of adults.

Community surveys performed by the Kaiser Family Foundation in 2006 and 2010 did not target health center users but did ask questions about access to them. Their findings demonstrate that more people reported having a usual source of care other than the emergency room (73 percent, up from 66 percent);[28] more people reported having a clinic in their neighborhood that offered free or reduced-price care (32 percent, up from 14 percent in 2008); and more people reported having used such a clinic (12 percent, up from 4 percent in 2008).[29]

Quality

These care sites are recognized for their quality by the National Committee for Quality Assurance (NCQA), a national entity that recognizes quality primary care, which employs evidence-based medicine, ensures good access to care, uses a population health approach, and coordinates care for patients.[30] As of 2010, thirty-seven of the network's community health sites had been recognized. A payment program that was part of the overall PCASG program gave bonus payments to providers who achieved recognition as a PCMH, dramatically facilitating the clinics' achievement of that status. In March 2010, the PCASG participating organizations—the Louisiana Public Health Institute and the Louisiana Health Care Quality Forum—received one of the NCQA's annual health quality awards in recognition of their work in building a high-quality primary care and behavioral health care network.[31]

Patient Experience

The Commonwealth Survey of community health center users also assessed patient experience. Seventy-four percent of New Orleans community clinic respondents reported confidence in the quality of their care; in contrast, only 39 percent of adults nationwide did so. Forty percent had an "excellent" experience; 90 percent reported better access to care; and 75 percent reported excellent patient-clinician communications.[32]

Cost-Effectiveness

The PCASG program has been regarded as both fiscally responsible and successful in developing a high-quality, cost-effective, and innovative health care foundation for the greater New Orleans area. Two reports on the program by the U.S. Government Accountability Office found that funding is responsibly used and that the program is achieving its original goals.[33]

An ongoing outcome evaluation of PCASG funding being conducted by the University of California at San Francisco is to be completed in 2011. This evaluation will give better information about the cost-effectiveness of services provided across the continuum of care. However, half of the population served is uninsured, and it will be impossible to accurately track its use of the health system in the absence of a unique identifying number. Nonetheless, the per-person cost to provide care for the nearly 150,000 uninsured patients seen each year is approximately $223. Assuming that 25 percent of those individuals would have visited the emergency room once annually, at an average cost of $1,000 for an emergency room visit, the program saved $112,032,000. The return on investment was safely $12 million.

Coordination and Integration of Health Services

The health centers are moving toward other structural changes aimed at improving efficiency and opening up opportunities for funding besides insurance payments. The organizations have developed alliances aimed at coordinating services and reducing redundancy. Part of the impetus for that is the recognition that horizontal links—including support for patients with complex or chronic conditions and those with mental health challenges—can improve efficiency and patient care. They have established a formal consortium to improve their collective effectiveness and to work cooperatively toward sustainability. The new organization, 504HealthNet, which currently includes seventeen of the new community health safety-net providers that have emerged since Hurricane Katrina, represents the majority of care providers in the community health safety net. Individually, these medical homes provide sophisticated, high-quality care, but they need to be integrated with one another and with the larger health system to optimize outcomes.[34] Integration becomes especially important as the broader New Orleans health care infrastructure is rebuilt with the investment of more than 1 billion dollars for a new public hospital, a hospital in New Orleans East, and a facility in St. Bernard Parish. The focus should remain on the care of the broader population, with efficiencies gained through shared planning, coordination of services, and quality programs. Added funding and technical infrastructure support for programs that integrate services horizontally and vertically will continue to be needed to support this network.

Implications for Future Policy

The development of the new distributed primary care network as the foundation for the redesigned health care system for post-Katrina New Orleans has been swift, but the security of the network and its innovations remains a challenge. Although some of the challenges are specific to the policy framework of Louisiana, others are common to other areas of the United States and to the world. Sustaining this investment and its continuing evolution will require ongoing payment policy innovations by government and private payers as well as broadening of the definition of FQHCs and workforce training to prepare skilled medical home teams.

Need for Sustained Gap Funding for the Primary Care Safety Net in the United States

The ideal long-term revenue stream will mirror those of the most robust community health networks and will be a mix of public and private funds, including gap funding for the care of uninsured individuals. Significant gap funding is needed for the community health providers in the New Orleans network until 2014, when health reform legislation is expected to take effect, extending insurance coverage to an estimated 80 percent of the population. Health care centers in the safety net, like those in New Orleans, will continue to need ongoing gap funding because under the current federal framework, the Affordable Care Act, there will still be substantial numbers of uninsured and underinsured people who will rely on the centers for care.[35] In addition, the centers will care for patients with greater medical and social needs, which require resources in addition to those provided by typical reimbursements. Enhanced funding to care for such high-risk populations will be an ongoing need for health centers, just as it is for hospitals.

A number of health care centers are moving toward recognition as federally qualified health centers, since historically that is the major tool available to the state and the federal government to provide additional funding and structural support to the low-income, socioeconomically disadvantaged, and working poor population. Such health centers can be an invaluable resource in the wake of disaster.[36] Of the current community health centers, only a limited number have obtained the FQHC designation, reflecting the larger picture in Louisiana. Competition is intense for FQHC grants. Unfortunately, some of the major providers in the network of community health primary care providers are ineligible under current rules, and others are so new that they are not able to meet the many requirements. Both federal and state support for this transition will be needed; such support could include technical assistance and operational support through enhanced reimbursement to providers in this valuable network.

Workforce Development

The local policy efforts aimed at addressing the historical shortage of primary care and community health professionals have largely been successful, although shortages persist. As in much of the nation, ongoing loan repayment programs aimed at recruiting and retaining community health professionals will be essential. In addition, expansion of health professional training in the community health setting may help to pique interest in community health as a career. Federal programs called for in the Affordable Care Act, such as teaching health centers, may help to improve interest and provide opportunities to expose physicians to community health practice.[37] The collaborative nature of the network in New Orleans, particularly between academia and community organizations, means that a number of the providers in the New Orleans network may meet eligibility criteria for this program.

Conclusion

Even with only early results, the network has been called a model for the nation because it has demonstrated success in developing patient-centered medical home facilities, integrating primary care and mental health services, and creating new payment models to support team-based, innovative primary care services. In addition, it has integrated workforce training and research, expanding economic opportunity and innovation in real world settings. Perhaps most significant, it has demonstrated itself to be a reliable mechanism for rapidly expanding capacity to provide primary care services for uninsured populations in a cost-effective and high-quality manner—something the entire nation will need to meet the expectations of health reform.

Following the flooding of New Orleans and surrounding parishes, a unique convergence of community and policy efforts resulted in an empowered and forward-thinking health sector reform movement that has led to transformational change. What had been the most ineffective health care system in the United States has become one that can serve as a model for others. The system has expanded from one that had only a single major safety-net primary care provider to a collaborative of more than twenty-five organizations that serve the community. The care provided within the system is better than that available before Katrina; more important, patients report receiving better care than the average American. This health network is demonstrating innovations including team-based care; successful integration of mental health and primary care services; attention to nonmedical aspects of health status, such as housing and literacy; and new ways to pay for primary care. From the devastation of Hurricane Katrina, a model of community health care has emerged for the nation.

Notes

1. Ruth E. Berggren and Tyler J. Curiel, "After the Storm: Health Care Infrastructure in Post-Katrina New Orleans," *New England Journal of Medicine* 354, no. 15 (2006): 1549–52; Karen B. DeSalvo, "Letter from New Orleans," *Annals of Internal Medicine* 143, no. 12 (December 20, 2005): 905–06; Karen B. DeSalvo, James Moises, and Joseph Uddo, "The Nine O'Clock Meeting," *Health Affairs* 25, no. 2 (2006): 483.
2. Louisiana State University Public Policy Lab, "Louisiana Health Insurance Survey 2005" (2005).
3. Karen B. DeSalvo, Paul Muntner, and Claude Earl Fox, "Community-Based Health Care for 'the City That Care Forgot,'" *Journal of Urban Health* 82, no. 4 (2005): 520–03.
4. Louisiana State University Public Policy Lab, "Louisiana Health Insurance Survey 2005."
5. Karen B. DeSalvo, "New Orleans Health Care after Katrina: One Year Out," *Johns Hopkins Advanced Studies in Medicine* 6, no. 7 (2006); "A Redesigned System of Care for the New Orleans Region," Louisiana Health Care Redesign Collaborative, Louisiana Secretary of Health Fred Cerise, chairman (2006) (www.allhealth.org/briefingmaterials/ConceptPaperforaRedesignedHealthCareSystem%E2%80%93CMSConceptPaper-710.pdf); Jane Stoever and Leslie Champlin, "Graham Center Article and Katrina Forum," *Annals of Family Medicine* 4, no. 2 (2006): 179–80.
6. Katherine Baicker and Amitabh Chandra, "Medicare Spending, the Physician Workforce, and Beneficiaries' Quality of Care," *Health Affairs* 7 (2004).
7. Ibid.; Karen B. DeSalvo, Benjamin Sachs, and L. Lee Hamm, "Health Care Infrastructure in Post-Katrina New Orleans: A Status Report," *American Journal of the Medical Sciences* 336, no. 2 (2008): 197–200.

8. Robin Rudowitz and others, "Health Care in New Orleans before and after Hurricane Katrina," *Health Affairs* 25, no. 5 (2006): w393–406.

9. Ibid.

10. LSU Health Sciences Center, "LSU Health Annual Report 2004" (2004) (www.lsuhospitals.org/About_LSU-HCSD/annual_reports.htm).

11. Ronald Horswell and others, "Disease Management Programs for the Underserved," *Disease Management* 11, no. 3 (2010): 145–52.

12. "Low-Income Uninsured Focus Groups Final Report: Health Insurance Flexibility and Accountability Waiver" (2004) (www.shadac.org/files/2004_LA_FG_Findings.pdf).

13. Rudowitz and others, "Health Care in New Orleans before and after Hurricane Katrina.

14. Louisiana State University Public Policy Lab, "Louisiana Health Insurance Survey 2005."

15. John K. Iglehart, "Spreading the Safety Net: Obstacles to the Expansion of Community Health Centers," *New England Journal of Medicine* 358, no. 13 (2008): 1321–23.

16. Rudowitz and others, "Health Care in New Orleans before and after Hurricane Katrina.

17. Leiyu Shi and others, "The Relationship between Primary Care, Income Inequality, and Mortality in U.S. States, 1980–1995," *Journal of the American Board of Family Medicine* 16 (2003): 412–22; Barbara Starfield, Leiyu Shi, and James Macinko, "Contribution of Primary Care to Health Systems and Health," *Milbank Quarterly* 83, no. 3 (2005): 457–502; George Burgess and others, "Straight Talk New Approaches in Healthcare," *Modern Healthcare* 36 (25) (2006): 57–60.

18. DeSalvo, "Letter from New Orleans"; Anjali Niyogi and others, "Restoring and Reforming Ambulatory Services and Internal Medicine Training in the Aftermath of Hurricane Katrina," *American Journal of the Medical Sciences* 332, no. 5 (2006): 289–91.

19. U.S. Government Accountability Office, "Federal Grants Have Helped Health Care Organizations Provide Primary Care but Challenges Remain" (Government Printing Office, 2009), p. 48.

20. Frederick P. Cerise and Dave A. Chokshi, "Orienting Health Care Reform around Universal Access," *Archives of Internal Medicine* 169, no. 20 (2009): 1830–32.

21. *Post-Katrina Health Care: Continuing Concerns and Immediate Needs in the New Orleans Region: Hearing before the Subcommittee on Oversight and Investigations of the Committee on Energy and Commerce, House of Representatives*, 110 Cong., 1 sess., March 13, 2007. Prepared statements and questions can be found at http://frwebgate.access.gpo.gov/cgi-bin/getdoc.cgi?dbname=110_house_hearings&docid=f:36572.pdf and at http://ftp.resource.org/gpo.gov/hearings/110h/36572.pdf.

22. U.S. Government Accountability Office, "Federal Grants Have Helped Health Care Organizations."

23. Jessica Zigmond, "Gaining in New Orleans: With Help from a Federal Grant, Wounded City Builds a Model Primary-Care System," *Modern Healthcare* 40, no. 3 (2010): 6–7.

24. "Greater New Orleans Community Health," Louisiana Public Health Institute (www.gnocommunity.org)

25. Maria Ludwick, Louisiana Public Health Institute, internal data, on file with author.

26. Kaiser Family Foundation, "New Orleans Three Years after the Storm: The Second Kaiser Post-Katrina Survey, 2008" (2008).

27. Michelle M. Doty and others, "Coming out of Crisis: Patient Experiences in Primary Care in New Orleans, Four Years Post-Katrina—Findings from the Commonwealth Fund 2009 Survey of Clinic Patients in New Orleans" (Commonwealth Fund, 2010).

28. Kaiser Family Foundation, "New Orleans Three Years after the Storm."

29. Kaiser Family Foundation, "New Orleans Five Years after the Storm" (2010).

30. National Committee for Quality Assurance, "Patient-Centered Medical Home" (2010) (www.ncqa.org/tabid/631/Default.aspx).

31. National Committee for Quality Assurance, "NCQA Honors Health Quality Leaders, Celebrates 20 Years of Improving Health Care Quality," news release, March 4, 2010 (www.ncqa.org/tabid/1145/Default.aspx).

32. Doty, "Coming out of Crisis."

33. U.S. Government Accountability Office, *Federal Grants Have Helped Health Care Organizations*; Debra Draper, *Hurricane Katrina: CMS and HRSA Assistance to Sustain Primary Care Gains in the Greater New Orleans Area* (U.S. Government Accountability Office, 2010).

34. Diane R. Rittenhouse, Stephen M. Shortell, and Elliot S. Fisher, "Primary Care and Accountable Care: Two Essential Elements of Delivery-System Reform," *New England Journal of Medicine* 361 (2009): 2301–03; Elliot S. Fisher, "Building a Medical Neighborhood for the Medical Home," *New England Journal of Medicine* 359, no. 12 (2008): 1202–05.

35. Mark A. Hall, "Focus on Health Care Reform: Approaching Universal Coverage with Better Safety-Net Programs for the Uninsured," *Yale Journal of Health Policy, Law, and Ethics* 11, no. 1 (2011): 9–19; Mark A. Hall, "Rethinking Safety-Net Access for the Uninsured," *New England Journal of Medicine* 364, no. 1 (2011): 7–9.

36. Leiyu Shi and Patricia B. Collins, "Public-Private Partnerships in Community Health Centers: Addressing the Needs of Underserved Populations," *Organizational Ethics* 4, no. 1 (2007): 35–42.

37. Richard E. Rieselbach, Byron J. Crouse, and John G. Frohna, "Teaching Primary Care in Community Health Centers: Addressing the Workforce Crisis for the Underserved," *Annals of Internal Medicine* 152, no. 2 (2010): 118–22.

5

Criminal Justice Reforms

Nadiene Van Dyke, Jon Wool, and Luceia LeDoux

Another hurricane is here! This time . . . it's raining bullets.

—Homemade sign held aloft during
2007's March for Survival

"Stop the Killing," "No More Excuses," and, simply, "Enough" demanded the signs held high during the March for Survival on January 11, 2007.[1] Three thousand people filed through the streets of downtown New Orleans, a cathartic demonstration by a citizenry weary of loss. Suited businessmen, groups of uniformed schoolchildren, mothers with infants in arms, elderly couples, and anti-crime activists converged on City Hall from diverse neighborhoods all over the city. Overflowing the steps of City Hall, march organizers commanded the microphone as stone-faced elected officials stood by silently.

Organized in response to the murders of Helen Hill, a local activist, filmmaker, and young mother, and Dinerral Shavers, snare drummer for the Hot 8 Brass Band and a high school band teacher, the unprecedented march sent a clear message that New Orleans' citizens' tolerance for crime had reached its limit.[2] At the same time, residents from neighborhoods in which human loss was a frequent, tragic occurrence reminded the city that every life counted, laying bare violent crime's class and racial divide.[3]

Anger over violent crime had been simmering for months. New Orleans, relatively crime free immediately following Hurricane Katrina, was rapidly regaining its position as the "murder capital" of the United States.[4] Between June 2006, when five youths were gunned down in a single attack in Central City, and January 2007, when Hill and Shavers were murdered, shootings and killings rose in frequency, again becoming a routine part of the city's landscape. Elected officials seemed unable to solve—and in some cases appeared unresponsive to—the problem.

Yet a movement was gaining momentum, both outside and within city government. The March for Survival was the most visible but far from the only element in the growing citizen response to rising violence. Between 2006 and 2008 a growing number of advocacy and civic groups placed public safety and justice on their agendas and demanded a role in improving the city's response to crime.[5]

Even as citizens dedicated themselves with impressive—and unprecedented—energy to demanding a safer and more just city, the criminal justice system struggled to respond effectively. New Orleans' criminal justice system had long been dominated by the political and financial interests of individual agencies under leaders who operated autonomously. The result was inefficient, ineffective, and unfair practices. Meaningful reform would require the development of a truly integrated system that employs proven practices and is guided by empirical analysis. While the chaos wrought by the storm provided a unique opportunity to reinvent a troubled criminal justice system, doing so would require a major change in the professional culture in which the New Orleans criminal justice agencies operated.

The New Orleans Criminal Justice System before Hurricane Katrina

New Orleans' reputation as a violent city was firmly established long before Hurricane Katrina. Since 1999 the city's murder rate had climbed steadily, and by 2005 it was 65.3 per 100,000 people, more than five times the national rate for comparably sized cities (see box 5-1).[6]

At the same time, 60 percent of arrests were for low-level offenses, and 67 percent of convictions were for simple drug possession, primarily of marijuana. Excessive numbers of low-level cases placed huge demands on the system and reduced resources available to address violent crime. The

**B O X   5 - 1 .   A Statistical Snapshot:
The New Orleans Criminal Justice System before the Storm**

New Orleans' criminal justice system operated ineffectively and inefficiently, both individually and as a system. Consider these pre-Katrina facts:

—In a city with a population just over 450,000, the police department made over 90,000 arrests in the year before the storm.[a]

—The United States had the highest incarceration rate in the world, and New Orleans had the highest incarceration rate in the country, double that of any other large city (1,480 per 100,000 residents).[b]

—New Orleans was the thirty-eighth largest city in the United States in 2005, yet Orleans Parish Prison (OPP) was the ninth-largest jail complex in the United States, housing an average of 6,846 people a day (including state and federal prisoners and prisoners from other parishes).[c]

—On any given day, 60 percent of OPP prisoners were being held on warrants for failure to appear or pay fees or on traffic or municipal charges.[d]

—For the period October 2003 through September 2004, only 5 percent of convictions in criminal district court were for violent offenses.[e]

—New Orleans had more police officers per capita than any other large U.S. city.[f]

—New Orleans spent approximately one-third of its general fund on public safety.[g]

a. Barry Gerharz and Seung Hong, "Down by Law: Orleans Parish Prison before and after Katrina," *Dollars and Sense* (March-April 2006) (www.dollarsandsense.org/archives/2006/0306gerharzhong.html).

b. ACLU National Prison Project, "Abandoned and Abused: Orleans Parish Prisoners in the Wake of Katrina" (2006) (www.aclu.org/prisoners-rights/abandoned-abused-complete-report).

c. Despite its name, Orleans Parish Prison is not a prison but a local jail. As such, it houses primarily individuals awaiting adjudication, along with some persons sentenced to less than one year and others alleged to have violated probation or parole. However, in an arrangement that is atypical in the nation but not uncommon in Louisiana, it also houses persons sentenced to multi-year prison terms under contract with the state department of corrections. David Morton, "Empire Falls: The Rise and Decline of the New Orleans Jail," *New Republic*, August 14 and 21, 2006 (www.tnr.com/article/politics/empire-falls); Gerharz and Hong, "Down by Law," ranked the jail as the eighth largest. See also "Orleans Parish Prison: A Big Jail with Big Problems," ACLU Fact Sheet, January 11, 2006 (www.aclu.org/prisoners-rights/orleans-parish-prison-big-jail-big-problems). For city rankings by population, see www.infoplease.com/ipa/A0763098.html.

d. Gerharz and Hong, "Down by Law."

e. Metropolitan Crime Commission, "Performance of the New Orleans Criminal Justice System 2003–2004" (August 2005) (www.metropolitancrimecommission.org/html/research.html).

f. Bureau of Justice Statistics, "Census of State and Local Law Enforcement Agencies" (2004) (http://bjs.ojp.usdoj.gov/content/pub/pdf/csllea04.pdf).

g. City of New Orleans, "Comprehensive Annual Financial Report" (December 2004) (www.nola.gov/Portals/BureauofAccounting/portal.aspx).

vast majority of those arrested were poor and therefore entitled to representation by a public defender, creating a huge burden on the chronically underfunded public defense system.[7] For those held on state misdemeanor or felony charges, it typically took sixty days for the police and the district attorney to move a case from arrest to a decision to prosecute, something many jurisdictions achieve in a day. The Metropolitan Crime Commission attributed the lengthy time frame to a "lack of communication and cooperation between the NOPD [New Orleans Police Department] and the district attorney's office."[8]

Orleans Parish Prison (OPP) had a long history of substandard conditions and treatment of inmates. Following a civil rights lawsuit filed in 1969, OPP had operated under a series of federal court consent orders that mandated standards in such areas as medical treatment and environmental conditions. Yet inmates, both before trial and after sentencing, continued to suffer inadequate medical care and abuse by deputies. In the year immediately preceding Katrina, a number of inmates died, both from beatings by deputies and from treatable medical conditions.[9]

Low prosecution and conviction rates reflected the system's difficulty in processing cases. The district attorney's office refused to prosecute 74 percent of all violent crime arrests, and only 5 percent of all convictions in the criminal district court were for violent offenses. In the end, only 39 percent of those arrested were convicted of a state offense, and two of every three of those convictions were for simple drug possession.[10]

The criminal justice system was not only ineffective and frequently unjust or abusive, it was also inefficient, vying with "general government" as the city's single largest general fund expenditure.[11] A significant portion of the system's funding came from fines and fees charged to defendants by every component of the system, creating a perverse incentive for its overuse. Borne disproportionately by individuals whose risk factors—poverty, poor education, lack of employment opportunities, mental illness, and substance abuse—made them more likely to be arrested, fines and fees financed the system on the backs of the city's most vulnerable residents.

Sporadic attempts to improve individual components of the system before Katrina did not result in sustained change. Reforms enacted by progressive police leadership, consultants' analyses of agencies' operations, and promises made by agency heads facing reelection either faded in the face of political changes or were never implemented.[12] It took the force of Katrina to ignite widespread demand for change across the system.

BOX 5-2. Effects of Hurricane Katrina on the New Orleans Criminal Justice System[a]

—The New Orleans Police Department lost its headquarters and three district stations; most of the department's guns and ammunition were destroyed; and much of the force's vehicle fleet was lost.

—The police force was greatly reduced: 80 percent of the officers lost their homes, and salaries were higher in other Southern cities. Two years later, the force was still down by 30 percent of the 2005 staff.

—At OPP nearly every electrical system was destroyed; half the vehicle fleet was ruined; computer equipment, bedding, and jumpsuits worth millions of dollars were lost; and the medical facility was completely destroyed. Most of the prison workforce left the prison and never returned.

—Inmates were scattered across the state and many of the jail's buildings were uninhabitable.

—The criminal district court building at Tulane and Broad, which housed the courtrooms, coroner's facilities, and evidence and property rooms, closed due to storm damage and remained closed until June 2006.

—Evidence for more than 3,000 cases lay under water at police headquarters and in the basement of the criminal district court. For two years, the city remained without an evidence storage facility.

—The crime lab was destroyed and remained nonoperational for nineteen months. Criminal justice agencies lost substantial revenues due to the absence of fines and fees and budget cuts in 2006 due to reductions in city revenues.

a. Brendan McCarthy, "Draft Is Rare Portal into NOPD: Unedited Text Details Department's Woes," *Times-Picayune*, November 18, 2007 (http://blog.nola.com/times-picayune/2007/11/draft_is_rare_portal_into_nopd.html); David Morton, "Empire Falls: The Rise and Decline of the New Orleans Jail," *New Republic*, August 14 and 21, 2006 (www.tnr.com/article/politics/empire-falls); Caterina Gouvis Roman, Seri Irazola, and Jenny W. L. Osborne, "After Katrina: Washed Away? Justice in New Orleans" (Washington: Urban Institute Justice Policy, 2007) (www.urban.org/publications/411530.html); and Brandon L. Garrett and Tania Tetlow, "Criminal Justice Collapse: The Constitution after Hurricane Katrina," *Duke Law Journal* 56, no. 127 (2006), pp. 127–78.

A Criminal Justice System Swept Away

Rising floodwaters caused the collapse of the criminal justice system and created a crisis during which hundreds of individuals effectively lost their constitutional rights for an extended period of time.[13] Facilities were uninhabitable, important documents damaged or destroyed, employees displaced, and equipment—everything from guns to computers to patrol cars—was either swept away or rendered useless (see box 5-2). For months, the system struggled to operate with a shortage of police officers, dozens of district attorneys and public defenders laid off, no adequate jail facilities or courts in which to hold hearings, no jury pool, and nowhere to store or process evidence. Years after the storm, the district attorney's office and municipal court operated in temporary rented space, trailers housed police officials as well as evidence, police stations lacked air conditioning, an uncertified crime lab operated without crucial equipment, and the records division of the police department shared space with the taxicab bureau. As of spring 2011, prisoners continued to be housed in tents, and the sheriff's staff was in temporary quarters.[14]

In the absence of a fully functioning criminal justice system, almost 8,000 prisoners did "Katrina time." Evacuated from the chaos that reigned as floodwaters engulfed the jail complex, prisoners were bused without records or identifying information to thirty-four facilities throughout Louisiana. There they waited, lost in the system without benefit of a lawyer or hearing, often unable to contact family members, whose whereabouts were unknown to them, and frequently held well beyond the release dates for their minor alleged offenses.[15] Not until eleven months after Katrina, with a backlog of 6,000 cases in criminal district court, did Judge Arthur Hunter declare "a state of emergency" and begin ordering the case-by-case release of detained suspects awaiting their day in court.[16]

Among the 8,000 prisoners evacuated from OPP were 150 juveniles transferred to the jail in advance of the storm. While exposed to the harrowing experience of the flood and evacuation, they were spared a lengthy exposure to the state's prisons. Due to the determined efforts of juvenile justice advocates and court officials, all but a few youth transferred to OPP for the storm had been released by October 2005.[17]

A Post-Katrina Opportunity to Reinvent Criminal Justice

Katrina and the ensuing flood caused complete disruption of the criminal justice system and eradicated many of the usual processes and procedures, facilities, and equipment that allowed the system to function. At that pivotal moment, an unprecedented decision point presented itself: whether to rebuild the system as it was or to reinvent the system using the best knowledge and standards of practice recognized by national experts in the field.

In May 2006, citizens elected four new reform-minded city council members with no previous political experience. As New Orleans' criminal justice system struggled to regain its footing and residents' demands for a safer city intensified, a respectful partnership between local civic and not-for-profit advocacy groups and the new council sparked an emerging synergy around criminal justice reform.

Less than one month after the election, the tragic murders of five young men in Central City prompted the creation of the City Council Criminal Justice Committee, and council member James Carter was appointed chair. With assistance from the Juvenile Justice Project of Louisiana and support and funding from the entire city council, Carter planned a city-wide crime prevention roundtable called Best Practices for New Orleans' Criminal Justice System.

More than 700 citizens registered for the September event, which was also attended by numerous federal, state, and local officials. Among the presentations by researchers and local and federal criminal justice agency leaders were those on good practices by the Vera Institute of Justice (Vera), Brown Group International's founder Lee Brown, and the Annie E. Casey Juvenile Detention Alternatives Initiative (JDAI). While a local columnist dismissed the event as "business as usual," Carter saw the roundtable as a way to promote cutting-edge research and empirically driven practices as the new standard. Indeed, the roundtable proved to give structure and focus to the impulse for criminal justice reform in New Orleans.[18]

In the following months and years, a diverse set of actors—government, civic, nonprofit, and grassroots—came together to undertake the tough task of "reinventing" key pieces of the criminal justice system to ensure that it would be more just, efficient, and effective. They did so in three ways: through citizen-led reforms that included the creation of innovative criminal justice programs and legislative changes, including establishing an independent police monitor and alternatives to incarceration; by improving the criminal justice system from within, through interagency partnerships to support systemic planning and implementation; and by top-to-bottom reform, as with the reinvention of public defense.

Building Innovative Criminal Justice Programs from the Ground Up

From the roundtable arose community-driven working groups to address improvements in the system and in public safety. The Corrections Working Group and the Court and Education Working Group, with dynamic leadership and committed members, developed two viable proposals for creating alternatives to incarceration.[19]

A joint proposal by both groups resulted in the development of the Tulane Tower Learning Center (TTLC), a collaborative venture of the Youth Empowerment Project, Delgado Community College, the criminal district court, and the city council, with assistance from numerous additional organizations.[20] The TTLC opened its doors in the spring of 2007, offering literacy training, GED preparation, and computer skills to court-referred adults and youth as well as the general population. Through TTLC, working group participants sought to enhance individuals' employment opportunities as a means of reducing their involvement in criminal activities.[21]

A second major effort by the Corrections Working Group, advised by a national consultant, resulted in the opening of the city's first Day Reporting Center (NODRC), a community-based nonresidential alternative to incarceration proven elsewhere to reduce the likelihood of reoffending. The pilot program offered enrolled clients individually tailored wraparound services including substance abuse counseling, educational and workforce development opportunities, and anger management and cognitive-based decisionmaking programs. The NODRC began accepting clients in February 2009 as a cooperative initiative involving three state and local agencies. Changes in state funding prompted the relocation of the program to facilities at OPP, where it currently operates under an agreement between the Orleans Parish Sheriff's Office and the Louisiana Department of Corrections.[22]

These two projects demonstrate the innovative potential of well-informed citizens, working collaboratively with the advice of experts and professionals, to develop appropriate and cost-effective, data-based responses to identified community needs. Noninstitutional, community-driven, and designed to address risk factors associated with criminal behavior, they were departures from existing public safety approaches. However, it is unclear whether it will be possible to ensure provision of the quality, outcomes, and stable funding needed to sustain such innovative approaches.

Creating Coalitions for Legislative Change

In early 2006, Safe Streets/Strong Communities formed to advocate for public safety and a transparent and accountable criminal justice system. Recognizing the frustration shared by many residents over police harassment and lack of professionalism, Safe Streets embarked on a determined campaign to establish an independent police monitor (IPM) in New

Orleans.[23] In other cities, independent police monitors provide "regular reports and analysis" of police department "activities, procedures, and practices" to "as wide an audience as possible."[24] With encouragement and advice from Safe Streets, Common Good, and Mary Howell, a civil rights attorney, council member Carter made establishing an independent police monitor a priority.

Drawing on technical expertise from the Police Assessment Resource Center, Carter developed an ordinance that established an independent police monitoring division within the Office of the Inspector General (IG). The ordinance passed the council unanimously in June 2008, supported by a strong coalition of advocacy organizations, community groups, and business and civic leaders. By design, a concurrent charter amendment established permanent funding for the IG's office. Placing the police monitor within the IG's office effectively ensured its permanence, making it immune to shifting political priorities. Strategically pairing a charter amendment guaranteeing permanent IG funding with the independent police monitor ordinance aligned proponents from diverse racial and socioeconomic backgrounds, giving both initiatives a broad base of support.[25]

The structure and funding for these reforms predated Hurricane Katrina, but insufficient pressure from citizens resulted in political inaction, and neither materialized. The rhetoric changed after the storm. Calls for transparency by an engaged citizenry combined with new leadership determined to make government responsive and accountable, trumping traditional institutional and political interests. Establishing the authority and autonomy of the IG and the IPM illustrates the potential of community activism, strategically mobilized and aligned with political leadership and expert technical assistance, to drive legislation based on good practices proven to be effective.

Improving the Criminal Justice System from Within

Following the roundtable, the city council engaged Vera to study New Orleans' criminal justice system. In June 2007, Vera presented "Proposals for New Orleans' Criminal Justice System: Best Practices to Advance Public Safety and Justice," to the city council.[26] System data analysis and key interviews shaped the report's findings: New Orleans' criminal justice system was not functioning as a system, its arrest rate was three times the national average, and it produced the highest detention rate in the country. While the emptying of the jail in the wake of the storm briefly altered the numbers, it did not change underlying practices. As a result, the detention rate rose inexorably even as Katrina's waters receded, remaining at three times the national average through 2010.[27]

The report prompted an immediate response. Three months after Vera's presentation, council member Carter convened leaders of all the criminal justice agencies for a weekend-long retreat to discuss its recommendations. There, agency representatives developed Vera's proposals into four actionable initiatives. In their "Statement of Commitment," they pledged to implement them and formed the Criminal Justice Leadership Alliance (CJLA) in order to do so.

CJLA working groups began meeting immediately, tasked with implementing the initiatives set out in the statement's substantive mandate.[28] The working group approach developed as a way to model systemic thinking and cooperative engagement, consensus building, and collaborative implementation. Meetings of agency leaders or their representatives were frequent and often provocative; they also offered a safe venue for dealing with issues in a forthright way. Despite the fact that they functioned as components of a criminal justice "system," agency actors had previously thought themselves free to operate autonomously within their separate realms. Through an iterative process of goal sharing and compromise, the initiatives developed in a way that reflected the interests of each agency, even as they met the needs of all and advanced the public good.

However, the process also revealed limitations. For some participants, the commitment to discuss change exceeded the commitment to make change. Also, there was an understandable reluctance to make necessary changes that would advance justice and efficiency but reduce agency revenues, such as the fines and fees generated from convictions for minor crimes. Finally, New Orleans' criminal justice agencies had limited capacity to develop and implement new practices. As a result, the CJLA refocused its efforts and prioritized one initiative.

The Expedited Screening and Disposition Initiative was launched in March 2009, after nearly a year of concentrated discussion and planning. Committed representatives from the police department, district attorney's office, public defender's office, clerk of court, and sheriff's office meticulously worked out a seamless agreement, including timelines for every step necessary to move a case from arrest to prosecutorial screening to arraignment. They built the data systems necessary to allow Vera researchers to monitor each increment of performance to ensure that the initiative was achieving its systemic goals. And they issued policies and trained their staffs to implement the new practices.

By late 2009 the result was a wholesale decrease in the time from arrest to the filing of the screening decision for all cases that did not involve a victim (30 to 40 percent of all state cases) from sixty-four days to five days, although as of early 2011 court delays continued to add another five days before a case was heard. That means that a person arrested on a nonvictim charge who is detained awaiting adjudication will have his or her day in court six times as fast as before the initiative. Expediting screening significantly reduces the social and financial costs of unnecessary detention.

Just as important, the leaders participating in the building and implementation of the expedited screening initiative used the knowledge gained in the work group and its processes to make other beneficial changes, such as the use of electronic transmission of police reports (previously driven every day from each police district to the district attorney's office), the assignment of public defenders to indigent defendants as close to the time of arrest as possible, the realignment of prosecutorial and defender staff to allow for continuity of attorney assignment, and the shifting of marijuana and other state misdemeanor cases to municipal court for even shorter arrest-to-arraignment times. Significantly, through the CJLA's focus on collective problem solving, the three principal agencies—police, prosecution, and public defense—have developed an ongoing forum for engagement on issues of systemic concern.

The Criminal Justice Leadership Alliance provides a model for supporting sustained change. Guided by expert technical assistance, the CJLA developed an infrastructure and methodology that identifies, nurtures, and implements system improvements, thereby filling a critical need for coordinated criminal justice policymaking in New Orleans. As of early 2011, no official centralized coordinating structure existed to direct agencies toward systemic decisionmaking or to compel the use of data to drive operations and determine outcomes. Without an institutionalized coordinating body with political autonomy and permanence, improvement efforts will be vulnerable to changes in leadership and shifting political priorities. Self-interested criminal justice agencies will continue to compete individually for resources rather than work collectively to advance the ability of the system as a whole to improve public safety.

Top-to-Bottom Reform of Public Defense

In the face of an almost complete collapse of the indigent defense system following Katrina, the Department of Justice's Bureau of Justice

Assistance (BJA) and the Southeast Louisiana Criminal Justice Recovery Task Force assessed indigent defense in New Orleans and concluded that the office needed $10 million to become fully functional. In mid-2006, with thousands of suspects awaiting court hearings and a total of six public defenders, the court also pressed for changes. Issuing a subpoena for Governor Kathleen Blanco to appear, Judge Arthur Hunter pleaded for additional state funds. The court also orchestrated the selection of a new local board, which brought in a management team that included Ronald Sullivan, a Yale Law School professor and former director of the Washington, D.C., public defender program.

The case for adequately funded, professional indigent defense in New Orleans was made. With a $580,000 state grant, a $2.8 million federal grant, and a $400,000 annual state appropriation, New Orleans' public defender's office began reinventing itself. Provision of office space, furniture, and computer equipment was among the changes. More significant, lawyers were required to give up their private practices and become full-time public defenders committed to serving their clients' needs rather than the institutional interests of the court.[29]

Bolstering local reform efforts, the legislature passed Act 307 in the 2007 regular session. The act created the Louisiana Public Defender Board (LPDB), which was charged with revitalizing public defense in Louisiana, including hiring and training state-level executive staff and establishing guidelines and standards of practice with concomitant penalties and disciplinary action for noncompliance. State appropriations for public defense rose to $28.5 million, a considerable increase over previous funding but not nearly enough to cover caseload demands.

In a city where the vast majority of defendants are indigent, the constitutionally protected right to counsel is a critical component of an effective criminal justice system. Post-Katrina emergency funding from state and federal sources enabled the creation of a reenvisioned office of the Orleans Public Defenders. Significant funding challenges remain, as local post-Katrina revenues have not reached the level necessary to sustain progress.

Reinvention in the Balance

As of early 2011, the criminal justice system faced huge obstacles, as evidenced by a comprehensive Department of Justice (DOJ) intervention with the New Orleans Police Department, a BJA review of criminal district court operations that reveals significant systemic problems, and a DOJ report ("findings letter") that alleges systemic violations of inmates' civil rights at Orleans Parish Prison (twenty-eight deaths since Katrina). In addition, stagnant state funding and declining local funding for public defense services pose a serious threat to that office and to system functioning overall. While attention from the federal government and assistance from national nonprofits and foundations offer the city an opportunity to make significant substantive improvements, city leaders must demonstrate a commitment to reform before the window of opportunity closes.

Several themes emerge. First, as illustrated by the Tulane Tower Learning Center, the Day Reporting Center, and the independent police monitor, collective activism by an informed citizenry and advocacy groups has enormous potential to drive change and set performance standards. Second, the crime prevention roundtable introduced a new criminal justice vocabulary to the city. Experts and professionals who presented at the summit used language emphasizing data-driven outcome measures and empirically proven practices that became the lexicon in working group discussions and community public safety discourse. Third, legislation became a powerful tool for directing change, especially when combined with community support and strong political leadership. And fourth, almost every example cited above relied on outside experts to advise and facilitate the change effort.

It remains to be seen whether decisionmakers will choose to reinvent rather than rebuild the system. The independent police monitor, which is autonomous, codified in law, and guaranteed a steady funding stream, will ensure greater police accountability and transparency unless a concerted assault on the legislation is successfully mounted. But every other initiative discussed so far is vulnerable to funding cuts and political caprice. Despite its success as a cost-effective, community-based alternative to incarceration, the state chose to remove the Day Reporting Center both geographically and administratively from the community and place it in the jail. Orleans Public Defenders and the Louisiana Public Defender Board face persistent—and increasing—funding crises. Significant ongoing gains made by the Criminal Justice Leadership Alliance face challenges due to chronic funding concerns and fluctuating political support.

The Louisiana Public Defender Board illustrates, however, how an organization with authority to allocate funds can effectively use that leverage to create change. New Orleans needs just such an agency to drive change in the criminal justice system and to ensure that criminal justice policy decisions are based on systemic thinking and public safety outcomes. The agency should financially support innovative programming and proven practices that increase both the effectiveness and the efficiency of the public safety system, such as TTLC and the Day Reporting Center, and that address real needs at significantly reduced costs. It should use funding to incentivize criminal justice system transparency, accountability, and professionalization, as exemplified by the independent police monitor and the LPDB. And it should support data-driven efforts to develop effective solutions for system improvement through interagency cooperative problem solving, such as that modeled by Vera.

The citywide discussion in late 2010 and early 2011 over the size of the rebuilt New Orleans jail suggests that there is reason to think that such progressive approaches may be gaining a foothold. Civic and community groups prompted Mayor Mitch Landrieu, in consultation with the city council, to form the Criminal Justice Working Group, which was tasked with making a recommendation regarding proposed plans to rebuild a dramatically expanded jail. Since the existing jail had been all but destroyed by the storm, working group members fully realized the need to build a new facility. However, after examining data and information provided by corrections experts and considerable community input, they also recognized that an oversized jail encourages unnecessary arrests and detention at great cost to taxpayers. In early 2011, the city council unanimously enacted an ordinance consistent with the working group's recommendation to authorize construction of a jail that would hold only 40 percent of the current jail population. While still larger than the national per capita facility, that reflected a dramatic reduction in jail size and a new vision for criminal justice practices in New Orleans.

Likewise, DOJ's support of systemic criminal justice reform has been pivotal. DOJ has not only used its enforcement authority to leverage change at NOPD and in the jail, it has partnered with nongovernmental organizations to drive a systemic reform process. Throughout 2010, both DOJ and concerned citizens and advocacy groups urged the mayor and the council to examine options such as developing a pretrial services program, finding other methods to eliminate the unnecessary use of detention, and ultimately planning for a smaller jail.

With the heightened public awareness of the criminal justice system's deficiencies following Hurricane Katrina, public safety became one of the most volatile issues facing the city. New coalitions between reform-minded politicians and citizen activists coalesced around this issue,

permitting empirically based model practices to emerge. Criminal justice system leaders, under pressure from diverse constituencies and with technical assistance from experts, developed a work group methodology that supported systemic thinking and problem solving and resulted in knowledge-based decisionmaking. These partnerships, if sustained, will be critical and may be sufficient to alter the course of criminal justice in New Orleans by basing policy on data and proven practices that support the public's interest in safety and justice rather than on political and institutional interests. Complex and multi-agency reform on this scale requires a long-term commitment. This is a marathon, not a sprint.

Notes

1. Homemade placard held aloft during the march. "New Orleans March, January 11, 2007, parts 1 and 2," April 2010 (www.youtube.com/watch?v=kznHArFw HYI&NR=1).

2. Ibid. Also, Laura Maggi and Gwen Filosa, "Enough! Thousands March to Protest City's Alarming Murder Rate: Officials Reviled in Public Show of Mass Outrage," *Times-Picayune*, January 12, 2007 (www.nola.com/news/t-p/frontpage/index.ssf?/base/news-7/1168585639261300.xml&coll=1).

3. David Winkler-Schmit, "Thou Shalt Not Kill—Pastor John Raphael's Crusade to Stop the Violence in Central City," *The Gambit*, May 18, 2009 (www.bestofnew orleans.com/gyrobase/Content?oid=oid%3A55677).

4. Maggi and Filosa, "Enough!"

5. Despite our best efforts, it would be impossible to include a complete list of all organizations. Examples include New Orleans Crime Coalition, Silence Is Violence, Innocence Project–New Orleans, Resurrection after Exoneration, Juvenile Justice Project of Louisiana, Safe Streets/Strong Communities, Friends and Families of Louisiana's Incarcerated Children, Juvenile Regional Services, and Voice of the Ex-Offender. Information on these and other organizations can be found at their websites.

6. Mark J. VanLandingham, "Murder Rates in New Orleans, LA, 2004–2006," *American Journal of Public Health* 97, no. 9 (September 2007): 1614–16 (http://ajph. aphapublications.org/cgi/content/full/97/9/1614); Steve Ritea and Tara Young, "How New Orleans Became the Nation's Murder Capital—Cycle of Death: Violence Thrives on Lack of Jobs, Wealth of Drugs," *Times-Picayune*, February 8, 2004, pp. A1 and A5; Brendan McCarthy, "Study: Murder Rate Is Even Higher," *Times-Picayune*, March 12, 2007 (www.nola.com/news/t-p/metro/index.ssf?/base/news-20/117367751715220. xml&coll=1). See also Statement before the Committee on the Judiciary, U.S. Senate, by Jim Letten, U.S. Attorney, "Violent Crime and the Criminal Justice System in New Orleans Following Hurricane Katrina," June 20, 2007 (http://judiciary.senate.gov/pdf/07-06-20LettenTestimony.pdf).

7. Heather Hall, "Katrina's Impact: Hurricane Brings Attention to Long Broken Public Defense System," *Cornerstone* 28, no. 1 (2006): 15–17 (www.lajusticecoalition. org/public+defense/katrinas+impact).

8. Metropolitan Crime Commission, "Analysis of the Process of State Misdemeanor and Felony Charges in New Orleans: Arrest through the Billing Decision" (2002), p.

2 (www.metropolitancrimecommission.org/html/research.html). The maximum time allowable by law was routinely exceeded.

9. Louis Hamilton, imprisoned at OPP, filed a class action lawsuit against the jail in 1969. In the intervening years the suit was modified a number of times. In 2009, the suit was dismissed at the request of the plaintiffs' attorneys. Yet the court retains jurisdiction over appended agreements governing per diem and lump-sum payments from the city to the sheriff to fund the jail. ACLU National Prison Project, "Abandoned and Abused: Orleans Parish Prisoners in the Wake of Katrina" (2006) (www.aclu.org/prisoners-rights/abandoned-abused-complete-report). See also Barry Gerharz and Seung Hong, "Down by Law: Orleans Parish Prison before and after Katrina," *Dollars and Sense* (March-April 2006) (www.dollarsandsense.org/archives/2006/0306gerharzhong.html).

10. Metropolitan Crime Commission, "Performance of the Criminal Justice System 2003–2004" (2005) (www.metropolitancrimecommission.org/html/research.html).

11. Metropolitan Crime Commission, "Analysis of the Process of State Misdemeanor and Felony Charges in New Orleans: Arrest through the Billing Decision" (2002) (www.metropolitancrimecommission.org/html/research.html); City of New Orleans Budget Books for 2002 through 2010; and "Comprehensive Annual Financial Report," City of New Orleans, December 2003 through 2008 (www.cityofno.com/Portals/BureauofAccounting/portal.aspx).

12. In the mid-1990s, under Superintendent Pennington's leadership, more than 350 police officers were "indicted, fired or disciplined for misconduct," significant organizational changes were made to the department, and the data-driven COMPSTAT model was instituted. Pennington's reforms coincided with marked reductions in crime, but gains dissipated beginning in 2005. Adam Nossiter, "2 Crime Busters for New Orleans," *New York Times*, December 5, 1996 (www.nytimes.com/1996/12/05/us/2-crime-busters-for-new-orleans.html?pagewanted=all). See also Ritea and Young, "How New Orleans Became the Nation's Murder Capital"; "APD Chief Richard Pennington to Resign," *Associated Press*, November 24, 2009 (www.myfoxatlanta.com/dpp/news/apd_chief_richard_pennington_to_resign_112409). On the prosecutorial side, implementation of recommendations made by Linder and Associates, a New York criminal justice consulting firm, at the request of then District Attorney Eddie Jordan, was derailed by the storm. Laura Maggi and Gwen Filosa, "OPDA Eddie Jordan Resigns," *Times Picayune*, October 30, 2007 (blog.nola.com/times-picayune/2007/10/sources_talks_underway_for_jor.html). During the 2004 campaign for criminal sheriff, the Orleans Parish Prison Reform Coalition outlined the "Nine Point Platform for Change" to raise the public's consciousness about the jail's conditions and operational problems. The sheriff endorsed the platform, but the changes were never implemented. White papers by the Orleans Parish Prison Reform Coalition, "Orleans Parish Prison—A Call for Reform" (2004) and "It Can Be Done: We Can Have a Safe Community Small Jail and Save Money" (2006).

13. Caterina Gouvis Roman, Seri Irazola, and Jenny W. L. Osborne, "After Katrina: Washed Away? Justice in New Orleans" (Washington: Urban Institute, 2007) (www.urban.org/publications/411530.html). Roman, Irazola, and Osborne give an excellent account of the devastation that the storm wrought on the criminal justice system. Brandon L. Garrett and Tania Tetlow, "Criminal Justice Collapse: The Constitution after Hurricane Katrina," *Duke Law Journal* 56, no. 127 (2006): 127–178.

14. Roman, Irazola, and Osborne, "After Katrina"; and Brendan McCarthy, "Draft Is Rare Portal into NOPD: Unedited Text Details Department's Woes," *Times-*

Picayune, November 18, 2007 (blog.nola.com/times-picayune/2007/11/draft_is_rare_portal_into_nopd.html). Immediately following the storm, the criminal district court and the jail began operations at the Amtrak Station in downtown New Orleans, with prisoners housed in cages behind the station. The jail opened in tent facilities on a limited basis in October 2005. In addition, judges held court hearings in other parishes where prisoners were being held.

15. Garrett and Tetlow, "Criminal Justice Collapse."

16. Gwen Filosa, "Judge Vows to Free Untried Inmates; State of Emergency Exists, Hunter Says," *Times-Picayune,* July 29, 2006, p. A1.

17. Juvenile Justice Project of Louisiana, "Annual Report 2005–2006." See also Juvenile Justice Project of Louisiana, "Treated Like Trash" (2006) (www.jjpl.org/PDF/treated_like_trash.pdf). While a full accounting of improvements in juvenile justice is not possible in this essay, it is important to note that juvenile justice underwent significant improvements following the storm. Juvenile justice advocates, spurred to action by the experiences of young people transferred to OPP in advance of the storm and the subsequent breakdown of the juvenile justice system, undertook two important initiatives. The first was the incorporation of Juvenile Regional Services (JRS) in 2006. Recognizing juvenile delinquency and law as a specialized body of knowledge, JRS's establishment created the nation's only independent entity that provides public defense for youth. Simultaneously, an active Juvenile Detention Alternatives Initiative (JDAI) supported by the Annie E. Casey Foundation provided a structural center for rebuilding a better and more responsive juvenile justice system, beginning with the involvement of families and the community. Broad system reform, made possible through JDAI in combination with clients' access to specialized legal advocates, has significantly improved justice outcomes for youth in New Orleans. Richard Mendel, "Two Decades of JDAI: From Demonstration Project to National Standard" (Baltimore: Annie E. Casey Foundation, 2009).

18. Lolis Eric Elie, "Can Summit Help City Cut Crime?" *Times-Picayune,* September 13, 2006, p. B1; Program for "New Orleans Crime Prevention Roundtable: Best Practices for New Orleans's Criminal Justice System," September 16, 2006.

19. Richard Webster, "Program Curbs Criminal Path," *New Orleans City Business,* November 19, 2007 (findarticles.com/p/articles/mi_qn4200/is_20071119/ai_n21125798/).

20. With initial financing from the city council, the TTLC was made possible by financial or in-kind contributions from Southern University at New Orleans; the Literacy Alliance of Greater New Orleans; the Lindy Boggs National Center for Community Literacy; the Carpenters' Union; Sunshine Career Counseling; Greater New Orleans, Inc.; Louisiana CURE; the Literacy Alliance of Greater New Orleans; and the Louisiana Department of Education.

21. Press release for the dedication of Tulane Tower Learning Center, Criminal District Court, Judicial Administrator's Office, August 8, 2007. See also Laura Maggi, "Literacy Program Pitched to Council: Judges Seek Financing to Aid Drug Offenders," *Times-Picayune,* November 14, 2006 (www.nola.com/news/t-p/frontpage/index.ssf?/base/news-18/1163487793320170.xml&coll=1).

22. "New Orleans Day Reporting Center Participant Handbook," revised March 2009. The NODRC opened as a cooperative program of Metropolitan Human Services District; the Louisiana Department of Safety and Corrections, Division of Probation and Parole, New Orleans District; and the City of New Orleans, which

provided funding for the consultant, Kevin Warwick of Alternative Solutions Associates, Inc., a firm recognized nationally for designing and developing community corrections programs.

23. Information sheet by Safe Streets/Strong Communities, "Crisis of Confidence: Persistent Problems within the New Orleans Police Department" (2006).

24. National Association for Civilian Oversight of Law Enforcement (NACOLE) Code of Ethics, adopted in "New Orleans Independent Monitor Policy" (2009) (www.sanjoseca.gov/ipa/NACOLECode%20of%20Ethics.pdf). See also New Orleans Independent Police Monitor website (www.nolaoig.org/main/inside.php?page=independent_police_monitoring). An independent police monitor was the top recommendation of the Police-Civilian Review Task Force formed under Mayor Morial. "Report of the Police-Civilian Review Task Force" (2002).

25. Council member Shelley Midura championed the effort to establish the Office of the Inspector General in New Orleans, authoring the ordinance that created the office in 2006.

26. "Proposals for New Orleans's Criminal Justice System: Best Practices to Advance Public Safety and Justice" (Vera Institute of Justice, 2007).

27. That statistic compares Orleans Parish Prison to jails nationwide and does not include the 30 percent of the jail's population that had been sentenced to state prison or was being held on federal charges.

28. The four initiatives addressed by the Statement of Commitment are pretrial release and expedited screening; substance use and mental health services; community service sentencing; and municipal court.

29. Fritz Esker, "Bench Relief: Judges, Lawyers Team Up to Solve Indigent Defender Problem," *New Orleans City Business,* May 22, 2006 (www.nacdl.org/public.nsf/PrinterFriendly/Louisiana084?openDocument); Gwen Filosa, "Judge Orders Blanco to Come to Court: He Seeks Answers as Poor Sit in Limbo," *Times-Picayune,* July 1, 2006 (www.nacdl.org/public.nsf/PrinterFriendly/Louisiana094?openDocument); and Mary Foster, "New Orleans Public Defender System Probed," *Associated Press,* February 12, 2006 (www.nlada.org/DMS/Documents/1139849124.24/15b40016246642f6.html).

6

Systemic Ethics Reform in Katrina's Aftermath

David A. Marcello

> *Their struggle . . . began as one of man against nature. It became one of man against man. For the flood brought with it also a human storm. Honor and money collided. White and black collided. Regional and national power collided. The collisions shook America.*
>
> —John Barry, *Rising Tide: The Great Mississippi Flood of 1927 and How It Changed America*

Hurricane Katrina inundated New Orleans on August 29, 2005.[1] Three weeks later, Hurricane Rita came ashore near Lake Charles. Together, these hurricanes delivered a devastating one-two punch.[2] But they ravaged more than the physical landscape of South Louisiana and the Gulf Coast region.[3] They also unsettled the established political order.

This chapter examines how state and local ethics reform took place in Katrina's aftermath. Accordingly, it is useful to clarify at the outset what is meant by the term "ethics reform." Ethics reform does not mean that people start behaving better. Ethics

The author gratefully acknowledges the research assistance of Thalia Reisin Ziffer, Public Interest Fellow at the Public Law Center.

reform means that systems are put in place to deal with people who are behaving badly. One sign of success in systemic ethics reform is when large numbers of citizens embrace and applaud that reform.

Three local ethics reforms had been legally authorized—and some legally mandated—in New Orleans' Home Rule Charter more than ten years before Katrina.[4] None had been properly implemented when Katrina struck; five years later, however, all were comfortably under way. Why and how the storm created such an opportunity for reform is the central focus of this chapter.

Systemic change also transpired in state ethics enforcement during the post-Katrina period. Some of the changes advanced the cause of ethics reform. Some had more ambiguous or mixed effects. Still others may have set back ethics reform—not by design but because of unanticipated consequences. Disasters are change agents, but the direction of change depends ultimately on the human choices made in a disaster's aftermath.

The key to enduring ethics reform is to put well-designed systems in place, fund them adequately, and allow them to function with some degree of independence. Good system design is the first step.[5] Every system then faces implementation challenges, such as funding and independence. Relying on a well-functioning system will produce good results more often than depending on well-motivated people—though well-functioning systems and well-motivated people produce the best results of all. Good systems enhance the efforts of good people.

The resilience of people who have been knocked down by disaster depends on more than their personal qualities of hardiness and fortitude. Resilience also depends on the presence of systems that can restore "normalcy" by resuming operations in the wake of a disaster. Post-Katrina recovery was impeded by the lack of sufficiently strong or well-designed ethical systems in the pre-Katrina period.[6] In one of the storm's ironies, however, the city and state may be better prepared to respond to future disasters because of systemic ethics reforms that were instituted as a consequence of the Katrina experience.

New Orleans Home Rule Charter Reform

Long before Katrina, New Orleans voters endorsed municipal ethics reform by overwhelmingly supporting revisions to the city's home rule charter in November 1995.[7] The charter changes, which took effect on January 1, 1996, mandated establishment of an Ethics Review Board; authorized the creation of an Office of Inspector General; and explicitly required, for the first time, competitive selection of professional service contractors.[8]

Despite the mandatory charter language approved by voters in 1995, all three ambitious ethics reforms remained mostly unrealized when Katrina blew through ten years later.[9] But Katrina's ill winds blew into being a whirlwind of civic activism and consequential political change that produced long-delayed ethics reforms before the storm's fifth anniversary.[10]

Three developments laid the foundation for reform. First, the failure of government at every level—city, state, and federal—to respond adequately during and after the storm prompted citizens to fill the vacuum by becoming more actively engaged in recovery and in reforming city government.[11] Second, disgust with government's performance translated into disgust with the performance of certain public officials, inspiring a new cadre of reform candidates to take voter dissatisfactions to the polls.[12] Third, the infusion of billions of dollars into the city's recovery raised red flags about the integrity with which those dollars would be administered, thereby laying the groundwork for increased scrutiny and systemic reforms.[13] These three spinoff effects of Katrina came together in a perfect storm to produce long-awaited ethics reform in New Orleans city government.

Ethics Review Board and Office of Inspector General

The Bring New Orleans Back Commission recommended creation of the Ethics Review Board (ERB) and Office of Inspector General (OIG) that had been authorized but never implemented under the revised home rule charter.[14] A candidate for the District A city council seat, Shelley Midura, made ethics reform the centerpiece of her campaign; when elected, she wasted no time in proposing an ordinance to deliver on that campaign promise.[15] Aided by the votes of other post-Katrina reform candidates elected to the "new" New Orleans City Council, an OIG ordinance passed in November 2006.[16]

The ERB convened its first meeting in January 2007—more than a decade after charter revisions that became effective in 1996 had called for its creation.[17] The ERB conducted a national search and selected New Orleans' first inspector general, Massachusetts native Robert Cerasoli, who relocated from his Boston-area home and began work in September.[18]

Civic support aided the growth and development of the OIG and ERB. Citizens for 1 Greater New Orleans hosted a forum at Loyola University in October 2007 to introduce the new inspector general to the community.[19] He worked steadily thereafter to bring the OIG message to thousands of area residents, making personal appearances before neighborhood organizations, civic groups, public bodies, and similar groups.[20] Newspaper editorials, op-ed articles, and letters to the editor celebrated a new era of ethics reform in city government.[21]

Public support for the OIG and ERB helped to secure further legislative and charter changes, strengthening both entities over the next year of operations. A broad coalition of civic groups and community organizations supported ordinance revisions that the city council approved in November 2007.[22] Citizens for 1 Greater New Orleans went to Baton Rouge with representatives of the OIG and ERB in the spring of 2008 and successfully sought legislation authorizing subpoena enforcement power.[23] Members of the Business Council of New Orleans and the River Region contributed to an informational campaign, and on October 4, 2008, voters approved a ballot proposition expanding the powers of the local ethics entities and dedicating in the charter a reliable annual source of funding to support their operations.[24]

Professional Service Procurement Reform

Reform of professional service procurements followed a more tortuous path. The 1994–95 Citizens' Charter Revision Advisory Commission originally recommended a single new competitive selection procedure, fixed by ordinance and broadly applicable to all of city government.[25] Instead, the mayor and city council opted for separate executive and legislative policies fixed by mayoral executive order and city council rule.[26]

Both mayoral executive order and council rule proved woefully inadequate when promulgated, since both established "in-house" evaluation groups to rate and rank respondents.[27] In-house evaluation groups appointed by the mayor and the city council are likely to remain wholly responsive to them, effectively serving as their alter egos.[28] When professional service procurements remain subject to the influence of elected officials, political patronage remains the order of the day.

The change agent for procurement reform was a well-regarded U.S. Attorney's Office that brought several high-profile prosecutions for public corruption, fueling public perceptions that something was seriously wrong with how city government handled procurements. A council member at large went to prison after accepting a bribe for a parking contract.[29] A former director of the Department of Property Management went to prison for accepting gifts from a contractor who received hundreds of millions in public funding.[30] Several political operatives who functioned outside government went to prison for their corrupt interactions with public officials; the public officials also were incarcerated.[31]

Press coverage of patronage practices in Mayor C. Ray Nagin's administration fostered public outrage over wasteful and corrupt use of public funds during a period of recovery and distress, when acute needs of neighborhood residents were going unmet while private contractors were living large at the public trough.[32] Voter distaste for patronage played an important role during the 2010 mayor-council elections, when many candidates pledged their support for procurement reform. Shortly after taking office in May 2010, Mayor Mitch Landrieu garnered widespread public praise when he signed four executive orders that instituted new procurement policies and signaled a new attitude of cooperation with the inspector general.[33]

State Ethics Reform

Katrina and Rita also had an impact on state politics, demonstrated most vividly by incumbent Governor Kathleen Blanco's decision not to seek reelection in 2007.[34] In the 2003 election, Louisiana voters gave Blanco a narrow electoral victory over her run-off opponent, Bobby Jindal, then lived to regret their decision during hurricanes Katrina and Rita and their aftermath when response and recovery efforts proved unimpressive among Louisiana voters.[35] Her signature recovery initiative, the Governor Kathleen Babineaux Blanco Road Home Program, extinguished whatever reelection hopes she may have entertained when it proved too expensive and too poorly administered to pave the "road home" for tens of thousands of displaced residents.[36] Feeling the effects of buyer's remorse, many former Blanco voters gravitated toward the candidate that they felt might have responded more successfully to the hurricanes' assaults, awarding Bobby Jindal an impressive first primary victory over all other candidates in the 2007 gubernatorial election.[37]

Governor Jindal made ethics reform the focus of a February 2008 special session, which convened within a month after his inauguration.[38] He secured most of his ethics reform agenda.[39] One major reform in the special session—a rigorous system of financial disclosure among different tiers of public officials—was made even more rigorous just months later in the regular session by extending disclosure requirements to include spouses of certain public officials.[40] The February 2008 special session produced ethics reforms that garnered extravagant national praise.[41] Over time, however, other voices from within the state proved less complimentary. Even the new ethics board chair criticized some of the changes and lobbied for their modification or repeal.[42]

Burden of Proof

The burden of proof under Louisiana's pre-Jindal ethics code called only for "substantial evidence" to support a finding of an ethics violation.[43] Governor Jindal's 2008 reform established "clear and convincing" proof as the evidentiary standard,[44] a demanding burden of proof that made it more difficult to enforce Louisiana's ethics code and that might have been questionably characterized as an "ethics reform." Conventional ethics reform usually demands more rigorous compliance with ethics code provisions—not a more rigorous burden of proof from ethics code enforcers.[45]

But the countervailing argument is a compelling one—that quasi-criminal punitive provisions ought not to be inflicted on the basis of a "substantial evidence" standard more often used in civil proceedings. Supporters of the Jindal ethics reform would maintain with some justification that the proper administrative burden of proof should indeed be clear and convincing evidence of a violation before violators are penalized with fines and threatened with suspension or termination of their contracts or employment.[46]

Disqualification of Board and Commission Members

Similar ambiguities accompanied a second major ethics reform, which governed the participation of appointed board and commission members in transactions involving a government entity. Throughout the four decades following its enactment, the ethics code applied a uniquely draconian provision to appointed board and commission members, requiring that they either divest themselves of any economic interest giving rise to a conflict of interest or resign their appointment to a government board or commission.[47] All other public servants—elected officials and public employees—could disclose a conflict and recuse themselves from participating in a transaction, but appointed board and commission members could not exercise the disclosure-and-recusal option.

A good example of how severely that provision worked in practice can be drawn from the experience of William Turner, who served as dean of the Tulane School of Architecture during the 1970s. His professional expertise was an obvious asset during his tenure as a member of the New

Orleans City Planning Commission (CPC), but his service ended when Tulane University applied for a zoning change that required CPC review and approval. Dean Turner could not recuse himself from participating in the transaction involving Tulane. His only choices were to resign his faculty position at Tulane or to resign from the commission. Not surprisingly, he chose the latter course of action, and the commission lost a valuable source of expertise.

Governor Jindal's 2008 ethics reform created a recusal option for appointed board and commission members for the first time.[48] Much can be said in favor of this reform, perhaps best illustrated by a hypothetical example. The chair of the New Orleans Ethics Review Board during its first three-and-a-half years of operation was Father Kevin Wildes, the president of Loyola University and a Jesuit priest whose training and specialization was in the field of ethics.[49] Father Wildes devoted many hours and performed very capably in his role as ERB chair. Under Louisiana's prior ethics regime, however, he might at any moment have been placed in an irreconcilable conflict of interest and forced to resign from the ERB simply by filing an ethics complaint against any member of the Loyola University community. Shrewd counsel could use a "strategic" ethics complaint to target certain ERB members for removal, preventing them from casting a vote against the lawyer's client in an unrelated ethics proceeding. The 2008 recusal option eliminated this opportunity for such a sordid abuse of ethics laws. Viewed in that context, the recusal option made very good sense.

Defenders of Louisiana's prior ethics regime also had valid arguments, however. They contended that appointed board and commission members should be subject to unique prohibitions because they occupy a unique position with regard to accountability. Other public servants are accountable to someone—elected officials to the voters, public employees to their supervisors. Once appointed, however, board and commission members are largely unaccountable to anyone, since they generally serve for a term of years and can be removed only for cause. That lack of accountability renders the situation ripe for "logrolling," or quid pro quo agreements: "I'll recuse myself this time with the understanding that you'll vote in my best interests, and the next time you have to recuse yourself, I'll be happy to reciprocate."

Here again, the merits of this particular ethics reform can be argued either way, depending on which policy position holds more beauty in the eye of the beholder.

Administrative Law Judges

A third ethics reform—very vigorously questioned by members of the State Board of Ethics—removed decisionmaking authority from the board and transferred it to a panel of three administrative law judges (ALJs).[50] The ethics board may have brought this particular reform upon itself by allowing its dual "prosecutorial" and "adjudicatory" roles to compromise the right of an accused individual to be heard and judged by an impartial decisionmaker.[51] Since the ethics board and its staff received and investigated complaints, evaluated them, and made a preliminary finding of ethical misconduct before bringing the matter to a public hearing, they could not credibly lay claim to the mantle of "impartiality" or dodge the charge of "prejudgment." The Louisiana Supreme Court held in 1989 that this confusion of roles violated the fundamentals of due process and ordered a change.[52] The ethics board's response—designating some staff attorneys to investigate and prosecute ethics complaints while some other staff attorneys counseled the board in its decisionmaking role—did not go far enough to create a "two-tier" separation of prosecutorial and adjudicatory functions. In 2008, the legislature did it for them.[53]

Louisiana already had a Division of Administrative Law populated by ALJs who heard and decided diverse agency proceedings involving welfare, employment, and similar matters.[54] The new Jindal ethics reform assigned the responsibility for hearing and deciding ethics complaints to a panel of three ALJs, removing that authority from the board of ethics and leaving the board with only the responsibility to investigate and prosecute complaints.[55] One feature of the new law was especially obnoxious to members of the ethics board; they were required to adopt the findings of the ALJs as their own and were prohibited from appealing an unsatisfactory outcome to the courts.[56] (In contrast, the target of an ethics proceeding could seek judicial review of an unfavorable decision by the ALJs.)[57] The ethics board chair prepared a substantial fifteen-page white paper detailing his dissatisfactions with the 2008 ethics reforms and urging the legislature to reconsider the decisions that it had reached in the special session two years earlier.[58]

Governor Jindal had garnered exceptional praise for his 2008 ethics reforms, and he was not of a mind to question the wisdom of those earlier decisions or to put his "ethics reform" legacy at risk by having the legislature reconsider those reforms. The legislature responded in a very limited fashion to the ethics board chair; the ethics board is no longer statutorily instructed to adopt the ALJs' decisions.[59] It is too soon to say how this further revision of the governor's initial reform will work in practice, but it is surely a less aggressive revision than the ethics board would have liked.

Consigning decisionmaking responsibility to a group of ALJs rather than to the ethics board was unquestionably a major systemic change, but its impacts arguably undermined two important values—diverse citizen representation, and the accumulation of agency expertise in administering ethics laws. An eleven-member ethics board composed of residents from all across the state exerts a stronger claim to "democratic legitimacy" than does a three-member panel of Baton Rouge–area ALJs whose composition changes from case to case. That constantly changing cast of characters—combined with their extensive caseload of non-ethics matters—also undermines the concept of accruing agency expertise, making courts less likely to give deference to administrative decisions rendered by a panel of ALJs.

A better approach to ethics reform might have left decisionmaking authority with the ethics board and created a separate system of investigation and prosecution in an office and staff operating independently of the board. That type of two-tier model is employed by the Louisiana State Bar Association in its attorney disciplinary proceedings.[60]

Overview of State Ethics Reforms

The new state ethics laws stand as powerful testimony to the disaster-based theory of "systemic change" at the heart of this chapter. Each change was sweeping and substantial, and some would simply have been unthinkable before Katrina. But this theory of change implies nothing about the content or direction of change, nor does it predict that systemic change will necessarily produce reform.

How are we to evaluate Governor Jindal's ethics changes in terms of principle—in terms of right or wrong? We might fairly conclude that neither supporters nor opponents can claim ownership of "right" or "wrong," nor does "truth" lie somewhere in between. Each of these three ethics "reforms" can be fairly debated from both sides, and the resolution of that debate depends utterly on policy choices that might be legitimately defended either way.

In evaluating these policy choices, we should be guided by measurable outcomes: In the years since their enactment, how have they worked in practice? The answer is—not that well. Imposing a rigorous new system of financial disclosure drove ethics board members and senior staff to resign en masse during the summer of 2008, which in turn led to an unhappily long season of inactivity while a new staff was hired and an entirely new board seated.[61] Transferring ethics decisions to constantly changing panels of ALJs undermined the concepts of agency expertise and democratic legitimacy by removing authority from a diverse eleven-member board.

The 2008 ethics changes shortened the prescriptive period from two years to one but did not address retroactivity, leaving it unclear whether matters that had been referred to investigation before the law changed required action by the ethics board within one year or two. Numerous other procedural questions—involving motions for summary judgment, discovery, and confidentiality issues—might all have been more thoroughly thought through than proved possible in a week-and-a-half-long special session held in February 2008, less than a month after the new administration took office. As a consequence, ethics administrators were still embroiled in time-consuming court proceedings to resolve procedural questions three years later.[62]

Substantive and implementation challenges continue to trouble the administration of ethics programs in Louisiana, as new members of the ethics board call for legislative changes that would reverse—and in their view, "reform"—some of the systemic changes pushed through by Governor Jindal.

By January 2010, civic and editorial commentary had begun to reflect a consensus about the efficacy of ethics reforms at the state level. The Public Affairs Research Council of Louisiana (PAR) characterized the reforms as a "mixed bag" and noted that "weakened enforcement" and "procedural pitfalls" placed "inordinate power in the hands of the governor."[63] A *Times-Picayune* columnist scoffed at Governor Jindal's 2008 ethics package, "when he emasculated the ethics code and called it the 'gold standard.'"[64] Katrina and Rita provoked systemic change at the state level, just as they did in New Orleans, but Governor Jindal steered the course of change in state legislation toward a somewhat more dubious destination.

Conclusion

Ten years after New Orleans' 1994–95 home rule charter revision process, the city still had no ethics review board, no office of inspector general, and no reform in procurement of professional services. Ten years of no progress—and no progress in sight—provides us with a good test case: We must credit Katrina as the catalyst that led to implementation of the ERB, OIG, and professional service procurement reform in post-Katrina New Orleans.

Disasters like Katrina inflict terrible trauma, and their physical devastation is often accompanied by comparable political upheavals within government. Post-Katrina political upheavals created an opportunity for systemic change, but systemic change itself is no guarantee of reform. Systemic change can have either positive or negative effects, and even well-designed changes can be well or poorly implemented. Governor Jindal's ethics changes provided many good examples of each type.

This chapter attributes post-Katrina ethics reform to the synergy arising out of high-profile prosecutions, press coverage, civic activism, and the political upheaval caused by an environmental catastrophe. The most important component of the cycle may well have been the political upheaval provoked by Katrina—a powerful reminder that "disasters are not only socially and physically disruptive; they are also political events."[65]

Because disasters introduce uncertainty into the established order, they create opportunities for change—change that is political as well as physical. How well or poorly we use these post-disaster opportunities remains very much a human enterprise and a test of the damaged community's resilience. To New Orleans' credit, post-Katrina ethics reforms generally strengthened the systems that safeguard public integrity, leaving a legacy of positive change in the wake of a devastating disaster.

Notes

1. Katrina delivered the wind and the rain to New Orleans' doorstep, but the flooding that inundated the city was a product of human error in the design and implementation of its flood protection systems, not an inevitable consequence of the hurricane:

> Katrina was an extraordinary act of nature, but what it precipitated was the most extraordinary manmade—not "natural"—disaster in the history of New Orleans. Long before Katrina ever made landfall, design failures by the Corps of Engineers, Congressional funding failures, and the fragmentation of responsibility among parochial levee protection bodies laid the awful groundwork (literally) for catastrophic levee failures and consequential losses in life and property.

David A. Marcello, "Housing Redevelopment Strategies in the Wake of Katrina and Anti-*Kelo* Constitutional Amendments: Mapping a Path through the Landscape of

Disaster," *Loyola Law Review* 53 (2007), pp. 827–28; omitted are footnotes 334–37, citing a report commissioned by the Corps of Engineers: American Society of Civil Engineers Hurricane Katrina External Review Panel, *The New Orleans Hurricane Protection System: What Went Wrong and Why* (2007) (www.asce.org/uploadedFiles/Publications/ASCE_News/2009/04_April/ERPreport.pdf). See also the definitive website for information about local levees: www.levees.org.

2. See, for example, Donald W. Davis, "The Aftermath of Hurricanes Katrina and Rita on South Louisiana" (www.epa.gov/OEM/docs/oil/fss/fss06/davis.pdf).

3. Douglas Brinkley, *The Great Deluge: Hurricane Katrina, New Orleans, and the Mississippi Gulf Coast* (New York: HarperCollins, 2006).

4. The Home Rule Charter of the City of New Orleans is the city's fundamental governing law—the equivalent of its "constitution." Under article VI, sections 4 and 6 of Louisiana's 1974 constitution, home rule jurisdictions (particularly pre-1974 home rule jurisdictions such as New Orleans) are protected from state laws that would alter the structure, powers, or functions of local government.

5. See, for example, William Lidwell, Kritina Holden, and Jill Butler, *Universal Principles of Design, Revised and Updated: 125 Ways to Enhance Usability, Influence Perception, Increase Appeal, Make Better Design Decisions, and Teach through Design* (Rockport Publishing, 2010).

6. For example, administration of the Road Home Program suffered significantly from multiple levels of anti-fraud protection built into the system (reportedly twenty levels; in comparison, Mississippi had four). Louisiana had such a bad reputation in ethics matters that public officials felt the need to protect themselves from the adverse consequences of fraud and abuse. If public confidence in state and local ethics systems improves in the future, that may alleviate the perceived need for extraordinary ethics protections and diminish administrative complexities such as those that burdened the road home program.

7. See "Orleans," *Times-Picayune*, November 19, 1995 (1995 WLNR 102490), which reported that 83,754 (68 percent) voted for charter reforms while 39,005 (32 percent) voted against. (WLNR references are to the Westlaw legal database, available by subscription at www.lawschool.westlaw.com.)

8. See sections 9-401, 9-402, and 6-308(5)(a) of the Home Rule Charter of the City of New Orleans.

9. Frank Donze, "Inspector General Plan May Get Vote; N.O. City Council to Discuss Today," *Times-Picayune*, September 20, 2006 (2006 WLNR 16316178): "A Wednesday story incorrectly reported that the New Orleans City Council failed to create an Ethics Review Board, appoint board members and enact an ethics code for city workers and contractors as mandated by a 1995 City Charter change approved by voters. The council took those steps in 1996 and 1997. The Ethics Review Board, however, never met and the staggered terms of all its members expired by 2003."

10. See, for example, "Women of the Storm" (www.womenofthestorm.net/) and "Citizens for 1 Greater New Orleans" (www.citizensfor1greaterneworleans.com/site/PageServer?pagename=home_2010).

11. See, for example, "Report: Katrina Response a Failure of Leadership," CNN, February 24, 2006 (www.cnn.com/2006/POLITICS/02/13/katrina.congress/index.html); Jed Horne, *Breach of Faith: Hurricane Katrina and the Near Death of a Great American City* (New York: Random House, 2006); *Hurricane Katrina: A Nation Still Unprepared*, Special Report of the Senate Committee on Homeland Security and

Governmental Affairs (Special Report 09-322) (2006), pp. 585–88 (www.gpoaccess. gov/serialset/creports/pdf/sr109-322/overview.pdf).

12. See, for example, Bruce Eggler, "Incumbents Lose Seats in 3 Districts," *Times-Picayune*, May 21, 2006 (2006 WLNR 8734158); Frank Donze, Gordon Russell, and Kate Moran, "Public Sours on Elected Officials," *Times-Picayune*, May 5, 2007 (2007 WLNR 8544219): "Renwick, who did the survey of 400 registered voters between March 30 and April 5 for WWL-TV, said that while he expected to see low [approval] numbers, he was taken aback by how low they were. 'This is clearly a product of frustration with the slow pace of recovery,' Renwick said. 'People are looking for someone to blame, and as long as these problems persist, incumbents will not be highly rated.'"

13. Public Affairs Research Council of Louisiana, "PAR Urges More Oversight for Aid Spending," June 8, 2006 (www.la-par.org/article.cfm?id=175&cateaid=2).

14. Bring New Orleans Back Commission, "Governmental Effectiveness Final Report," January 19, 2006 (www.bringneworleansback.org/Resources/Government Effectiveness.pdf).

15. Bruce Eggler, "Ethics Board, Inspector General Deferred; Council Sets Aside Midura Proposal," *Times-Picayune*, June 23, 2006 (2006 WLNR 10891375): "Fulfilling a campaign promise, recently elected City Councilwoman Shelly Midura tried at Thursday's council meeting to start the process of adding two features to city government that were authorized by a sweeping 1995 revision of the City Charter but never implemented: an Ethics Review Board and an Office of Inspector General."

16. Bruce Eggler, "Inspector General Plan Passed," *Times-Picayune*, November 3, 2006 (2006 WLNR 19107563).

17. See Bruce Eggler, "Council Ratifies Ethics Appointees; Board, Inspector General Are to Ferret Out Corruption, Waste," *Times-Picayune*, January 11, 2007 (2007 WLNR 605144).

18. Bruce Eggler, "City Names Official to Probe Fraud; He Founded Group of Inspectors General," *Times-Picayune*, June 13, 2007 (2007 WLNR 029800).

19. See "Ethics Reform History" (www.citizensfor1greaterneworleans.com/site/PageServer?pagename=Ethics_reform_story).

20. Frank Donze and Gordon Russell, "Turf Check, N. O.'s Inspector General Is Taking the Time to Know His New City," *Times-Picayune*, March 1, 2008 (2008 WLNR 4101095).

21. See, for example, Michael Cowan, "A New Day for New Orleans," *Times-Picayune*, December 23, 2008 (2008 WLNR 24579331): "On Dec. 17, Inspector General Robert Cerasoli submitted his first public report to the mayor and the public, a document inauspiciously entitled 'Interim Report on the Management of the Administrative Vehicle Fleet.' It's not the Magna Carta or the Gettysburg Address, yet I believe it signals the beginning of the end of the waste, corruption and insider dealing that have crippled New Orleans under white and black administrations alike, destroying economic opportunity and feeding social mistrust"; Laine Lazar, "IG Brings Hope to City," *Times-Picayune*, November 30, 2007 (2007 WLNR 2367970); David Marcello, "Finally, City Tackles Real Ethics Reform," *Times-Picayune*, January 7, 2008 (2008 WLNR 332397).

22. New Orleans Ordinance M.C.S. No. 22,888 (November 1, 2007); Bruce Eggler, "Council Grants Inspector General His Own Attorney; He Won't Have to Rely on City Attorney," *Times-Picayune*, November 2, 2007 (2007 WLNR 21656479).

23. "Briefing Book, News and Views from the Capital," *Times-Picayune*, February 14, 2008 (2008 WLNR 2838792); La. R. S. §33:9611 (2008) (Act. No. 18, H.B. 80,

First Extraordinary Sess. [La. 2008]); Bill Barrow, "Inspector General Gains Clout; Secrecy Measure Defeated in Senate," *Times-Picayune,* February 26, 2008 (2008 WLNR 3802286).

24. Brian Friedman, "Officials Supporting Inspector General Ordinance; Charter Change Established Office," *Times-Picayune,* September 21, 2008 (2008 WLNR 17940755); New Orleans Ordinance Calendar No. M-08-573 (October 2008).

25. See James C. Brandt, letter to the editor, "Two Significant Changes Proposed for Charter," *Times-Picayune,* January 30, 1995 (1995 WLNR 982405); Home Rule Charter of the City of New Orleans, "Mayor's Charter Revision Advisory Committee: Committee Recommendations" (December 15, 1994) (on file with author or see New Orleans Public Library, Public Archives).

26. Section 6-308(5) of the Home Rule Charter of the City of New Orleans; Home Rule Charter of the City of New Orleans, "Mayor's Recommendations: Amendments to the Charter" (March 16, 1995) (on file with author or see New Orleans Public Library, Public Archives).

27. New Orleans City Council Rule 45; Executive Order MHM 96-020 (September 5, 1996).

28. Council Rule 45, section 7, established an in-house Selection Review Committee that consisted of "the Council Chief of Staff, the Council Research Officer and either the Council Fiscal Officer or the Director of Council Utilities, depending on the type of professional service to be performed." Executive Order MHM 96-020, section 8 (September 5, 1996), established in-house evaluation groups drawn from members of the unclassified service, who held employment at the pleasure of the mayor. The chief administrative officer or an executive assistant could also appoint "other persons with specialized knowledge or expertise" from the community at large or the university community, but those "outsiders" would be chosen by mayoral representatives—if chosen at all: "Nothing herein shall be construed to require these additional raters." The system preserved mayor and council control over patronage practices.

29. Frank Donze, "Thomas Expected to Plead Guilty; New Orleans Councilman Oliver Thomas Could Resign Monday," *Times-Picayune,* August 12, 2007 (2007 WLNR 15584730); "The Case against Thomas," *Times-Picayune,* August 14, 2007 (2007 WLNR 15726311).

30. Gordon Russell and Frank Donze, "Letter Reveals Private Deals; Feds Contend Document Will Show Broader Pattern of Corruption," *Times-Picayune,* January 9, 2007 (2007 WLNR 397456); Gwen Filosa, "Barre, DeCay Must Forfeit Pensions; Judge Orders Pair to Pay $1 Million," *Times-Picayune,* January 8, 2009 (2009 WLNR 350241).

31. See, for example, Stephanie Grace, "Two Sides of Stan Barre?" *Times-Picayune,* November 6, 2007 (2007 WLNR21906569); Laura Maggi, "Guilty on 4 Counts: In a Split Verdict, Mose Jefferson Is Convicted of Bribery and Obstruction of Justice," *Times-Picayune,* August 22, 2009 (2009 WLNR 16383246).

32. See, for example, Gordon Russell, "Probe Looks at N.O. Pastor, Sources Say, Feds Suspect He Received Kickback as S&WB Member," *Times-Picayune,* November 15, 2009 (2009 WLNR 25679753); James Gill, "Trash Contract Gets Smellier All the Time," *Times-Picayune,* October 26, 2006 (2006 WLNR 18505618): "If the Ray Nagin administration is, as advertised, on the up and up, how come contracts get awarded on the down low?"; David Marcello, "Contracts Should Be Done in the Open," *Times-Picayune,* May 15, 2011 (2011 WLNR 9698159).

33. Executive Order MJL 10-02 (June 3, 2010); Executive Order MJL 10-03 (June 3, 2010); Executive Order MJL 10-04 (June 3, 2010); Executive Order MJL 10-05 (June 3, 2010).

34. Ed Anderson and Robert Travis Scott, "Blanco Bows Out of Race; Slow Recovery Takes Toll on Governor. Blanco: Politics a Distraction from Duties," *Times-Picayune,* March 21, 2007 (2007 WLNR 5357909).

35. "Dive in Blanco's Popularity Reflected in Post Storm Poll, Vitter Rises, Landrieu and Bush Stand Pat," *Times-Picayune,* November 30, 2005 (2005 WLNR 19279766): "Louisiana voters have taken a dim view of Gov. Kathleen Blanco's performance since Hurricane Katrina hit the state, with fewer than one out of five voters saying they would definitely vote to re-elect her to office, according to polls conducted before and after the storm by Southern Media & Opinion Research." See also "Briefing Book, News and Views from Louisiana," *Times-Picayune,* October 21, 2007 (2007 WLNR 17554884): "Hurricanes Katrina and Rita have done more than wreck lives and property in Louisiana. They also appear to have put a major dent in Gov. Kathleen Blanco's public approval rating."

36. Robert Travis Scott, "Road Home Snag Broke Blanco," *Times-Picayune,* March 22, 2007 (2007 WLNR 5422429).

37. See, for example, Jan Moller, "Jindal Wins," *Times-Picayune,* October 21, 2007 (2007 WLNR 20668636); Chris Cillizza, "Louisiana: Is Jindal's Win a Sign of GOP Turnaround Nationally?" *Washington Post,* October 21, 2007: "Jindal ran on a reform platform and against the entrenched Democratic political establishment, a message that resounded in a state full of angry survivors of the 2005 storms."

38. Bill Barrow and Jan Moller, "Jindal's Special Session Agenda Is Heavy on Ethics; Financial Disclosure Sought for All Offices," *Times-Picayune,* February 2, 2008 (2008 WLNR 1997425).

39. Jan Moller and Bill Barrow, "Ethics Session Ends with Solid Results," *Times-Picayune,* February 26, 2008 (2008 WLNR 3802007).

40. Act No. 1, H.B. 1, 1st Extraordinary Sess. (La. 2008); Act No. 162, H.B. 842, Regular Sess. (La. 2008).

41. Ed Anderson and Robert Travis Scott, "Ethics Law Changes to Take Effect One by One; Effects Will Extend to Officials Statewide," *Times-Picayune,* February 27, 2008 (2008 WLNR 3824995).

42. Robert Travis Scott, "Chief Wants Ethics Board to Hear Cases, Jindal Proposal to Shift Duties Draws Criticism," *Times-Picayune,* February 12, 2008 (2008 WLNR 2676170).

43. Acts 1979, No. 443, § 1, eff. April 1, 1980, amended by Acts 1980, No. 579, § 1; Acts 1980, No. 580, § 1: La. R.S. 42:1141(D): "(11) If the investigation of an ethics body fails to disclose any substantial evidence to support the charges, the ethics body shall make an official determination of its findings and thereupon close its file on the charges."

44. Act No. 23, H.B. 41, 1st Extraordinary Sess. (La. 2008): La. R.S. 42:1141(C)(4)(e): "If the public hearing of the ethics adjudicatory panel fails to disclose clear and convincing evidence to support the charges, the ethics adjudicatory panel shall make an official determination of its findings, and thereupon the Board of Ethics shall close its file on the charges."

45. Jan Moller, "After a Year of Hurricanes and Public Firestorms, Gov. Bobby Jindal Faces Tougher Challenges," *Times-Picayune,* January 11, 2009 (2009 WLNR

544746): "Although the ethics law changes won Louisiana flattering national publicity and helped clean up the state's long-running reputation for moral laxity, they also could make it harder to prosecute public officials by raising the legal standard for winning a conviction. The new system requires 'clear and convincing' proof to establish an ethics violation, whereas the previous law called for only 'substantial' evidence of a violation." Robert Travis Scott, "Watchdog Seeks Reversal of Change in Ethics Laws; Standard of Proof for Violation at Issue," *Times-Picayune,* November 3, 2009 (2009 WLNR 21902700).

46. See, for example, Robert Travis Scott, "Ethics Changes Called into Question; Some Say Burden of Proof Is Too High," *Times-Picayune,* April 27, 2008 (2008 WLNR 7808277).

47. See Bill Barrow, "Board Member Recusal Bill Signed, Board Sidesteps Conflicts of Interest," *Times-Picayune,* July 8, 2008 (2008 WLNR 12763726).

48. Act No. 685, Regular Sess. (La. 2008): La. R.S. 42:1120.4.

49. Wikipedia, "Kevin Wildes" (http://en.wikipedia.org/wiki/Kevin_Wildes); http://president.loyno.edu/about-president.

50. See, for example, Jan Moller, "Panel OKs Revamp of Ethics Board, Measure May Hit House Floor Friday," *Times-Picayune,* February 13, 2008 (2008 WLNR 2758154).

51. See, for example, Robert Travis Scott, "Watchdogs Oppose Ethics Proposal; Bill Alters Who Hears Enforcement Cases," *Times-Picayune,* February 19, 2008 (2008 WLNR 3199640); Robert Travis Scott, "House, Senate Reach Deal on Judging Ethics Cases; Under Bill, Board Loses Judicial Power," *Times-Picayune,* February 26, 2008 (2008 WLNR 3726097): "House Bill 41 by House Speaker Jim Tucker, R-Algiers, would remove the State Board of Ethics as the judge in cases of alleged violations and give that power to a panel of administrative law judges. . . . The ethics board would retain its role as investigator and prosecutor of ethics cases. . . . 'It's curious as to why this wasn't done years ago,' said Sen. Rob Marionneaux."

52. *Ga. Gulf Corp.* v. *Bd. of Ethics for Public Employees,* 543 So.2d 173, 176-180 (La. 1997), citing *Allen* v. *La. Bd. of Dentistry,* 543 So.2d 908 (La. 1989).

53. Act No. 23, First Extraordinary Sess. (La. 2008).

54. La. R.S. 49:992.

55. Act No. 23, 1st Extraordinary Sess. (La. 2008), amending Section 42:1141(C).

56. Act No. 23, 1st Extraordinary Sess. (La. 2008) added to Section 1141(C) a new subparagraph (5): "If the ethics adjudicatory panel determines that a violation has occurred and prescribes authorized penalties or other sanctions, the Board of Ethics shall, within forty-five days of the issuance of the determination by the ethics adjudicatory panel, issue a decision adopting the determination of the ethics adjudicatory panel."

57. La. R.S. 42:1142(A): "Whenever action is taken against any public servant or person by the board or panel or by an agency head by order of the board or panel, or whenever any public servant or person is aggrieved by any action taken by the board or panel, he may appeal therefrom to the Court of Appeal, First Circuit."

58. State of Louisiana Board of Ethics, "White Paper on the Effects of Act 23 on Louisiana's Ethics Program" (adopted August 26, 2009) (www.ethics.state.la.us/pub/laws/WhitePaperAct23_08252009.pdf).

59. Act No. 1002, S.B. 310, Regular Sess. (La. 2010), amending Section 1141(C)(5).

60. See Louisiana Attorney Disciplinary Board, "An Emphasis on Ethics and Professionalism" (www.ladb.org/about_the_board.asp).

61. It took four months to fill vacant board and staff positions, and the "backlog of cases wasn't cleared until April 2009." Penny Font, "Fool's Gold: Gov. Bobby Jindal Might Have Declared Sweeping Ethics Reform to 'Set the Gold Standard,' but Board Members Say Significant Problems Remain," *Baton Rouge Business Report* at 28, November 30, 2010.

62. See, for example, Marsha Shuler, "Judge Says His Ruling Could Hamstring Ethics Law Enforcement," *The Advocate,* November 8, 2010, quoting Judge William Morvant, who "begrudgingly" held that enforcement of campaign finance laws was transferred from the ethics board to ALJ panels with the 2008 ethics changes: "It's going to hamstring the ability of the Ethics Board. . . . If the goal was to streamline this and make its function easier, it sorely missed its point" (www.2theadvocate.com/blogs/politicsblog/106907774.html).

63. Public Affairs Research Council of Louisiana, "The Unfinished Business of Ethics Reform" (January 2010) (www.la-par.org/Publications/PDF/EthicsReform_01272010.pdf).

64. James Gill, "Ethics in the Legislature? That's a Laugh," *Times-Picayune,* February 7, 2010 (2010 WLNR 2581877). See also other editorial commentary in January-February listings under "PAR in the News: 2010" (www.la-par.org/parnews.cfm).

65. Gregory Button, *Disaster Culture: Knowledge and Uncertainty in the Wake of Human and Environmental Catastrophe* (Walnut Creek: Left Coast Press, 2010).

7

Bringing New Orleans Home: Community, Faith, and Nonprofit-Driven Housing Recovery

Kalima Rose

There is no doubt that the loss of home and all that went with it—the dispersion of families, neighbors, social networks; the loss of family records and cultural histories to the flood waters; and the loss of loved ones—was the most wrenching and traumatizing part of Hurricane Katrina and the floods of 2005. Over 200,000 households faced major or severe damage to their homes.[1] In New Orleans alone, 134,000 housing units—70 percent of all occupied units—suffered damage from Katrina and the subsequent flooding.[2]

In the five years following that loss, residents, friends, families, neighborhoods, organizations, volunteers, students, university faculties, governments, philanthropies, developers, legal aid providers, and all manner of faith institutions rose up to help recreate what was lost in a city loved by so many. This multitude of actors worked to address the catastrophic loss by rebuilding homes, neighborhoods, and communities—and by doing so, delivering hundreds of thousands of acts of healing. In the process,

Laura Tuggle contributed to this article during her tenure as staff attorney of the Housing Law Unit at Southeast Louisiana Legal Services. She has since become general counsel for the Housing Authority of New Orleans.

new civic partnerships have emerged; culture bearers have come home; and residents have become urban planners, organizers, and community developers. The best of the recovery has built on cultural strengths, historic and creative architectural design, an energy conservation ethic, and safer and more sustainable homes and communities. The greatest challenges of the recovery stem from the absence of the 110,000 residents who have not returned—leaving many neighborhoods underpopulated and many homes and buildings blighted, with the deepest losses among African American residents. This chapter documents the multifaceted response—from community, faith-based, and advocacy organizations and the Obama administration—that arose to move housing recovery forward and bring New Orleanians home.

Promise in the Face of Huge Challenges

New census numbers provide a sobering benchmark in the recovery trajectory: a quarter of the 189,896 housing units in New Orleans, or 47,738, were vacant in 2010. While the challenges of blight and shrinking population are at the top of the city's official agenda, there have also been huge strides in recovery and rebuilding of homes and neighborhoods over the last five years, due largely to the emergence of diverse community and neighborhood developers.[3] This new community capacity—both home-grown and transplanted—continues to address the unfinished business of the recovery in partnership with those still working to recover their lives and homes. And while the handful of organizations that focused on community development before the storm grew and strengthened after Katrina, dozens of new organizations and networks of organizations rose up to focus on particular neighborhoods and on more vulnerable populations. These organizations have taken on each wave of redevelopment in the neighborhoods that they serve and have increasingly focused on the heavily flooded, mostly African American communities that have been the slowest to recover. They have helped homeowners navigate the frustrating bureaucracy of the state's homeowner recovery program, the Road Home, and have contributed millions of hours of volunteer sweat equity to help thousands of owners overcome the gaps in the program. They have pressed the owners of blighted properties to take action and negotiated with redevelopment authorities for properties and land use rights under their control to enact new neighborhood visions. They have built new rental homes for seniors, for people rendered homeless by the floods, and for some of those displaced from public housing. And they have filed lawsuits to apply civil rights law to remedy the disproportionately slow recovery faced by African Americans.

These organizations grew out of deep love of the city and their neighbors, their quest for cultural continuity, and their desperate need to reweave the social fabric frayed by the scattering of their people. The population of New Orleans fell from 455,188 before Katrina (July 2005) to 208,548 one year later (July 2006)[4]—a loss of over half of the city's population. Five years later, the population stood at 343,829, or 75 percent of the pre-Katrina population.[5] With slightly more than 118,000 African American residents who have not returned, African American communities have had the hardest time bouncing back, and their share of the city population fell from 66.7 percent in 2000 to 59.6 percent in 2010.[6] These organizations continue to be critical to changing that reality.

They have been innovators at every turn, facing intractable challenges and nevertheless finding a way forward. They have pushed for and won on multiple fronts: rebuilding sustainable, green, affordable homes; forging relevant systems of counseling and case management; and pressing for rental subsidies, additional grants, and matching resources when residents' housing needs continued to be unmet. They have partnered with (or grown from) philanthropic organizations to show the public sector the way, and they have pushed government to be more effective, accountable, and transparent. And they have continued to focus on the disproportionate impact on African American communities and their right to return. They have looked beyond housing recovery to push for the opening of schools, health clinics, grocery stores, transportation services, and parks in their communities. And they have played leadership roles in planning for their communities and rebuilding for long-term resilience.[7]

History of the Challenge

New Orleans is a city of unique neighborhoods with long histories, deep loyalties, and family lineages that go back generations. As in many older cities in America, segregation had been growing in the decades prior to Katrina, fueled largely by a city losing population and white residents moving out to surrounding suburban parishes. So, while the percentage of people in poverty stayed relatively constant between 1970 and 2000, at 26 to 28 percent of the population, by 2000, the number of census tracts identified as "extreme poverty" grew from 28 to 40—a two-thirds increase.[8]

The entities charged with addressing the housing conditions of poverty were failing—at the city, state, and federal levels. The Housing Authority of New Orleans (HANO), the agency responsible for providing housing and community development services to low-income people, had been characterized as a poorly functioning organization since 1977.[9] Its main strategy for addressing concentrated poverty before Katrina was primarily the decommissioning and redevelopment of troubled public housing complexes. That strategy largely consisted of moving the majority of families into other high-poverty communities (by the use of housing choice vouchers), thereby making the former public housing *less* poor but not providing greater opportunity for the people who moved. In 1996, the federal government took HANO into receivership.[10] During the decades of management decline, HANO helped reinforce the perception of public housing as a poorly run government program. Under a revolving door of receivers, HANO continued after Katrina to mismanage its own affairs even as it was handed the huge tasks of rehousing its residents, repairing and redeveloping its hurricane- and flood-damaged properties, and serving a vastly expanded population reliant on housing subsidies.[11] Under those conditions, federal, state, and local officials supported the lockout of residents and demolition of almost 3,000 occupied public housing units[12]—a large share undamaged—despite residents calling for a phased redevelopment in the face of catastrophic housing losses in the city.

Meanwhile, the city of New Orleans faced its own challenges of underperformance matched by an overall weak housing finance and development system. Federal resources meant to address poverty often lined the pockets of ineffective developers or were left unspent; when they addressed real housing needs, it was not always in ways that leveraged broader neighborhood change.[13] The pre-Katrina New Orleans community development sector was uneven. There were a few strong organizations, but others were shells for graft. While there were good first-time homebuyer programs, they were not complemented by a robust system of community development finance. There was little dynamic leveraging of public funds with private sector action. Public policies deployed in other parts of urban America to invest in declining neighborhoods and foster inclusion—housing trust funds, community land trusts, inclusionary zoning, and housing needs assessments—were not used in the New Orleans area to address housing opportunity. The system of code enforcement was completely broken, meaning that tenants lived in substandard properties with no recourse and neighbors had to tolerate eyesores and real dangers due to lack of maintenance and abandonment. Moratoriums on multifamily housing development were spreading across the region, partly in reaction to the actions and perceptions of the housing authority and partly due to the long-standing practice of racial exclusion. The U.S. Department of Justice was called in to investigate violations of fair housing law.

Similar challenges faced the state. In 2004, Governor Kathleen Babineaux Blanco had formed the "Solutions to Poverty" network to try to tackle the roots of persistent poverty across the state.[14] In every region of the state, community leaders identified quality affordable housing as a critical need. Yet in 2004, the state had comparatively little experience, infrastructure, or resources with which to foster a robust program for affordable housing development. No meaningful funding was allocated to the state's housing trust fund. There was no statewide housing advocacy network, unlike in at least forty other states.[15] There were no statewide policy mechanisms for directing affordable homes into all the state's parishes.

Just as state leaders prepared to address the challenge, hurricanes Katrina and Rita and the breached levees destroyed more than 200,000 homes. In the weeks after the storm, the Louisiana Recovery Authority was formed to ultimately steer $13 billion in housing recovery funding. A legislature historically indifferent to housing policy would vote to approve proposed plans. And the Louisiana Housing Finance Agency, which had been allocating $8 million a year in low-income housing tax credits, found itself responsible for directing a congressional allocation of $170 million in tax credits.[16] Overall, that represented $1.7 billion in equity over ten years to repair and replace damaged multifamily rental housing across southern Louisiana.[17]

That set of dynamics set the stage for the transformations that community developers and neighborhood leaders would set in motion in the post-Katrina years. While their progress has been deep, their continued work for the next decade will be critical to the long-term prosperity of New Orleans. These actors will be the key to restoring the homes that disaster-impacted residents need to fully participate in the community, and they will be the key to ensuring that the housing is linked to other neighborhood and regional opportunities. The challenges of recovery from a catastrophic disaster are only magnified when compounded by poverty.

Major Developments since Hurricane Katrina

From the beginning of discussions on recovery, residents wanted to rebuild their communities to be better—stronger, safer, and more equitable. Neighborhood leaders were called to action when Mayor Ray Nagin's Bring New Orleans Back Commission announced in November 2005 that to prove their viability, heavily flooded neighborhoods would have to have enough returned residents in the next four months to "warrant" city investment. These leaders arose from the swirling political chaos and began driving the effort to get what their communities needed:

—Neighborhood recovery that included homes, infrastructure, services, and amenities

—Greater economic opportunity

—Affordable, sustainable, energy-efficient homes.

With those goals in mind, community leaders and their partners have advanced housing and community recovery against formidable odds.

Rise of Strong Community-Based Groups Reviving Key Neighborhoods

The intentional and spirited approach of diverse local communities and their leaders have forged renewal from the ruins. Patricia Jones, executive director of the Ninth Ward Neighborhood Empowerment Network Association (NENA), has built a formidable organization to take on her community's Herculean challenge. "At this point," she said, "we have to own what we are dealing with."[18] (See figure 7-1 on repopulation of neighborhoods). For NENA, with the 2010 census showing only 2,842 residents returned (down from 14,008 in 2000), it means counseling families one by one; coordinating action; challenging the state and its agencies to move resources; working with the New Orleans Redevelopment Authority to transfer land for redevelopment so that whole blocks can be brought back and residents can be clustered; and fighting for the infrastructure to support a neighborhood.

NENA has pioneered a community land trust to leverage subsidies and ensure the affordability and sustainability of the land, homes, and businesses that they rebuild.[19] On community infrastructure, they have had to mount a three-year campaign because only one of six schools to be financed through FEMA funds has been rebuilt and the community is desperate for a high school. Bus service is still at a fraction of pre-Katrina levels. They are fostering small, community-serving businesses so that money will circulate in the community. And they are focused on getting

FIGURE 7-1. **Percent Change in Population, by Neighborhood, New Orleans, 2000–10**

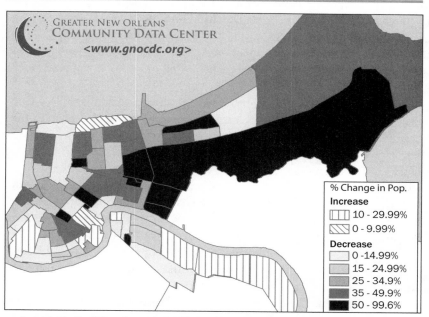

Source: Greater New Orleans Community Data Center analysis of data from the U.S. census, 2000 and 2010.

their own African American contractors on projects—confronting the ongoing frustration that statutory goals for local contracting and hiring are not being met.

NENA's focus on "clustering"—bringing back an entire block at a time and anchoring commercial amenities and infrastructure—is a strategic effort that community developers have adopted across the more damaged and blighted portions of the city. Groups are employing a range of strategies: property swaps; building new homes on property owners' lots with sweat equity; counseling distressed owners to draw on every available resource in a range of confusing options; creating lease-to-own strategies for renters with federal Section 8 housing rental vouchers; and using federal Neighborhood Stabilization Program funds to create opportunities for first-time homebuyers by rehabbing properties sold to the state by homeowners who opted not to return. It has been no small act of fortitude to navigate the bureaucracy and come up with the creativity, financing, patience, and humor that have been required, especially when the majority of homeowners in the Ninth Ward had financing gaps that averaged $75,355.[20] Residents are still awaiting settlement of a lawsuit brought by the NAACP Legal Defense Fund, the Greater New Orleans Fair Housing Action Center, and the National Fair Housing Alliance, that found discriminatory impact on African American homeowners due to the formula used to calculate grants based on a pre-storm assessment rather than damage estimates.

Further up in the Upper Ninth Ward, Branford Marsalis, Harry Connick Jr., and New Orleans Habitat for Humanity channeled over 18,000 volunteers to build seventy-two affordable ownership homes and ten senior apartments in Musicians Village, on eight acres across several blocks.[21] The homes ring the blocks, with performance grounds and open space as their collective backyard. Construction recently began on the Ellis Marsalis Center for Music, dedicated to the development of the next generation of New Orleans musicians. "With this Center we celebrate this most vital part of our culture," said Branford Marsalis.[22]

Project Home Again, a nonprofit developed by the Leonard and Louise Riggio Foundation, took on the recovery of a neighborhood in Gentilly, an older working- and middle-class African American community that was badly flooded. The organization worked through a land swap model, allowing any low- or moderate-income family with property in the area to swap for a lot in their construction zone, where they in turn got a new, modest, two- or three-bedroom, elevated, energy-efficient Craftsman home. Seventy homes now make up a beautiful, colorful neighborhood that has gone further than most in ensuring safety, sustainability, and the preservation of historic community social connections. And they have shown how to make an affordable, scalable model that has expanded to include former renters as well.

Organizations like these have played the most significant role in helping homeowners who did not get enough rebuilding resources—or were victims of contractor fraud—to return.[23] A property-based survey by Beacon of Hope of the most damaged neighborhoods found that 32 percent of the recipients who had received Road Home funds were still not back in their homes[24] (a total of as many as 10,000 homes),[25] making organizations like Project Home Again and NENA critical to both family and neighborhood recovery.

Other organizations have worked to support public housing residents locked out of their homes in the four largest city public housing complexes after Katrina by the Housing Authority of New Orleans. The public housing residents' councils, their allies at Southeast Louisiana Legal Services, community organizations that border each of the complexes, and community development agencies played critical roles in working to keep displaced residents connected to the redevelopment process in the five years after Katrina. The wrenching December 2007 city council vote to demolish 4,529 apartments marked a low point in groups working for the "right to return" for displaced renters. Today, three of the four complexes are back on line as mixed-income developments, with 1,660 homes in total.[26] While the new buildings are beautifully designed mixes of different architectural compositions and sizes, with only 807 of them affordable to former residents, they constitute a serious reduction in the overall number of homes serving displaced residents.

Strong Neighborhood Networks

Kysha Robinson, Fred Johnson, Carol Bebelle, and Don Boutte are only a few of the hundreds of citizen leaders who have focused on the recovery and opportunity structures of Central City—a historic neighborhood that met the definition of extreme poverty prior to Katrina. The Central City Renaissance Alliance, the New Orleans Neighborhood Development Collaborative, the Neighborhood Development Foundation, the Ashe Cultural Arts Center, the Gulf Coast Housing Partnership, and Churches Supporting Churches have all worked individually and collectively with dozens of partner organizations since Katrina to take on each recovery challenge in turn. Their efforts illustrate how progressive, successive community development can begin to transform entire neighborhoods. They created the Community Benefits Coalition to negotiate with developers. They advocated for opening schools in Central City and won both a new early childhood center and a KIPP charter school associated with the redevelopment of the recently opened Harmony Oaks (formerly C. J. Peete public housing). They rallied political support for locating the Louisiana Civil Rights Museum in Central City. They supported the expansion of the Ashe Cultural Arts Center, a community cultural anchor, and Cafe Reconcile, a workforce development social enterprise, which serve their own neighborhood residents as well as residents from across the city. They established co-located offices of the Central City Renaissance Alliance, the Louisiana Association of Nonprofit Organizations, the Good Work Network, and Idea Village on historic O. C. Haley

Boulevard—all mission-driven organizations to foster the redevelopment
of the area and to help small businesses build their economic assets.

These enterprises are adjacent to the area where the New Orleans
Redevelopment Authority will soon be breaking ground to build new
offices, and the beautiful Muses mixed-income rental housing development is now open for tenants.[27] Local and national foundations all
invested in their growing success. And now community developers Jeri-
cho Road and the New Orleans Neighborhood Development Collaborative are tackling both pre- and post-Katrina blight in the neighborhoods
and working aggressively with neighbors, strategically buying problem
properties to "tip" blocks one at a time for first-time homebuyers and
rental assistance voucher holders.[28]

These networked consortiums of nonprofit partners, working together
for recovery, are replicated across New Orleans neighborhoods. New
City Partners, a network of over fifty organizations, is putting in place
the transit, schools, housing, greenways, and small business corridors
to revive the Lafitte, Tremé, and Gravier neighborhoods and support
the in-progress redevelopment of the Lafitte public housing complex.[29]
Members of the group have worked to win federal grants for streetcar
extensions and sustainable communities planning, and they are pushing
for the dismantling of the interstate highway that decimated the historic
commercial district of Tremé, one of the important early free black communities in the United States. The Obama administration, through HUD
and the Department of Transportation, has aided their efforts by aug-
menting the original disaster resources with additional funding to extend
streetcar lines, further public housing redevelopment, and study the dismantling of the interstate. The "comprehensive" development approach
being pursued by the Obama administration in communities of high poverty is being pioneered in these New Orleans neighborhoods.

Greater Attention to Economically Integrated Housing and Neighborhoods

More economic integration of housing has been pursued in almost all
new rental housing development. The Louisiana Housing Finance Agency
radically changed its development policies and priorities to foster income
mixing, the integration of permanent supportive housing for people
with disabilities in every development, and energy efficiency standards
in many of the more than 4,289 new and rehabbed apartments that have
come on line.[30] Several of the developments have been nominated for
national quality awards.[31] Some developments reused historic buildings

in the central business district; others took pre-Katrina planned market-rate developments and used tax credits to include affordable units. The Small Rental Property Program funded the repair of 2,157 rental units in one- to four-unit buildings, providing affordable rentals across diverse damaged neighborhoods.[32] While not adequately replacing thousands of public housing units or reducing the despair of residents locked out of their homes after Katrina, the redeveloped public housing provides a variety of housing and affordability levels, from senior housing to public housing to affordable home ownership.

While all of these are promising advances, they do not equal the scale of the housing lost or provide enough affordable homes to those who lost a home that they could afford before Katrina. Rents are still about 40 percent higher than before, and residents, neighborhood leaders, housing advocates, HUD, HANO, and the Louisiana Recovery Authority have had to continually readjust and work out new avenues to try to meet the needs of those still not safely housed.

Expanding the Affordable Housing Tools to Serve Vulnerable Populations

When the Louisiana Recovery Authority set out its Road Home plan for renters in 2006, it set goals for the Louisiana Housing Finance Agency to create as many as 33,000 affordable rental housing units with as many as 9,000 highly affordable units for households earning less than 40 percent of the area median income. Seventy percent of those units were intended to restore lost rental housing in Orleans Parish.[33] Because of many unanticipated constraints, just under 4,300 units have come on line in New Orleans under these programs to date.[34] Constraints included higher construction costs; the national economic downturn, which collapsed the value of the tax credits; and persistent resistance to affordable developments by the myriad state and local actors who are involved in some part of the programs.[35]

While the need for more affordable rental homes persists, Louisiana housing advocates have been effective in ensuring that many seriously disabled residents who lost their homes during the flood find permanent housing. The development of the Louisiana Permanent Supportive Housing Program (PSH) shows great promise as a national model for the delivery of affordable housing with support services to severely disabled households. When fully implemented, it will provide about 3,000 highly affordable homes to disabled households earning less than half of the New Orleans area median income.[36]

In a bold move engendered by disability advocates and faith-based leaders, the Louisiana Housing Finance Agency (LHFA) imposed the unprecedented requirement that all developers seeking community development block grant (CDBG) piggyback funds paired with Gulf Opportunity Zone low-income housing tax credits set aside at least 5 percent of their units as permanent supportive housing.[37] The Louisiana Recovery Authority set aside $72.9 million of Road Home CDBG funds to provide for supportive services to disabled households for up to five years. But the projects still needed PSH vouchers to provide a deeper subsidy for the most vulnerable populations, such as those on supplemental security income (SSI) with incomes at about 20 percent of median income. Unity of Greater New Orleans led a three-year advocacy effort in partnership with a wide array of government and nonprofit partners to win a 2008 congressional appropriation to provide permanent housing vouchers for this program.[38]

While still in its infancy, the PSH program shows great promise in improving the lives of those fortunate enough to be admitted to it.[39] The 535 disabled residents living in the new tax credit developments in New Orleans are extremely pleased by the high quality of housing in the new developments. Martha Kegel, director of Unity of Greater New Orleans, said, "This initiative created something incredibly positive in the aftermath of one of our nation's greatest tragedies, providing a way for some of the most vulnerable residents of our region to get the housing and supports they needed."[40]

The Federal Role

While the replacement of permanent housing has been far slower than anticipated, both Congress and the Obama administration stepped up to allocate more rental assistance to many households. After a disaster, FEMA typically provides short-term rental assistance under its Individual Assistance Program, which was not income based or means tested. But due to the catastrophic nature of losses from hurricanes Katrina and Rita and the subsequent floods, FEMA was still providing rental assistance or other temporary housing assistance to about 45,000 families in early 2007, when the program was due to expire. Because hardly any replacement housing was back on line, FEMA announced that it would extend rental payments for an additional eighteen months, with HUD taking over administration of housing assistance.

FEMA estimated that 79 percent of the displaced families were renters and about 19 percent homeowners before the disaster. Their median annual income was about $14,000. The idea that most families with incomes that low could transition to self-sufficiency by the end of the Disaster Housing Assistance Program (DHAP) was unrealistic. While thousands of participants were able to transition to other permanent housing options by the end of the program, thousands of others faced possible homelessness without permanent housing voucher assistance.

On September 30, 2008, Congress appropriated $85 million to provide permanent housing choice vouchers for eligible families that still needed housing assistance beyond the end of DHAP Katrina. Congress later appropriated another $80 million to provide additional permanent housing assistance to those still in trailers as of June 24, 2009, and to other disaster-impacted populations.[41] Shaun Donovan, secretary of HUD, and Janet Napolitano, security of the Department of Homeland Security, twice extended the program to ensure that the 4,400 eligible families could be transitioned.

The assessment of need and alignment of resources has been more consistent under the Obama administration.[42] In addition to funding PSH vouchers and vouchers under the DHAP conversion, HUD notified HANO in 2010 that its voucher program would be funded at about $162 million, which would support almost 17,000 vouchers, including about 4,000 additional vouchers.[43] HUD's commitment of additional voucher resources to New Orleans provides creative matching of resources: with market-rate housing vacancies in New Orleans near 13 percent as of September 2009 and tens of thousands on affordable housing waiting lists, the additional vouchers can help to house those on the waiting lists and to fill the market-rate properties that have been restored by their owners.[44]

Reform of the Troubled Housing Authority

Another bright spot was the decision of HUD in October 2009 to remove HUD staff as HANO's administrative receiver and to contract with the private management company of Gilmore Kean to manage the day-to-day operations of the agency.[45] Known for turning around the notorious Washington, D.C., housing authority, firm principal David Gilmore completed a ninety-day assessment that was extremely candid about HANO's dysfunctional management, and HUD set a course to fix HANO within a three-year period and return it to local control.[46]

Under Gilmore Kean's leadership, a twelve-member local advisory board of civil rights, legal aid, community development, health, and tenant council leaders was appointed. HANO quickly required all of its $34.6 million in American Recovery and Reinvestment Act (ARRA) funding to be used to supplement many stalled recovery projects,[47] won a CHOICE neighborhoods implementation competition to redevelop its last aging public housing complex, and began to restore some of the confidence of some resident leaders.

HANO has taken proactive and creative steps to get its vouchers leased up, giving priority to the housing needs of the homeless, the disabled, and domestic violence victims through partnerships with nonprofit agencies to ensure that vulnerable populations have access to housing vouchers. It is working to "project base" as many of the new vouchers as possible, with the aim of putting vacant units back on the market as long-term affordable housing.[48] Cynthia Wiggins, tenant council president at Guste Community Housing and president and CEO of Guste Homes Resident Management Corporation, sees all of these as good signs. "Hopefully the Housing Authority can get on the same page with the new mayor [Landrieu] to change mindsets and make the neighborhoods right," she said.[49]

The Private, Philanthropic, and Local Role

Combining the place-based approach of neighborhood recovery with the people-based approach of providing housing support to vulnerable residents continues to transform the recovery. The community developers of the new Harmony Oaks development apply a case management approach to helping residents access training and services that will allow them to increase the economic strength of their households. Urban Strategies, a national nonprofit that provides such services to public housing redevelopment communities, is now applying its services to a Central City neighborhood beyond Harmony Oaks where residents have similar needs.

Philanthropy has played an invaluable role in investing in the initiatives, the leadership, and the physical development and human capital that are making transformation possible. The Louisiana Disaster Recovery Foundation; the Greater New Orleans Foundation; the Patrick F. Taylor Foundation; the Ford, Surdna, Rockefeller, Kellogg, Marguerite Casey and Annie E. Casey foundations; Oxfam America; and many others have invested individually, and collective philanthropic support has come through the Community Revitalization Fund at the Greater New Orleans

Foundation. This fund fosters the local leadership that is bringing the best parts of the city back. The growing collective action has powered the development of physical and human infrastructure that will stand as critical capacity for years to come, and it can only bode well for delivering on the aspirations of the city's returning and recovering residents.

Cautions and Implications for Future Policies and Actions

Despite the progress made, serious cautions remain for many residents and many neighborhoods.

When the Louisiana Recovery Authority (LRA) presented its Road Home plan for renters in 2006, it set goals to replace a portion of the 82,000 rental homes damaged or destroyed with 31,000 to 36,000 below-market-rate rental housing units under the multifamily and small rental repair programs. In its action plan to HUD, the LRA noted that 55 percent of damaged homes in New Orleans were rental units and that 20 percent of those units (16,000) were affordable to extremely low-income households.[50]

In September 2009, HANO opened its voucher waiting list for about two weeks, the first time that the list had been opened to the general public since July 2001. The agency, which estimated that it had about 4,000 vouchers to issue, received 28,960 preapplications.[51] Over 83 percent, or 20,336 households, had incomes at or below 30 percent of area median income. These families were simply priced out of the private rental market, and they could not afford rents in the recovery programs that offered shallow subsidies, such as the low-income housing tax credit program or the Road Home small rental repair program, which are currently redeveloping rental homes (see table 7-1).

When Mayor Landrieu gave his first State of the City address in June 2010, he emphasized housing: "[K]ey to the health of our city is affordable housing. . . . In addition, blight is a major issue for all of us . . . with over 55,000 blighted properties in the city. Over a quarter of residential addresses—27 percent—are still unoccupied, becoming breeding grounds for crime and plummeting property values."[52]

With over 10,000 homeowners who chose to rebuild their homes but have not been able to complete the job and with over 28,000 households on waiting lists for affordable rental homes, the city will continue to need the creative community developers that are bringing back the Tremé, the Ninth Ward, Gentilly, Mid-City, Broadmoor, New Orleans East, Central

TABLE 7-1. Examples of Renters Who Need a Deeper Subsidy after Katrina

Resident needing affordable housing	2010 HUD fair market rent (FMR)	2010 low-income housing tax credit rent (LIHTC) with owner paying utilities	2010 Small Rental Property Program (SRPP) rent with owner paying utilities	Affordability gap
Eloise M. (71-year-old senior) Monthly income: $1,034 Affordable rent: $310	1 bedroom $840	1 bedroom $689	1 bedroom $616	FMR: $530 LIHTC: $379 SRPP: $306
Florence S. (two children/disabled family) Monthly income: $674 Affordable rent: $202	2 bedroom $982	2 bedroom $826	2 bedroom $742	FMR: $780 LIHTC: $624 SRPP: $540
Maria C. (five children/full-time worker at $7.00 an hour/40 hours a week) Monthly income: $1,213 Affordable rent: $364	3 bedroom $1,261	3 bedroom $933	3 bedroom $743	FMR: $897 LIHTC: $590 SRPP: $490

Source: Compiled by Southeast Louisiana Legal Services from various sources. Client examples come from organizational files. Rental data sources are as follows: U.S. Department of Housing and Urban Development, "2010 Fair Market Rents" (www.huduser.org/datasets/fmr.html); Novogradac and Company, "Rent and Income Limit Calculator" (www.novoco.com/products/rentincome.php); the Road Home, "2010 Maximum Rents by AMI Tiers" (www.road2la.org/rental-docs/2010_SRPP RentLimits.pdf).

City, and other neighborhoods. These community leaders must be key strategists in how to combine resources best to address both blight and housing challenges together. They have two post-Katrina advocacy venues from which they collectively advance their shared agenda: the Louisiana Housing Alliance, a nonprofit formed in 2007 to do statewide housing advocacy, and the Greater New Orleans Housing Alliance, a peer learning and advocacy network of local housing organizations.

The 2010 census confirmed what many already knew about unreturned residents and unrepaired properties, and these leaders and the Obama administration continue to work to ensure that state and federal authorities do not rescind or reallocate any unspent recovery funds. They are working to keep these resources focused on unmet housing needs, neighborhood rehabilitation, blight reduction, and community opportunity infrastructure. They are especially focused on applying the funds to remediate the disproportionately severe impact on African American neighborhoods and residents.

They also are focused on rebuilding the other components of their neighborhoods: small businesses, access to fresh food, new schools, new transit infrastructure, and workforce development pathways that can address the roots of too many residents' low incomes.

Work in Progress

The world knew that New Orleans and its incredible people and culture were worth saving. It also knew that it wanted the recovery to leave the city economically stronger. The city's equity-focused changemakers continue to carry the mantle of this work. And while much has been accomplished in the five-plus years since the worst urban disaster in modern American history, those focused on addressing the disparities in the recovery deserve the nation's support to finish the job of building an equitable, thriving place that can bring home all who want to return and prosper.

Notes

1. Kalima Rose, Annie Clark, and Dominique Duval-Diop, "A Long Way Home: The State of Housing Recovery in Louisiana 2008" (PolicyLink, 2008). Over 150,000 homeowners applied for rebuilding funds from the Road Home Program (Louisiana Recovery Authority data, June 26, 2008), and FEMA estimated that 82,000 rental units received major or severe damage (FEMA estimates released February 2006).

2. Greater New Orleans Data Center, "Hurricane Katrina Impact," news release, April 15, 2010 (www.gnocdc.org/Factsforfeatures/HurricaneKatrinaImpact/index. html).

3. The Greater New Orleans Housing Alliance (GNOHA) was formed in the spring of 2007. It is a collaborative of forty nonprofit housing builders and community development corporations and twenty-nine housing advocacy groups, financial institutions, and government agencies that are working to rebuild the hardest-hit neighborhoods in New Orleans. The Neighborhoods Partnership Network (NPN) is a citywide network of neighborhoods that was established after Hurricane Katrina to facilitate neighborhood collaboration, increase access to government resources and information, and strengthen the voices of individuals and communities across New Orleans. Together, these networks bring development expertise, neighborhood planning, and strong advocacy.

4. Allison Plyer, "Neighborhood Recovery Rates: Resiliency of New Orleanians Shown in Neighborhood Repopulation Numbers" (Greater New Orleans Community Data Center, 2010) (www.gnocdc.org/RecoveryByNeighborhood/index.html).

5. Greater New Orleans Community Data Center, "Census Population Estimates 2000–2009 for New Orleans MSA," 2010 (www.gnocdc.org/census_pop_estimates. html).

6. Allison Plyer and Elaine Ortiz, "Who Lives in New Orleans and the Metro Area Now? Based on 2008 U.S. Census Bureau Data" (Greater New Orleans Community Data Center, 2009) (www.gnocdc.org).

7. See essays in *New Orleans Index at Five: Reviewing Key Reforms after Hurricane Katrina* (Washington: Brookings Institution and Greater New Orleans Community Data Center, 2010) (www.gnocdc.org/TheNewOrleansIndexAtFive/).

8. Alan Berube and Bruce Katz, "Katrina's Window: Confronting Concentrated Poverty across America" (Brookings, 2005). "Extreme poverty neighborhood" is defined as one in which at least 40 percent of the residents have family incomes below the federal poverty level.

9. David Gilmore, *Operational Assessment of the Housing Authority of New Orleans* (U.S. Department of Housing and Urban Development, 2010).

10. Judy England-Joseph, *Public Housing: HUD's Takeover of the Housing Authority of New Orleans*, GAO/T-REC-96-212 (U.S. General Accounting Office, 1996).

11. Gilmore, *Operational Assessment of the Housing Authority of New Orleans.*

12. Annie Clark and Kalima Rose, "Bringing Louisiana Renters Home: An Evaluation of the 2006–2007 Gulf Opportunity Zone Rental Housing Restoration Program" (PolicyLink, 2007).

13. As reported by community housing organizations in a U.S. Department of Housing and Urban Development forum at Greater New Orleans Foundation, April 9, 2010.

14. See "Louisiana Solutions to Poverty: Engaging Ideas, Empowering People, Enhancing Lives" (Governor's Summit on Solutions to Poverty Summary Report and the First Annual Solutions to Poverty Initiative Roadmap and Action Plan, 2005) (www. dss.state.la.us/assets/docs/searchable/OFS/solutionsToPoverty/GovernorsSummit STOPReport.pdf).

15. National Low Income Housing Coalition State Affiliates, "State Partners and State Level Information" (www.nlihc.org/partners/map.cfm).

16. The tax credits were partnered with $667 million in disaster community development block grant funding administered by the Louisiana Office of Community Development to provide for a mix of income levels in the new and repaired developments.

17. Clark and Rose, "Bringing Louisiana Renters Home."

18. Interview by author, March 30, 2010.

19. Ibid.

20. Rose, Clark, and Duval-Diop, "A Long Way Home," p. 47. Grant awards calculated on prestorm value severely underfinanced the cost of rebuilding, as damage estimates averaged double the prestorm value of Lower Ninth Ward homes. Since this analysis, the Louisiana Recovery Authority (LRA) has provided additional compensation grants to owners who earned less than 80 percent of the area median income and had not received the maximum $150,000 award, helping some of the Ninth Ward households.

21. New Orleans Area Habitat for Humanity (www.nolamusiciansvillage.org/ about/). Including the seventy-two homes in Musicians' Village, New Orleans' Habitat has helped over 300 households become homeowners since Katrina. See www. habitat-nola.org/.

22. New Orleans Habitat Musician's Village (www.nolamusiciansvillage.org/news/detail.asp?id=95).

23. A 2008 review of Louisiana Recovery Authority data by PolicyLink found that Orleans parish homeowners receiving Road Home funds had an average gap of $54,586 between resources received to rebuild and costs of replacement. Rose, Clark, and Duval-Diop, "A Long Way Home," p. 47. The state subsequently got approval from HUD to award approximately 20,000 homeowners who earned less than 80 percent of median income additional compensation grants, which will help some of the affected households finish rebuilding. Louisiana Recovery Authority, "Progress Report, February 2010," p. 5 (www.lra.louisiana.gov/index.cfm?md=pagebuilder&tmp=home&nid=50&pnid=15&pid=69&fmid=0&catid=0&elid=0&ssid=0&printer=1).

24. David Hammer, "Road Home Rebuilding Covenants Have Had Mixed Results, Review Suggests," *Times-Picayune*, April 18, 2010.

25. Louisiana Recovery Authority, "Progress Report, February 2010." As of January 1, 2010, grants had been awarded to 45,309 Orleans parish homeowners.

26. Doug MacCash, "The Architecture of New Orleans' Rebuilt Public Housing Gets Mixed Reviews," *Times-Picayune*, February 13, 2011; and Clark and Rose, "Bringing Louisiana Renters Home," PolicyLink, June 2007, p. 30.

27. NORA will build new offices in Central City if the state Bond Commission approves their bonding application.

28. Una Anderson (executive director, New Orleans Neighborhood Development Corporation), interview with author, June 18, 2010.

29. See partnerships and asset mapping of community at "NEWCITY Partnerships" (www.providencecommunityhousing.org/NEWCITYflyer_03.03.09.pdf).

30. Louisiana Housing Finance Agency, "Housing Pipeline Report, Orleans Parish," a presentation to the Housing Task Force, Transition New Orleans, March 19, 2010.

31. Volunteers of America's the Terraces on Tulane senior housing development and the Crescent Club master-planned, mixed-use community of extremely low-, very low-, low- and moderate-income homes developed by Domain Cos are both finalists in the 2010 Affordable Housing Finance Readers Choice Awards.

32. "Status of Small Rental Property Program, Louisiana Recovery Authority," PowerPoint presentation to U.S. Department of Housing and Urban Development, July 8, 2010, p. 11.

33. Louisiana Housing Finance Agency, "Housing Pipeline Report, Orleans Parish."

34. Louisiana Office of Community Development, Division of Administration, and the Louisiana Recovery Authority, "The Road Home Housing Program's Action Plan Amendment of Disaster Recovery Funds" (www.doa.la.gov/cdbg/dr/plans/Amend1-RoadHome-Approved_ 06_05_11.pdf).

35. A recent inventory compiled by the Greater New Orleans Fair Housing Action Center found eleven developments in the greater New Orleans metropolitan statistical area that had been denied development permits, had land rezoned to prevent their development, or had multifamily building moratoriums imposed to prevent their development. Other developments are stuck in the state bond commission, where refusals to hear requests for bonding are sustained. And when the bottom fell out of the national low-income housing tax credit market, Congress agreed to make the credits refundable from the Treasury Department, but the department ruled that this did not include disaster tax credits, leaving the deals without financing.

36. Congressional funding for 3,000 PSH vouchers was obtained in June 2008, almost three years after Katrina. The Supplemental Appropriation Act of 2008 (P.L. 110-252) provided $20 million in federal project-based voucher funding for 2,000 vouchers and $50 million in Shelter Plus Care vouchers for 1,000 vouchers for a five-year period; 1,890 vouchers are planned for New Orleans.

37. Costs of construction escalated during the recovery, when the Great Recession compromised many investors' commitments to projects, bank credit tightened, and developers did not propose projects at the higher levels of affordability.

38. UNITY of Greater New Orleans, *Homeward Bound Newsletter,* vol. 2, no. 2 (2010).

39. As of this writing, about 535 households had moved into PSH homes in New Orleans and an effective partnership between federal, state, and nonprofit agencies is involved in operating the program, including HUD, the newly created Louisiana Housing Authority, Unity of Greater New Orleans, the Louisiana State Department of Health and Hospitals, six local lead agencies, the Louisiana Housing Finance Agency, the Louisiana Office of Community Development, and numerous nonprofit agencies that provide case management services to participants.

40. UNITY of Greater New Orleans, *Homeward Bound Newsletter,* vol. 2, no. 2.

41. Congress allocated the funds under the Consolidated Appropriations Security, Disaster Assistance, and Continuing Appropriations Act, 2009 (P.L. 110-329). See U.S. Department of Housing and Urban Development, "2009 Supplemental Appropriation Sec. 1203 Vouchers (THU to HCV)" (www.hud.gov/offices/pih/publications/sec1203.cfm).

42. John Washek, Edgemere Consulting, interview by author, May 28, 2010. Washek is a consultant with Gilmore Kean, the new HUD receiver for the Housing Authority of New Orleans.

43. As of July 16, 2010, HANO had reported that within the prior ninety days, it had issued about 4,000 vouchers. However, under HUD voucher funding rules, HANO will be funded in 2011 based on the number of vouchers that are actually under lease, not simply issued, as of September 20, 2010. While voucher funding formulas are quite complicated, it is basically a "use it or lose it" system. Some adjustments can be requested by a housing authority for vouchers leased up through December 31. If a significant number are not leased up, the subsequent revocation of funding would be a catastrophic loss for New Orleans, given the unmet targets for affordable rental housing replacement.

44. Allison Plyer and others, "Housing Production Needs: Three Scenarios for New Orleans: Annual Report November 2009" (Greater New Orleans Community Data Center, 2009), p. 10 (www.gnocdc.org/HousingProductionScenarios/index.html).

45. U.S. Department of Housing and Urban Development, "HUD Names New Leadership at Housing Authority of New Orleans," news release, October 2, 2009 (portal.hud.gov/portal/page/portal/HUD/press/press_releases_media_advisories/2009/HUDNo.09-198).

46. U.S. Department of Housing and Urban Development, "HUD Report Shows Serious Shortcomings in HANO Operations," news release, February 18, 2010 (portal.hud.gov/portal/page/portal/HUD/press/press_releases_media_advisories/2010/HUDNo.10-034).

47. Katy Reckdahl, "HANO Proves Doubters Wrong, Lines Up Plans for Stimulus Money," *Times-Picayune,* March 17, 2010 (www.nola.com/politics/index.ssf/2010/03/hano_proves_doubters_wrong_lin.html).

48. Project-based Section 8 attaches the subsidy to a unit rather than a tenant, providing long-term affordability of the unit.

49. Interview by author, July 1, 2010.

50. Louisiana Office of Community Development, Division of Administration, and the Louisiana Recovery Authority, "The Road Home Housing Program's Action Plan Amendment of Disaster Recovery Funds."

51. Reported unduplicated applications. U.S. Department of Housing and Urban Development, Office of Public and Indian Housing, *Annual Plan for Fiscal Year Beginning 10/2010* (2010), p. 8 (www.hano.org/Postings/PHA%20Plan.pdf)..

52. Mayor Mitchell J. Landrieu, *State of the City Address: Eyes Wide Open,* July 9, 2010 (http://media.nola.com/politics/other/landrieu-speech-2010.pdf).

8

Evacuation Planning for Vulnerable Populations: Lessons from the New Orleans City Assisted Evacuation Plan

John L. Renne

M ass evacuations due to natural disasters and anthropogenic events, including accidental and terrorism-related disasters, have become an increasingly important topic in the United States, especially since the September 11 terrorist attacks in 2001 and Hurricane Katrina in 2005. Given these events, many planners and policymakers realize the importance of evacuation planning, particularly for vulnerable populations, in creating resilient cities. Vulnerable populations include but are not limited to people who are unable to self-evacuate in a car and those with specific or functional needs. Moreover, vulnerability is dynamic, and it can be created by a disaster, impacting tourists and residents who might not consider themselves vulnerable until they cannot provide their own means of evacuation before, during, or after a disaster.

I would like to acknowledge the Federal Transit Administration for providing a grant to study the issues discussed in this chapter. I would also like to thank all the members of our team who contributed to the research that this chapter is based on, including Thomas Sanchez, Todd Litman, Jacky Grimshaw, Brian Wolshon, Pamela Jenkins, Shirley Laska, Robert Peterson, and Peter Bennett. Robert Peterson was instrumental in researching and drafting the preliminary text on the New Orleans City Assisted Evacuation Plan. I also wish to thank John Kiefer, Elisa Nichols, and Deborah Matherly, who have guided my understanding of these issues. Any errors or omissions are solely the responsibility of the author.

While some people might become vulnerable as a result of a disaster, many cities have large populations of carless residents, defined as anyone not having access to an automobile for any reason. Given past failings and the fact that such a large percentage of urban renters in large cities do not have access to vehicles, there is an opportunity for America to become better prepared and more resilient by examining and reformulating policies to reduce social exclusion in evacuation planning for vulnerable populations. During the evacuation of New Orleans for Hurricane Katrina, an estimated 1 million people fled by automobile within forty-eight hours, which was one of the largest evacuations in U.S. history.[1] That success was overshadowed by the fact that many of the carless, which included vulnerable populations such as independent elderly residents, were unable to leave.[2] The social exclusion of carless and vulnerable populations in emergency preparedness and evacuation planning efforts prior to Hurricane Katrina represents a key environmental justice issue that requires a national policy response.[3]

The evacuation of New Orleans during Hurricane Gustav in September 2008 went relatively unnoticed by the media despite being one of the most successful evacuations in U.S. history. The city of New Orleans, Jefferson Parish, and the state of Louisiana executed the City Assisted Evacuation Plan (CAEP), with only minor problems.[4] This plan, which can serve as a national model, resulted from a two-and-a-half-year planning process that included nonprofit and private organizations as well as hundreds of stakeholders from all levels of government.

Overview of Evacuation Planning for Carless and Vulnerable Populations

Across the nation, approximately 10 million households do not have access to automobiles. As shown in table 8-1, one-in-five (20 percent) rental households across the country do not have access to a vehicle. The carless are heavily concentrated in selected large cities. The average carless rate for rental households across San Francisco, Washington, Miami, Chicago, New Orleans, Baltimore, Boston, New York, and Philadelphia is 57 percent. Two-thirds (68 percent) of renters in New York City do not have access to a vehicle.

Vulnerability extends beyond not having access to a vehicle. Many poor households that have cars might not be able to afford to evacuate due to the cost. Those with medical needs might not be able to withstand

TABLE 8-1.   **Percent of Households without Vehicle Availability, by Housing Tenure, for Selected Cities across the United States**

Percent

City	Owner-occupied housing units without vehicles	Renter-occupied housing units without vehicles	All occupied housing units without vehicles
San Francisco	9	43	30
Washington, D.C.	15	51	35
Miami	8	25	19
Chicago	11	41	27
New Orleans	7	30	18
Baltimore	13	48	30
Boston	13	47	35
New York City	27	68	54
Philadelphia	20	49	33
Average for selected cities	19	57	42
United States	3	20	9

Source: Greater New Orleans Community Data Center compilation of 2009 American Community Survey one-year estimates, U.S. Census Bureau.

a long journey in a car. The failure of planning efforts in New Orleans prior to Katrina resulted in the deaths of over 1,800 people, who were disproportionately elderly: 71 percent of the victims were over the age of sixty and 47 percent were over the age of seventy-five.[5] Global media focused on the approximately 30,000 people stranded and suffering for days at the Superdome and the New Orleans Convention Center. Thousands more were airlifted or rescued from their rooftops by boats.

Since Hurricane Katrina, a number of articles and reports have highlighted the need for better planning and preparedness when it comes to evacuating vulnerable populations. Although literature addressing evacuation planning for carless and vulnerable populations is found mainly in the fields of emergency management and sociology, in recent years the topic has gained attention in the disciplines of transportation, planning, engineering, and health and human services.

In a report that studied the emergency response and evacuation plans of fifty-six states and territories and the seventy-five largest urbanized areas, the U.S. Department of Homeland Security (DHS) found that plans were not sufficient to handle catastrophic events and that mass evacuation is a significant weak spot. The study noted that 18 percent of state plans and only 7 percent of urban area plans were "sufficient in incorporating all available modes of transportation into emergency plans."[6]

A seminal study by Wolshon, Urbina, and Levitan only briefly addressed evacuation planning for low-mobility groups;[7] however, a cross-national historical study of evacuations found that rail, bus, and walking were "used by many" in twenty-two of twenty-seven disasters.[8] A review of plans for cities in New York state, including Albany, Buffalo, Rochester, and Syracuse, found that each had a carless population of more than 25 percent but failed to consider multimodal evacuation planning.[9] In a report to Congress, the U.S. Department of Transportation (DOT) and the DHS found that plans to evacuate people with special needs during catastrophic hurricanes were virtually nonexistent.[10]

In 2006, a U.S. Government Accountability Office (GAO) report found that one of the greatest challenges to evacuating people is the identification of transportation-disadvantaged populations. Moreover, understanding special needs and providing transportation for people with such needs was noted as a major challenge: the populations are diverse, constantly changing, and hard to assess since their needs vary widely—some need basic transportation while others need specialized equipment, such as buses with wheelchair lifts. The report also identified legal barriers as a major challenge. For example, liability concerns of transit agencies were identified as a reason that some do not want to become involved in evacuation planning. The GAO notes that state and local governments are not well prepared—"in terms of planning, training, and conducting exercises—to evacuate transportation-disadvantaged populations, but some have begun to address challenges and barriers."[11] It found that only 10 percent of state plans and 12 percent of urban area emergency plans addressed evacuating these populations.

After examining the thirty-eight largest urbanized areas in the United States, the Transportation Research Board (TRB) Committee on the Role of Public Transportation in Emergency Evacuation recommended including transit providers and social service agencies in the creation of emergency evacuation plans.[12] Moreover, TRB recommended creating memoranda of understanding between agencies and across jurisdictions to clarify roles and responsibilities and perhaps reduce liability concerns. They also recommended training for operators, better public information, and preparedness drills and exercises.

Finally, this author, along with Thomas Sanchez and Todd Litman, published a report in which we recommended that emergency plans should be evaluated on the basis of their effectiveness in serving vulnerable populations.[13] We called for the inclusion of evacuation planning and disaster response for all hazards as part of nonemergency transportation planning efforts. Building resiliency and redundancy within the transportation system, including infrastructure, is vital to becoming better prepared. That includes managing and staging resources, cross-training personnel, and educating the public, especially at-risk populations.

Federal Policy on Emergency Preparedness and Evacuation Planning

While there is a dearth of evacuation planning focusing on carless and vulnerable populations at the local level, federal policy—which includes no mandates for pre-disaster planning, especially for vulnerable populations—also is limited. The predominant policy statement guiding emergency management at the federal level in the United States is that "all disasters are local." If local governments cannot handle the magnitude of a disaster, state government must either provide the necessary resources or seek assistance from the federal government. The federal government's focus in emergency preparedness efforts is on response, with minimal guidance on planning for mass evacuations that require multiple modes of transportation. When it comes to transportation planning for nonemergencies, the federal government requires metropolitan planning organizations (MPOs) to engage in regional transportation planning. Policy includes a number of elements related to daily transportation needs, but MPOs are not required to engage in evacuation planning.

Evacuation response (not to be confused with evacuation planning) falls under the domain of the Federal Emergency Management Agency (FEMA), a division of the Department of Homeland Security. FEMA organizes emergency responses as stipulated within the National Response Framework (NRF). Under the NRF, emergency support functions (ESFs) dictate the role of federal agencies in an emergency response to state and local governments when FEMA receives a request for assistance. While ESF 1 focuses on transportation, which includes prevention, preparedness, and response, it does not go as far as mandating that local governments and transit agencies create evacuation plans for vulnerable populations.

Local jurisdictions, regions, and states can find resources for crafting evacuation plans in the FEMA Pre-Disaster Mitigation (PDM) program, which provides grants to states, territories, Indian tribal governments, communities, and universities for hazard mitigation. Funds are awarded on a competitive basis. In 2010, FEMA awarded 186 PDM grants. While none of them had "evacuation" or "transportation" in the title, many of them were called "multi-hazard mitigation plan." However, without studying the plans it is difficult to know how many of them include an evacuation component.[14]

The New Orleans City Assisted Evacuation Plan: A Best-Practice Case for Carless and Vulnerable Populations

Immediately after Hurricane Katrina, the city of New Orleans, in cooperation with a variety of public, nonprofit, and private stakeholders, including state and federal agencies, created the City Assisted Evacuation Plan. The CAEP was tested during Hurricane Gustav in 2008 and serves as a best-practice case for evacuation planning for carless and vulnerable populations.

Louisiana is under constant threat from hurricanes. Prior to Hurricane Katrina, evacuation plans in New Orleans and at the state level focused solely on automobile-based evacuations, known as contraflow plans, in which inbound highways reverse direction so that all lanes force vehicles to leave the city, thus increasing the capacity for outbound traffic. After Katrina, New Orleans, in collaboration with neighboring suburban Jefferson Parish and the state of Louisiana, expanded on the contraflow plans and developed the CAEP, which addressed vulnerable populations, including but not limited to tourists and elderly, carless, homeless, and poor residents and those with medical needs.

In Louisiana, evacuation planning is a responsibility shared by the parishes and the state government. Under the State of Louisiana Emergency Operations Plan, developed by the Governor's Office of Homeland Security and Emergency Preparedness (GOHSEP), emergency support function 1, transportation, calls for defined pickup locations in each of the state's sixty-four parishes. It is the responsibility of each parish to transport persons needing evacuation assistance to the pickup locations by implementing its Parish Emergency Operations Plan—in the case of New Orleans, the CAEP.

The city of New Orleans Office of Emergency Preparedness developed the CAEP along with a significant public education campaign to inform residents that evacuation assistance was available to those who could not self-evacuate.[15] The CAEP functioned to pick up people throughout

New Orleans at various locations, including four senior centers, thirteen general public locations, two hotels, and paratransit residential locations. Once at a designated pickup spot, people were transported to staging areas. Jefferson Parish had pickup locations that fed into the same staging areas in New Orleans. People were also allowed to arrive directly at one of the staging areas to join the public evacuation. The hotel pickup locations were intended for tourists who already had airline tickets; their staging area was the Louis Armstrong International Airport, and their evacuation was coordinated with the airlines, which agreed to bring in extra planes to evacuate tourists early. Tourists without cars or airline tickets entered the CAEP as members of the public through general public pickup locations.

At the general public pickup locations, evacuees were transported on local buses to their staging area, the New Orleans Arena (NOA); their evacuation then became dependent on the evacuation planning of the state of Louisiana through GOHSEP, and their destination was confidential for security reasons. However, emergency planners realized that secrecy discouraged people from evacuating, and the policy has since been revised.

The senior center pickup locations and paratransit residential pickups were intended for seniors or persons who need medical resources (NMRs). Each NMR is allowed to be accompanied by one caregiver. During Hurricane Gustav, their staging area was the Union Passenger Terminal (UPT) and their mode of transportation was Amtrak, destined for Memphis, Tennessee. Memphis was chosen, despite being 200 miles beyond Jackson, Mississippi, because an agreement had not been reached between officials in New Orleans and Jackson. People requiring a higher level of medical assistance were transported to the Belle Chasse Naval Air Field, other helicopter interceptor sites, or other airfields.

The city of New Orleans estimated that nearly 18,000 people used the CAEP during Hurricane Gustav. An estimated 14,000 people could travel through the NOA staging area, and 6,000 seniors or NMRs could travel through the UPT staging area. An additional 5,000 to 50,000 tourists could be in the city at any given time. However, the city of New Orleans takes into consideration that most tourists have cars or, at least, return airline tickets. The plan designated two hotel pickup locations and used local charter buses to move tourists to the airport. This phase of the plan began at H-58, fifty-eight hours before the hurricane made landfall on the Gulf Coast.

The CAEP began with a process called "leaning forward" as early as eighty-four hours before the hurricane's coastal landfall. That process included the preparation of the staging areas and transportation assets. At H-54, the CAEP took effect, and general public and senior center pickup locations opened, designated buses began running evacuation services (two buses per pickup location), and forty more buses continued to offer limited regular service. At that time, 100 state-contracted buses arrived at the NOA ready to transport people from the city to shelters. The paratransit service began residential pickups at the same time.

Paratransit operations were coordinated by the 311 Center under the residential evacuation assistance pickup (REAP) operations plan. The 311 Center functioned as the control center for the operations. The city of New Orleans promoted pre-registry with the 311 system, but evacuees needing residential assistance were able to call 911 or 311 at the onset of the emergency. Call center operators screened the callers to determine their needs. The information was then passed to the area commander, who dispatched a bus, ambulance, or other appropriate form of transportation. The operations of REAP continued until everyone requesting assistance received it. Broadening the definition of "residential" in the REAP, the area commander sent buses to locations where seniors often congregate, in addition to the seventeen planned pickup locations, such as homeless shelters.

The CAEP included a hospital and care centers evacuation operations plan that was closely coordinated with ESF 8 of the Louisiana Emergency Operations Plan, resulting in transportation by ambulance. Each hospital had previously developed plans to shelter in place, partially evacuate, or completely evacuate. In addition, each hospital initiated one of the three plans at different storm levels. For example, Children's Hospital had a stay-in-place plan for category 3 and 4 hurricanes and a full evacuation plan for a category 5 hurricane. On the other hand, University Hospital initiated a full evacuation for a category 3 hurricane.

The Louisiana Department of Health and Hospitals requires an evacuation plan before nursing home and home health agencies can be licensed. It was unclear, however, if those plans have overbooked local transportation resources. To limit potential conflict, the CAEP has developed contracts with coach buses from outside the city, thereby leaving local companies available for local nursing home contracts.

The CAEP also included a pet evacuation plan. The city of New Orleans anticipated offering shelter for up to 10,000 pets; however, while the number of pets boarded during Gustav was less, the actual number is not known. Since pets were not allowed in American Red Cross shelters, they must be sheltered separately. The Louisiana Society for the Prevention of Cruelty to Animals (SPCA) has developed extensive planning to pick up pets at both the UPT and NOA staging areas. Pets that were confined in carriers or were muzzled were allowed on the local transit buses that brought evacuees to the staging areas. The SPCA then bar-coded the pets to facilitate the reuniting of pets with their families after the storm.

A study of CAEP participants during Hurricane Gustav found that almost three-quarters were satisfied with their experience and would use the CAEP again. Moreover, more than 70 percent rated their experience as good or better.[16] The evaluation also identified areas that could be improved, but the overall conclusion was that the CAEP was successful in evacuating vulnerable and carless populations using multiple modes of transportation.

The CAEP in New Orleans resulted from the lack of such a plan during Hurricane Katrina, with results that attracted negative national attention. Miami–Dade County had a similar experience after Hurricane Andrew in 1992, and planning efforts increased in New York City following the September 11, 2001, terrorist attacks. The experience after Katrina led the city of New Orleans, Jefferson Parish, and the state of Louisiana to work closely, with assistance from the federal government, to develop an important social safety net. While the CAEP was multimodal and focused on vulnerable and carless populations, it was not truly a regional plan. The planning process was led by emergency managers in New Orleans working closely with emergency managers in Jefferson Parish. Together, they coordinated mainly with state officials. Perhaps a more regional effort would allow for the inclusion of all suburban areas, not just two parishes, into the planning process.

Lessons for the Inclusion of Carless and Vulnerable Populations during Disaster Planning

American cities need to become more resilient by crafting evacuation plans that are more inclusive of carless and vulnerable populations. The federal government does not mandate transportation planning for emergencies the same way that it does for daily travel. However, FEMA's ESF 1 includes language supporting prevention and preparedness. Local, state, and other jurisdictions also have the opportunity to receive pre-disaster hazard mitigation grants to support these endeavors; however, the extent to which PDM grants are being used to support evacuation planning, especially for carless and vulnerable populations, is unknown.

Since Hurricane Katrina, few local jurisdictions around the nation have crafted evacuation plans for carless and vulnerable populations. That is worrisome considering the large percentage of people in major cities, especially renters, low-income families, and elderly residents, who might not have access to a vehicle for self-evacuation.

The case study of the New Orleans CAEP identifies how vulnerable and carless populations can be included in an evacuation plan. The CAEP's effectiveness led to the inclusion of these communities during the evacuation of New Orleans for Hurricane Gustav in 2008, resulting in increased environmental justice during an impending disaster, which is arguably the most important time.

Cities around the United States should look to New Orleans and the CAEP as an example of a proactive and inclusive government approach to evacuation planning. The plan was not the result of a federal mandate; it was based on the initiative of a local government, working in partnership with many stakeholders, to ensure that the disaster of Katrina was not repeated. Its success was evident during Hurricane Gustav in 2008.

The federal government needs to realize that planning for the inclusion of vulnerable populations during disasters requires regional evacuation planning. The cultures of emergency managers and transportation planners rarely cross, but interaction has become more common in recent years. Current policy, which asserts that all disasters are local, ignores history. While some cities, like New Orleans, may proactively create plans that include carless and vulnerable residents, most will likely ignore evacuation planning for these people, thereby failing to capitalize on the opportunity to become more resilient. Thus, until the federal government mandates that regional planning efforts address carless and vulnerable populations, current emergency management and transportation policies will continue to exclude the members of society that most need assistance during the most trying times.

Notes

1. Brian Wolshon and Ben McArdle, "Temporospatial Analysis of Hurricane Katrina Regional Evacuation Traffic Patterns," *Journal of Infrastructure Systems* 15 (2009): 12–20; John Renne, Thomas Sanchez, and Todd Litman, "National Study on Carless and Special Needs Evacuation Planning: A Literature Review" (University of New Orleans Transportation Center, 2008) (www.planning.uno.edu/docs/CarlessEvacuationPlanning.pdf).

2. Clare Cahalan and John Renne, "Safeguarding Independent Living: The Role of Transportation Planning and Policy in Evacuating the Elderly and Disabled," *In Transition* 14, no. 1 (2007): 7–12, 29–31.

3. Social exclusion is defined here "in the wider context of increasing levels of car dependence across the general population, at the expense of the increasing minority of households who do not have access to a car or individuals who cannot drive." See Karen Lucas, Sophie Tyler, and Georgina Christodoulou, "Assessing the 'Value' of New Transport Initiatives in Deprived Neighbourhoods in the UK," *Transport Policy* 16 (2009): 115–116.

4. Some have reported unpleasant conditions in the shelters (for example, evacuees not being treated with dignity; lost luggage; and delays in returning home).

5. AARP, "AARP Offers Tips to Help Older Americans Prepare for Emergencies," *news release,* September 6, 2006 (www.aarp.org/research/presscenter/press currentnews/preparing_for_emergencies.html).

6. U.S. Department of Homeland Security, *Nationwide Plan Review: Phase 2 Report* (2006) (www.dhs.gov/xlibrary/assets/Prep_NationwidePlanReview.pdf), as cited in Committee on the Role of Public Transportation in Emergency Evacuation, *The Role of Transit in Emergency Evacuation* (Washington: Transportation Research Board of the National Academies, 2008), p. 143 (http://onlinepubs.trb.org/onlinepubs/sr/sr294.pdf).

7. Brian Wolshon, Elba Urbina, and Marc Levitan, *A National Review of Hurricane Evacuation Plans and Policies* (Baton Rouge: Louisiana State University Hurricane Center, 2001).

8. Wilbur Zelinsky and Leszek Kosinski, *The Emergency Evacuation of Cities: A Cross-National Historical and Geographical Study* (Savage, Md.: Rowman and Littlefield, 1991).

9. Daniel Hess and Julie Gotham, "Multi-Modal Mass Evacuation in Upstate New York: A Review of Disaster Plans," *Journal of Homeland Security and Emergency Management* 4, no. 3 (2007) (www.bepress.com/jhsem/vol4/iss3/11).

10. *A Report to Congress on Catastrophic Hurricane Evacuation Plan Evaluation* (U.S. Department of Transportation and Department of Homeland Security, 2006).

11. *Transportation-Disadvantaged Populations: Actions Needed to Clarify Responsibilities and Increase Preparedness for Evacuations* (U.S. Government Accountability Office, 2006).

12. *The Role of Transit in Emergency Evacuation* (Transportation Research Board, 2008).

13. Renne, Sanchez, and Litman, "National Study on Carless and Special Needs Evacuation Planning."

14. *Pre-Disaster Mitigation Fiscal Year 2010 Selections* (Federal Emergency Management Agency, 2010) (www.fema.gov/library/viewRecord.do?id=4316).

15. The CAEP is based on over 100 agreements between the city of New Orleans and outside entities in the public and private sectors. Since these agreements are subject to change each year, the CAEP constantly evolves. This chapter summarizes the nature of the CAEP during Hurricane Gustav in 2008. In 2010, Amtrak and the city of New Orleans failed to reach an agreement, so transporting people by rail out of New Orleans is no longer part of the CAEP.

16. John Kiefer, Pamela Jenkins, and Shirley Laska, *City-Assisted Evacuation Plan Participant Survey Report* (University of New Orleans, Center for Hazards Assessment, Response, and Technology, 2009).

9

Come On in This House: Advancing Social Equity in Post-Katrina Mississippi

Reilly Morse

I'm beggin' you, come on in this house.[1]

The staggering spectacle of Hurricane Katrina's destruction of the Mississippi Gulf Coast—entire coastal communities obliterated, tens of thousands of houses demolished, lives washed away—was not even a day old when it was overtaken by the levee failures and drowning of the nearby city of New Orleans. "If the levees had held in New Orleans," wrote the *New York Times,* "the destruction wrought on the Mississippi Gulf Coast . . . would have been the most astonishing storm story of a generation."[2] As major news outlets increasingly erased Mississippi from the Katrina narrative, a Biloxi newspaper's front page editorial, "Mississippi's Invisible Coast," called them to account: "Please, tell our story. Hear the voice of our people and tell it far and wide."[3] Unfortunately, both Mississippi's unimaginable destruction and its recovery appeared destined to become a footnote.

Unlike New Orleans, the Mississippi Gulf Coast region had no widely known identity to capture the national imagination. Some disaster response volunteers admitted that they had not realized Mississippi even had a coastline. Most were surprised to learn that Biloxi had been settled in 1699 and served as the capital of French Louisiana before the founding of New Orleans.[4] But what the coastal region lacked, the state of Mississippi possessed in abundance: a powerful, bitter grip upon this nation's historical imagination. Rooted in a slave labor economy, quick to secede from the Union, embittered by its defeat, Mississippi was the quintessential unreconstructed segregationist state. The state's reputation for racism and violence was reinforced by the bombings, burnings, arrests, and assassinations during the civil rights movement.

Against that backdrop, the Mississippi coast's fundamental challenge was to stake out a distinctive, empathetic public identity. Within two months after Katrina's landfall, local leaders undertook an aggressive planning effort to deliver a blueprint for recovery to Mississippi's governor, Haley Barbour, before the end of 2005. Meanwhile, Governor Barbour persuaded Congress to award Mississippi federal disaster aid that was unprecedented in size and in the degree of control that the terms of the award surrendered to a state.

Mississippians have worked hard to improve the state's reputation through their response to Hurricane Katrina and to replace the legacy of racism, poverty, and ignorance with a more optimistic, cooperative, and problem-solving image. For the Barbour administration, that effort was expressed as refusal to succumb to victimhood and adoption of a state-driven recovery agenda that made wise use of federal disaster dollars. For community advocates, that approach was a call to change inherited racial disparities in housing and poverty and to extend to all of the state's people the power to decide the state's priorities. In a long, hard fight, organizers and advocates made some advances in the fairness and inclusiveness of Mississippi's housing recovery. The final breakthrough came after advocates persuaded fresh leadership at the federal and the state level to confront past mistakes and come into the houses of those who fell through the cracks.

The Sip[5]

Hurricane Katrina assaulted a coastal landscape that reflects classic southern patterns of settlement. A nineteenth-century railway connecting New Orleans to Mobile laid down a racial dividing line separating white beachfront homes from black neighborhoods.[6] Elsewhere, whites pushed black communities out of town and into low-value, flood-prone swamplands and creeks.[7]

Katrina pushed a massive dome of water into the Mississippi Sound and slammed tsunami-like waves into the entire ninety-mile-long Mississippi coast.[8] The eye of the storm traveled north along the Mississippi–Louisiana border, bringing wind gusts of up to 130 miles an hour and tidal surges of up to twenty-eight feet that obliterated virtually all populated portions of Hancock County.[9] The surge flattened homes along the twenty-six-mile-long mostly white beachfront portions of Harrison County and shoved enormous piles of wreckage several blocks inland to the railroad tracks.[10] The railbed functioned as a levee holding back the tidal waves but not the hurricane-force winds, which tore apart older black "back of town" communities immediately to the north.[11] The Biloxi peninsula was encircled by the surge, which continued westward through a network of waterways and flooded backwater black communities.[12] In Jackson County, the city of Pascagoula suffered widespread surge and wind damage, but the black-majority town of Moss Point, situated on relatively high ground away from the shore, experienced heavy wind-storm damage.[13]

By the time Katrina moved on, 238 Mississippians had died and the Gulf Coast area was left in complete devastation.[14] More than 220,000 dwellings in Mississippi received some damage, including 61,000 with major to severe damage and 159,000 with lesser damage.[15] By the following spring, when FEMA's temporary housing program became fully operational, over 100,000 south Mississippians were living in 39,000 FEMA trailers.[16]

Less than two months after the storm, a team of more than 100 planners, architects, and other experts crowded into the only casino hotel still open to conduct a marathon six-day planning session known as the Mississippi Renewal Forum.[17] Those in attendance felt a mix of euphoria and anxiety. The planners' operating assumption was that the Gulf Coast was now a blank slate, ready to be transformed into a new vision of itself.[18]

The Governor's Commission for Recovery, Rebuilding, and Renewal developed a framework for taking a comprehensive approach to meeting Mississippi's challenges.[19] The commission called on the rebuilding effort to observe the principles of social and intergenerational equity; place priority on addressing the needs of low-income/low-wealth residents in all housing initiatives; invite the public to participate in shaping policy; conduct a detailed housing needs assessment; and share data widely.[20]

Skin Game[21]

During this period, Governor Barbour lobbied Congress to ensure that Mississippi received all the disaster aid that it requested, even at the expense of other states.[22] The federal response took the form of an award of a community development block grant (CDBG) to Governor Barbour's office, and, in an unprecedented act of fiscal federalism, the legislation required the Department of Housing and Urban Development (HUD) to issue waivers at Mississippi's demand of any HUD program requirements except those regarding compliance in four core areas: fair housing, nondiscrimination, labor standards, and the environment. Traditionally, CDBG funds carry a requirement that at least 70 percent be spent in ways that benefit primarily persons of low and moderate income, but Governor Barbour had insisted that the rule was out of place in a comprehensive disaster recovery program.[23] The final bill authorized HUD to reduce the target to 50 percent or to waive it altogether on a showing of compelling need.[24]

In February 2006, HUD awarded Mississippi $5.05 billion of an $11 billion appropriation, leaving only $6.2 billion for Louisiana, which had three times the residential damage.[25] Governor Barbour found himself solely in charge of a sum equal to Mississippi's annual budget, without any state legislative or federal agency checks and balances. Using the powers of his office and his political clout, he blocked bills that would have asserted state legislative oversight.[26]

Once the allocation was announced, Governor Barbour requested that HUD waive the requirement that any percentage whatsoever of the $5 billion be spent to benefit lower-income households.[27] When that failed, he requested that HUD waive the requirement for his first recovery expenditure, a $3.2 billion grant program offering a $150,000 compensation grant to homeowners situated above the federal flood plain whose hazard insurance did not cover storm surge damage.[28]

HUD had put alternative public participation requirements into place that allowed an abbreviated public notice and comment period,[29] and Barbour's proposed expenditure occasioned the first major call to action by advocacy organizations, which had been gathering themselves into informal alliances. Broadly speaking, the groups clustered into one of the following categories: affordable housing and housing counseling organizations, social justice advocates, case management and direct service providers, grassroots community organizers, and racial or policy constituent groups.[30] Some had been working in state or on the coast for years, while others were newly created; some were very small community-based organizations, while others claimed larger geographic service areas; and some were national advocacy or human rights organizations, while others were state or local legal services groups. Overall there was a wide range of focus areas, core competencies, missions, and priorities, with no consistent focal point.

When the first disaster housing program to provide aid only to insured homeowners with uncovered surge losses was put out for public comment, this informal network of national, regional, and local advocates took its first step toward coordinated action. It submitted 1,750 comments opposing the program, which became known as Phase I, and issued a lengthy legal critique through its attorney partners.[31] In summary, the objections were that the program needed to be more inclusive, covering anyone with hurricane-damaged homes, that there needed to be assistance for renters, and that HUD should not waive the requirement that 50 percent of the funds go to persons of low and moderate income. HUD approved Mississippi's plan without revisions but acknowledged the failings of Phase I by stating that Mississippi

> has agreed to examine other housing needs and to pursue other sources of funding to provide assistance for other compelling housing needs, such as for homeless and special needs populations, for low-income renters, and for uninsured low-income homeowners. . . . [Approval of the waiver is granted] provided that the state . . . give reasonable priority for the balance of its funds to activities which will primarily benefit persons of low and moderate income.[32]

HUD's conditional approval did influence Mississippi's housing programs to a degree. The state's next three affordable housing programs targeted low-income residents, but things did not go smoothly. Mississippi's second housing assistance program, referred to as Phase II, originally proposed to provide only $50,000 per flood-damaged household, only one-third of the maximum amount given to Phase I homeowners.[33] By this time housing advocates had formally created an alliance known as the Steps Coalition,[34] and, in their first direct engagement, persuaded the Barbour administration to increase the maximum amount to $100,000.[35] The Steps Coalition attempted to continue collaborating, but the Barbour administration was no longer interested.

Up the Line[36]

Mississippi's piecemeal release of disaster recovery programs made oversight difficult since there was no agreed baseline and no way to weigh alternatives. The state did not fulfill the first housing task recommended by the Governor's Commission for Recovery, Rebuilding, and Renewal: to conduct a detailed housing needs assessment. The Barbour administration also did not pursue any of the participatory policy development proposals recommended by the commission. Instead, the governor put the Mississippi Development Authority (MDA) in charge of the overall disaster recovery program, and it developed policy on its own. The result was that Mississippi skirted public accountability on program design and performance for several years.

Housing advocates used the state public records law in the summer of 2007 to compel Mississippi to produce the HUD quarterly disaster recovery grant reports (DRGRs).[37] Using that information, the Steps Coalition released its first oversight report, which stated that HUD had allowed Mississippi to disregard the requirement to assist low-income residents for $4 billion of $5.5 billion in disaster recovery funds.[38] The report, released on the second anniversary of Katrina, received coverage by *Salon*[39] and *Media Matters for America*[40] and started the first national media critique of the Barbour administration.

National attention increased within weeks when Governor Barbour announced his intention to divert $600 million from housing recovery to the expansion of the State Port at Gulfport.[41] Reports in three national papers,[42] a profile on *Bill Moyers' Journal*,[43] and a *New York Times* editorial[44] criticized the Barbour administration's actions. Representatives Barney Frank (D-Mass.) and Maxine Waters (D-Cal.) wrote HUD secretary Alphonso Jackson, urging him to reject Mississippi's diversion of funds.[45] The Steps Coalition unveiled its "People before Ports" campaign and submitted over 2,000 citizen complaints plus legal objections to the proposal.[46] Local questions were raised about Mississippi's progress in the *Biloxi Sun Herald*: "We need housing numbers we can crunch with confidence."[47] While this editorial did not directly oppose the port diversion, its call for accountability and transparency legitimized the debate.

In January 2008, Secretary Jackson wrote Governor Barbour to reluctantly accept the $600 million plan for the port but, echoing the Steps Coalition's objections, Jackson stated, "I remain concerned that this expansion does indeed divert emergency federal funding from other more pressing recovery needs, most notably affordable housing."[48] In a subsequent congressional hearing, Jackson said:

> Well, I don't think that everything has been provided to low- and moderate-income people that should be provided for housing or infrastructure. . . . But had I had my druthers, I probably would have said, sir, I don't think we should be using this money and I would not approve it. But I didn't have that kind of authority.[49]

Additional opportunities to advance the Steps Coalition's campaign came in a series of congressional oversight hearings. In the first hearing before Representative Waters's subcommittee, the MDA spokesman promised dramatic production of housing, defended the diversion of funds, and announced that a housing needs assessment would be performed.[50] Other testimony accused the state of exaggerating its performance and ignoring the needs of low-income renters and owners of wind-damaged homes.[51]

As a result, thirteen members of the House recommended legislation to bar Mississippi from diverting the CDBG funds from housing to the State Port:

> First, the State has only devoted 55 percent of its CDBG funds for direct housing recovery programs. Second, the state has frequently sought and received waivers of the low-and-moderate-income requirement for CDBG funds. Third, the State explicitly excluded wind damage from its homeowner assistance grant program.[52]

Unfortunately, that initiative failed to garner enough support to move forward.

Hear Me Holler

In the summer of 2008, the Gulf Coast Business Council (GCBC) submitted to Governor Barbour a ten-point memorandum for addressing unmet needs for at least 8,000 to 10,000 affordable homes and 6,000 rental units.[53] The GCBC asked the Steps Coalition to support the recommendations, a request that was a sign of the coalition's growing influence. At the top of the list was the appointment of a "Coast Housing and Redevelopment Czar." Thanks to Governor Barbour's embrace of the recommendation and subsequent selection of Gerald Blessey for the job, the center of gravity of policy moved outside the governor's office in Jackson.

Blessey, a former Biloxi mayor with strong affordable housing experience and solid social policy credibility, opened valuable lines of communication with the social justice community.[54]

On the day of Blessey's appointment, the Steps Coalition released its second annual advocacy report, "Hurricane Katrina: Is Mississippi Building Back Better than Before?"[55] According to Steps, Mississippi continued to have more than 75 percent of its funds exempt from income targeting. The state's completions of affordable housing were not meeting projections, particularly in small rentals. The report added that Louisiana had spent a greater percentage of its disaster aid than Mississippi, particularly on programs benefiting lower-income residents.[56] This was an important counterpoint to the prevailing national view that Mississippi was outperforming Louisiana in disaster recovery.[57]

Two developments concerning Mississippi's housing disaster recovery took place between the Democratic sweep of the presidential and congressional elections in 2008 and the end of the Bush administration. First, a lawsuit was filed on behalf of the Mississippi Conference NAACP and other organizations and individuals challenging HUD's approval of Mississippi's diversion of disaster housing funding.[58] Second, HUD officials in the Bush administration reexamined all of the income-target waivers granted to Mississippi and rescinded those covering $1.2 billion in economic development, community revitalization, and infrastructure.[59]

In early 2009, more than three years after Katrina, Governor Barbour finally released the Mississippi Housing Data Report (MHDP), a detailed assessment of damage and housing recovery progress performed by the Compass Group, a national housing policy firm, and local planning districts.[60] Overall, the report forecast that the state's existing housing programs would produce a surplus of single-family homes and apartments across all affordability categories above pre-Katrina levels and that the gap between demand and supply would be substantial due to the area's lagging population recovery.[61] Coast leaders and state media celebrated this report as definitive proof that the Barbour administration's existing housing programs were more than sufficient to ensure a comprehensive recovery, despite the diversion of housing funds to the State Port.[62]

One questionable MHDP forecast was that over 2,000 households would permanently reside in Mississippi cottages, durable modular shotgun dwellings built as an alternative to the infamous FEMA trailer,[63] but residents in touch with housing advocates described numerous barriers to placing the cottages on permanent sites.[64] Another problem in the report's analysis was the omission of low-income homes with wind damage from the tracking criteria of the first MHDP report. Housing advocates were skeptical that the state would meet the forecasts for other programs on which the MHDP's predictions of success rested, such as the long-term workforce housing program, but they lacked data to disprove the claims.

Cold in Hand[65]

Over the summer of 2009, discussion began with local leaders to determine whether Governor Barbour would be willing to find common ground on the extent and nature of the remaining need for housing. Meanwhile, the Steps Coalition released its third report, "Hurricane Katrina: Has Mississippi Fallen Further Behind?"[66] Steps noted that Mississippi continued to lag behind Louisiana in spending disaster relief, and its housing allocation had decreased while Louisiana's increased.[67] Using graphs and bar charts, Steps showed that Mississippi had spent less, later and more slowly, on lower-income residents than on wealthier homeowners and businesses.[68] Steps listed the need to rescue households outside of existing housing recovery programs as the top challenge facing Mississippi.[69]

Three weeks after the report's release, the *New York Times* published an editorial, "Mississippi's Failure," which endorsed the Steps report's conclusions and significantly raised the organization's credibility.[70] The editorial outraged the *Jackson Clarion Ledger,* which retorted that New York City had no basis to complain since HUD funds had restored New York City's piers following the 9/11 attack.[71] But the *Biloxi Sun Herald* thought differently, writing that "as our recovery enters the home stretch, we need to reappraise our housing programs."[72] For the first time, the *Sun Herald* endorsed extending disaster assistance to low-income owners of wind-damaged homes. In December, the Department of Justice contacted the Mississippi plaintiffs' attorneys to schedule a time to open negotiations. Then, in January 2010, before any meetings could be scheduled, the district court issued a ruling granting HUD's motion to dismiss the Mississippi case. The court observed that the objection to the diversion of the funds "may be well founded as a policy matter" but that the plaintiffs lacked legal standing to bring the case.[73] Plaintiffs appealed the dismissal and announced plans to file an administrative complaint.[74]

Cutting Heads[75]

In the spring of 2010, Governor Barbour agreed to a meeting between
MDA, HUD officials, and Mississippi advocates. A consensus emerged
to develop estimates of the remaining unmet needs and then to determine
ways to cover the cost. HUD officials also agreed to visit Mississippi to
assess local conditions. Over the next several months, MDA conducted a
survey of open cases to estimate the size and cost of unmet needs. Meanwhile, the Mississippi plaintiffs' counsel developed maps to identify any
geographic patterns. In the field visit, after meeting and touring the area
with business leaders, the HUD team accompanied housing advocates on
a tour of damaged homes of residents who were outside of existing case
management programs.

As the fifth anniversary approached, local activists had feared that
Mississippi again would be overlooked by national media, but renowned
film director Spike Lee ignited hope when he decided to include Mississippi voices in his sequel to the Katrina documentary, *When the Levees
Broke*.[76] In July 2010, at a congressional hearing on the Fair Housing
Act, the Mississippi Center for Justice (MCJ) released a report, "Hurricane Katrina: How Will Mississippi Turn the Corner?"[77]

This report contained maps of clusters of unmet needs for housing in
nonwhite communities north of the railroad tracks in Gulfport and Moss
Point.[78] The report challenged Mississippi's use of its "Adopt a Katrina
family" website soliciting donations from bake sales and lemonade stands
for housing repairs when it had nearly $2 billion in unspent federal disaster
funds.[79] MCJ called for the state to fund an unmet needs strategy to address
an estimated 5,000 households.[80] The early release of MCJ's report enabled
the advocates' views to appear in the *Root*'s "Bake Sales for Biloxi,"[81] on
National Public Radio,[82] and on the front page of the *Washington Post*,
which ran an article headlined "Uneven Katrina Recovery Efforts Often
Offered the Most Help to the Most Affluent."[83] On the fifth anniversary of
Hurricane Katrina, HBO aired the first segment of Spike Lee's *If God Is
Willing and Da Creek Don't Rise*, which used an MCJ advocate to explore
the disparity between states and the diversion of disaster aid.[84]

Crossroads[85]

HUD, Mississippi officials, and housing advocates thereafter developed
a framework agreement to provide $93 million for housing assistance to

4,400 households with identified needs, to implement an outreach program, and to reserve an additional $40 million for the needs of additional households.[86] The agreement included households with unrepaired wind damage, residents seeking to permanently occupy cottages, and very low-income renters.[87] Its geographic reach extended 100 miles inland to Hattiesburg and Laurel.[88] Finally, on a rainy day in a civic center in a predominantly black neighborhood in Gulfport, new HUD secretary Shaun Donovan, Governor Barbour, and the Mississippi Center for Justice held a press conference announcing that in return for this $133 million housing program, the Mississippi plaintiffs' appeal of HUD's decision on diversion of housing resources would be dismissed.[89] The following day, the *New York Times* published an editorial, "For Katrina Victims, Relief at Last,"[90] a sentiment to which the *Sun Herald* added, "A Fine Final Effort to Meet Housing Needs."[91] Ten weeks later, more than 17,000 households across nine counties had applied for assistance.[92]

"Ain't No Use Sitting There Crying, 'Cause Crying Won't Ease Your Mind."[93]

In Mississippi, as in other parts of the South, the social justice infrastructure that existed before Katrina was underdeveloped in the areas of alliances, research, and resources.[94] Considering its relatively weak capacity, Mississippi's advocacy community performed above expectations in overcoming the trauma of disaster and responding to the challenges of recovery. It remains uncertain whether its performance can be sustained in the face of crises from the 2008 recession to the BP oil disaster, but the post-Katrina work demonstrates a possible path to success.

By uniting under one alliance known as the Steps Coalition, Mississippi coast organizers and activists connected a variety of campaigns to promote fairness and inclusiveness to a single name and brand while preserving their own autonomy and priorities. This alliance afforded a means to align national advocacy groups with local organizations and project a more powerful identity to political leaders and the public at large. The sharing of data and resources about individual case solutions, civic engagement, and policy advocacy helped the alliance to better critique and navigate the complex array of disaster response programs.

Spotlighting Mississippi's underserved populations in the national media was a top priority, and it required advocates to locate the most powerful and vivid embodiments of injustice.[95] Over time, the Steps

Coalition increasingly wove human examples into its annual reports to attract national media attention to the systemic failures of the state's disaster programs. Other strategies included organizing a march for affordable housing at the reopening of Biloxi's largest casino, having the "People before Ports" team present at the first 2007 gubernatorial debate, and having a slogan-covered FEMA trailer, dubbed the Katrina-RitaVille Express, driven across the nation by a Mississippi activist.[96] The common message was that the chronic poverty and racial discrimination experienced by disadvantaged communities before Katrina explained the disparity in post-Katrina resilience between segments of society.

Mississippi's social justice infrastructure was strengthened by national allies such as the National Low Income Housing Coalition and Oxfam America, which brought local organizers to Washington, D.C., to train them in how to inform Congress and the administration on the issues. Over time, that approach opened up opportunities to testify in congressional hearings and meet with administration officials. As local organizers from different states gathered for these activities, the seeds were planted for regional partnerships and state-by-state comparisons of policy and performance.

It was essential to create room for discussions with the political establishment and demonstrate a data-driven, problem-solving approach to controversies. At times, social justice advocates may resist the opportunity to negotiate with business and political leaders for fear of being accused of selling out. Finding ways to preserve the coalition's integrity while negotiating with nontraditional partners was key to changing the direction of Mississippi's housing disaster recovery.

The best advocacy actions in the world will mean nothing unless someone in government exercises the power to stand up for invisible people. By the same token, the most responsive public officials cannot exercise their powers until advocates and organizers deliver a solution that is backed up with hard data and compelling stories. Persistent effort prepared Mississippi's social justice alliance to seize the opportunity after Governor Barbour appointed a Gulf Coast housing director and after more responsive leadership took control at HUD.

Notes

1. Junior Wells, *Come On in This House,* album released September 24, 1996.
2. Campbell Robertson, "Coastal Cities of Mississippi in the Shadows," *New York Times,* December 12, 2005, p. A-1.

3. Stan Tiner, "Mississippi's Invisible Coast," *Sun Herald,* December 14, 2005, p. A-1.

4. Charles Sullivan and Murella Powell, *The Mississippi Gulf Coast: Portrait of a People* (Sun Valley, Calif.: American Historical Press, 1999), p. 12.

5. A colloquial abbreviation for Mississippi.

6. Sullivan and Powell, *The Mississippi Gulf Coast,* p. 103.

7. Derrick Evans, "A Brief Summary of Turkey Creek's History and Its Importance to Local, State and National Heritage" (Turkey Creek Community Initiatives, 2006) (www.turkey-creek.org/Content/10000/A_BRIEF_HISTORY_OF_TURKEY_CREEK.html).

8. Richard D. Knabb, Jamie R. Rhome, and Daniel P. Brown, "Tropical Cyclone Report: Hurricane Katrina," December 20, 2005, pp. 8–10 (www.nhc.noaa.gov/pdf/TCR-AL122005_Katrina.pdf).

9. Knabb, Rhome, and Brown, "Tropical Cyclone Report," pp. 8–9; for wind speed conversions, see Disaster Center, "Conversion Table for Knots to Miles per Hour" (www.disastercenter.com/convert.htm).

10. Governor's Commission on Recovery, Rebuilding, and Renewal, "After Katrina: Building Back Better than Before," December 2005, p. 21 (hereafter Governor's Commission Report) (www.mississippirenewal.com/documents/Governors_Commission_Report.pdf).

11. Reilly Morse, "Hurricane Katrina: How Will Mississippi Turn the Corner?" Mississippi Center for Justice, July 2010, p. 4 (www.mscenterforjustice.org/glomer/upload_repo/docs/reports/Interim%20Housing%20Report%20Hurricane%20Katrina%20at%205.pdf); see also Governor's Commission Report, p. 58.

12. Knabb, Rhome, and Brown, "Tropical Cyclone Report," p. 9.

13. Morse, "Hurricane Katrina: How Will Mississippi Turn the Corner?" p. 4.

14. Knabb, Rhome, and Brown, "Tropical Cyclone Report," pp. 11–12.

15. Federal Emergency Management Agency and U.S. Department of Housing and Urban Development, "Current Housing Unit Damage Estimates: Hurricanes Katrina, Rita and Wilma," February 12, 2006, p. 12 (www.dhs.gov/xlibrary/assets/GulfCoast_HousingDamageEstimates_021206.pdf).

16. FEMA, "Mississippi: 1604, Individual Assistance Program Global Report," December 4, 2008, p. 2 (on file with author).

17. "Historic Mississippi Renewal Forum Begins," news release, Mississippi Renewal Forum, October 12, 2005 (www.mississippirenewal.com/info/day01.html).

18. Governor's Commission Report, pp. 21–22.

19. Ibid., pp. 153–175.

20. Ibid., pp. 63, 164, 168.

21. A skin game is a game that is rigged against the player.

22. The law contained a requirement that no state receive more than 54 percent of the overall appropriation. See Department of Defense Appropriations Act, 2006, Public Law 109-148, December 30, 2005, 119 Stat. 2780, 2780. See also exchanges between Senator Mary Landrieu, HUD special adviser Fred Tombar, and Governor Barbour in *The Role of the Community Development Block Grant Program in Disaster Recovery, Hearing before the Senate Homeland Security Ad Hoc Subcommittee on Disaster Recovery,* 111 Cong., 1 sess., May 20, 2009, pp. 27–31.

23. 119 Stat. 2780. Written testimony of Governor Haley Barbour, *Role of Community Development Block Grant Program,* p. 103.

24. 119 Stat. 2780.

25. See exchanges between Senator Landrieu and Louisiana Recovery Authority director Paul Rainwater, *Role of Community Development Block Grant Program,* pp. 29–30.

26. Governor Haley Barbour, Veto Message for House Bill 1320, "An Act to Provide for the Tracking of Certain Federal Grant Funds That Are to Be Provided to the State of Mississippi for Assistance to Homeowners Whose Homes Were Damaged or Destroyed by Hurricane Katrina," March 15, 2006 (http://billstatus.ls.state.ms.us/documents/2006/html/veto/HB1320.htm). See also Derrick Johnson, "The Accountability Gap: Unanswered Questions Two Years Later," Mississippi Conference NAACP (www.naacpms.org/files/The_Accountability_Gap.pdf).

27. "Additional Waivers Granted to and Alternative Requirements for the State of Mississippi under Public Law 109-148," HUD, October 24, 2006, *Federal Register* 71, no. 62, p. 372: "HUD is not granting the state's request that all of its activities be carried out under the national objective of urgent need because such a waiver would effectively grant an overall benefit waiver for the entire grant."

28. "Waivers Granted to and Alternative Requirements for the State of Mississippi's CDBG Disaster Recovery Grant," HUD, June 14, 2006, 71 *Federal Register* 34457.

29. "Allocations and Common Application and Reporting Waivers Granted to and Alternative Requirements for CDBG Disaster Recovery Grantees under the Department of Defense Appropriations Act, 2006," HUD, February 13, 2006, 71 *Federal Register* 7666, 7668.

30. Affordable housing and counseling groups included Mercy Housing and Human Development, Back Bay Mission, and Visions of Hope. Social justice advocacy groups included Oxfam America, Lawyers' Committee for Civil Rights under Law, Mississippi Center for Justice, and American Civil Liberties Union. Grassroots community organizers included Amos Network and Southern Echo. Racial and constituency advocacy groups included Mississippi Conference NAACP, Boat People SOS, NAVASA, Mississippi Immigrant Rights Alliance, and Coalition for Citizens with Disabilities.

31. MDA Partial Action Plan for Katrina Recovery Homeowner Grant Program, Phase 1, "Public Comments," p. 18 (http://msdisasterrecovery.com/documents/hap3606%20final.pdf); letter to MDA and HUD from Lawyers' Committee for Civil Rights under Law, March 17, 2006, on file with author.

32. "Waivers Granted to and Alternative Requirements for the State of Mississippi's CDBG Disaster Recovery Grant," 71 *Federal Register* 34457.

33. MDA Partial Action Plan for Homeowner Assistance Program, Modification No. 4, Phase II (public comment version), on file with author.

34. "New Coast Group Organizes: Steps to Aid in Coast Recovery," July 27, 2006, news release, on file with author.

35. MDA Partial Action Plan, Phase II (final version), p. 7. "The Grant Cap Has Been Increased to $100,000" (http://msdisasterrecovery.com/documents/HAP%20Phase%20II%20Mod%204%20Final.pdf.)

36. A railroad term meaning that a person is going north.

37. *Emergency CDBG Funds in the Gulf Coast: Uses, Challenges, and Lessons for the Future, Hearing before the House Financial Services Subcommittee on Housing and Community Opportunity,* 110 Cong., 2 sess. (May 8, 2008) (testimony of Reilly Morse, Exhibit H) (http://financialservices.house.gov/ hearing110/hr050808.shtml).

38. Steps Coalition, "Mississippi CDBG Recovery Fund Report Card and Recommendations," August, 2007 (revised January 2008), p. 2, on file with author.

39. Tim Shorrock, "Hurricane Recovery, Republican Style," *Salon,* August 29, 2007 (www.salon.com/news/feature/2007/08/29/gulf_coast).

40. "Media Ignored Mississippi's Use of Waivers to Redirect Funds Designated for Low-Income Katrina Victims," *Media Matters for America,* August 30, 2007 (http://mediamatters.org/research/200708300010).

41. MDA Amendment 5, Port of Gulfport Restoration Program, September 7, 2007, 2 (on file with author).

42. Sheila Byrd, "Idea to Divert Katrina Housing Funds to Port Draws Fire," Associated Press, September 12, 2007 (www.chron.com/disp/story.mpl/nation/5130884. html); Leslie Eaton, "In Mississippi, Poor Lag in Hurricane Aid," *New York Times,* November 16, 2007, p. A-1 (www.nytimes.com/2007/11/16/us/16mississippi.html?_r=1&oref=slogin); Peter Whoriskey, "Biloxi's Recovery Shows Divide," *Washington Post,* November 25, 2007 (www.washingtonpost.com/wp-dyn/content/article/2007/11/24/AR2007112400616.html).

43. "Recovery Gone Wrong?" *Bill Moyers Journal,* November 16, 2007 (www.pbs.org/moyers/journal/11162007/profile.html).

44. "Mississippi's Misplaced Priorities," editorial, *New York Times,* June 26, 2008 (www.nytimes.com/2008/06/26/opinion/26thu4.html).

45. Letter from Representatives Frank and Waters to HUD Secretary Jackson, October 17, 2007 (http://www.nlihc.org/doc/Frank-Waters-letter-on-MS-CDBG.pdf).

46. See "Recovery Gone Wrong?"

47. "We Need Housing Numbers We Can Crunch with Confidence," editorial, *Biloxi Sun Herald,* December 19, 2007, p. C-4.

48. *Emergency CDBG Funds in the Gulf Coast, Hearing before the House Financial Services Subcommittee on Housing and Community Opportunity* (testimony of Reilly Morse, Exhibit I).

49. See exchange between Representative Capuano and HUD Secretary Jackson, *Oversight of the Department of Housing and Urban Development, Hearing before the House Financial Services Committee,* 110 Cong., 2 sess. (March 11, 2008), p. 9 (http://frwebgate.access.gpo.gov/cgi-bin/getdoc.cgi?dbname=110_house_hearings&docid=f:41728.pdf).

50. *Emergency CDBG Funds in the Gulf Coast, Hearing before the House Financial Services Subcommittee on Housing and Community Opportunity,* pp. 11–13; appendix, pp. 218 (testimony of Jack Norris) (http://frwebgate.access.gpo.gov/cgi-bin/getdoc.cgi?dbname=110_house_hearings&docid=f:43696.pdf).

51. *Emergency CDBG Funds in the Gulf Coast, Hearing before the House Financial Services Subcommittee on Housing and Community Opportunity,* pp. 39–42; appendix, p. 253 (testimony of Reilly Morse).

52. Letter from Representative Frank and others to Representative Obey, June 16, 2007, on file with author.

53. Recommendations of the Housing Working Group of Gulf Coast Business Council, August 8, 2008, on file with author.

54. WLOX News, "Gerald Blessey Named Mississippi Coast Housing Director," August 28, 2008 (www.wlox.com/Global/story.asp?S=8918978).

55. "Is Mississippi Building Back Better than Before?" *Steps Coalition,* August 2008 (www.stepscoalition.org/images/uploads/2008StepsReport.pdf).

56. Ibid., pp. 3, 5, 7–9.

57. Larry Copeland, "In Mississippi, Katrina Recovery Gaining Steam," *USA Today,* July 25, 2006 ("As maddeningly slow as the recovery seems to trailer-bound Missis-

sippians, it's moving faster than in New Orleans—much faster.") (www.usatoday.com/news/nation/2006-07-24-miss-rebuilds_x.htm); Michael Kunzleman, "Louisiana Katrina Victims Still Awaiting Cottages," *Associated Press*, July 18, 2008 ("The delays also bolster a perception that Mississippi has been more effective than Louisiana in employing federal aid in Katrina's aftermath.") (www.foxnews.com/wires/2008Jul18/0,4670,KatrinaCottages,00.html).

58. *Mississippi Conference NAACP et al.* v. *HUD*, No. 1-08-cv-02140-JR (DC DC) (December 10, 2008); "Mississippi State Conference NAACP Files Suit against HUD over Diversion of Hurricane Recovery Funds," press release (www.naacp.org/press/entry/mississippi-state-conference-naacp--files-suit-against-hud-over-diversion-of-hurricane-recovery-funds--/).

59. 73 *Federal Register* 75733, December 12, 2008. The programs whose waivers were rescinded include $606 million in regional infrastructure and $650 million in economic development and community revitalization. The actual amounts vary because of later reallocations to other programs.

60. Compass Group LLC and South Mississippi Planning and Development District, "Mississippi Housing Data Project," January 2009 (http://smpdd.com/housing/MississippiHousingDataProjectExecutiveSummary.pdf).

61. Ibid., p. 3.

62. Michael Newsom, "New Study Looks at Housing on the Coast," *Sun Herald*, February 11, 2009, p. A-1. The MHDP's work for MDA received a national award from the National Association of Development Organizations (http://msdisasterrecovery.com/documents/81709_Housing_Study_award.pdf).

63. MHDP, December 2009 Update, p. 11 (http://smpdd.com/housing/MississippiHousingDataProject_Dec31Update.pdf); Mississippi Alternative Housing Pilot Program (http://www.mscottage.org/reservist/).

64. "Removing Discriminatory Zoning Barriers," Mississippi Center for Justice, 2008 (http://mscenterforjustice.org/featured-article.php?article_id=141).

65. "Cold in hand" means that a person is broke.

66. "Hurricane Katrina: Is Mississippi Falling Further Behind?" Steps Coalition, August 2009 (www.stepscoalition.org/downloads/news/headlines/k+4_report.pdf).

67. Ibid., pp. 3–4.

68. Ibid., pp. 4–5.

69. Ibid., p. 8.

70. "Mississippi's Failure," editorial, *New York Times*, September 21, 2009 (www.nytimes.com/2009/09/21/opinion/21mon1.html).

71. "Port: HUD Funds Built New NYC Piers," editorial, *Jackson Clarion Ledger*, September 23, 2009 (http://www.portofthefuture.com/News.aspx?NewsID=96) .

72. "As Our Recovery Enters the Homestretch, We Need to Reappraise Our Housing Programs," editorial, *Biloxi Sun Herald*, September 26, 2009, on file with author.

73. *Mississippi Conference NAACP et al.* v. *HUD*, Memorandum Opinion, January 8, 2010, p. 5, on file with author.

74. "Group Appeals Dismissal of HUD Suit," *Sun Herald*, February 24, 2010 (www.mscenterforjustice.org/news-article.php?article_id=154) .

75. "Cutting heads" refers to a competition between two guitarists to outplay each other.

76. WLOX News, "Spike Lee Films Documentary in South Mississippi," March 4, 2010 (www.wlox.com/global/story.asp?s=12080861).

77. *Protecting the American Dream (Part III): Advancing and Improving the Fair Housing Act on the 5-Year Anniversary of Hurricane Katrina,* Hearing before the House Judiciary Subcommittee on the Constitution, Civil Rights, and Civil Liberties, 111 Cong., 2 sess., July 29, 2010. (http://judiciary.house.gov/hearings/pdf/Morse 100729.pdf).

78. Morse, "Hurricane Katrina: How Will Mississippi Turn the Corner?" pp. 4, 20–21.

79. Ibid., p. 3.

80. Ibid., pp. 4–5.

81. "Bake Sales for Biloxi," *The Root,* August 13, 2010 (www.theroot.com/views/bake-sales-biloxi?page=0,0).

82. Debbie Elliott, "A Hard Fight for a Political Voice in Biloxi," National Public Radio, August 23, 2010 (featuring map) (www.npr.org/templates/story/story.php?storyId=129375373).

83. Michael Fletcher, "Uneven Katrina Recovery Efforts Often Offered the Most Help to the Most Affluent," *Washington Post,* August 27, 2010, p. A-1 (www.washington post.com/wp-dyn/content/article/2010/08/26/AR2010082606858.html).

84. "If God Is Willing and Da Creek Don't Rise," documentary, HBO (www.hbo.com/documentaries/if-god-is-willing-and-da-creek-dont-rise/synopsis.html).

85. An intersection where a deal is struck in exchange for one's soul.

86. Letter from HUD Secretary Shaun Donovan to Governor Haley Barbour, October 1, 2010, on file with author.

87. Ibid. See also WLOX, "Federal Assistance Is Coming to the Coast," November 14, 2010 (www.wlox.com/Global/story.asp?S=13501477).

88. Ibid.

89. "A Special Thanksgiving for Mississippi's Gulf Coast," Bridge the Gulf Project (http://bridgethegulfproject.org/node/186).

90. "For Katrina Victims, Relief at Last," editorial, *New York Times,* November 17, 2010 (www.nytimes.com/2010/11/17/opinion/17wed3.html?_r=1&ref=opinion).

91. "A Fine Final Effort to Meet Housing Needs," *Sun Herald,* November 14, 2010 (http://bit.ly/euG9Yt).

92. Trang Pham-Bui, "Response to New Housing Grant Program 'Exceeded Expectations,'" WLOX News, February 1, 2011 (www.wlox.com/Global/story.asp?S=13951141); status report from Mississippi Development Authority, on file with author.

93. Junior Wells, "Come On in This House."

94. "Social Justice Organizing in the U.S. South," Institute for Southern Studies, April 2009, pp. 13–16 (www.southernstudies.org/iss/Southern%20Scan%20Apr09.pdf).

95. The injustice of Mississippi's exclusion of owners of wind-damaged homes was illustrated by the story of Irene Walker. When Katrina's tidal surge swept in, the Chamberlains, a white family, waded out of their Gulfport home and crossed the railroad into a predominantly black neighborhood, where Irene Walker offered them shelter until the storm blew over. The Chamberlains received a $150,000 homeowner grant from the state plus insurance, but Mrs. Walker received no assistance, because her home suffered only wind damage. This story was first told in MCJ's fifth anniversary report but then was used in a *Washington Post* lead story (see n. 83) and became the centerpiece of HUD Secretary Donovan's remarks at the unveiling of the Neighborhood Home Program (http://portal.hud.gov:80/hudportal/HUD?src=/press/speeches_remarks_statements/2010/Speech_11152010).

96. KatrinaRitaVille Express National FEMA Trailer Tour (http://krvexpress.org/).

10

A Tale of Uneven Comebacks: Community Planning and Neighborhood Design on the Mississippi Gulf Coast

Mukesh Kumar

The devastation wrought by Hurricane Katrina on the Mississippi Gulf Coast was soon followed by optimistic public statements regarding recovery and renewal. The Mississippi Renewal Forum, organized by the Governor's Commission on Recovery, Rebuilding, and Renewal and the Congress for New Urbanism in October 2005, brought visions of a better future for the coast. The so-called design charrette sought to provide clarity on directions for rebuilding, largely influenced by the principles often found in the new urbanism paradigm. But experiences along the Gulf Coast since then have varied according to local preferences for urban forms instead of adhering to the common vision proposed in the design charrette. Those preferences range from emphasis on compact traditional neighborhoods to sprawling and highly commercial casino-based economic growth.

This chapter presents an analysis of planning efforts in municipalities along Mississippi's Gulf Coast. These municipalities form the Mississippi Gulf Coast Urbanized Areas, from Waveland on the western edge to Moss Point and Pascagoula on the eastern edge. The experiences of these communities have been quite varied, sometimes as a result of federal and state policies but often for local reasons. This analysis of planning efforts on the Mississippi Gulf Coast partially explains the uneven nature of comeback efforts and outcomes and draws insights that may be helpful in planning for rebuilding after future disasters.

The rebuilding and recovery efforts on the Mississippi Gulf Coast in the wake of Hurricane Katrina, while unique at the time, were also remarkably similar in their rhetoric to earlier experiences in the history of cities. American examples include the San Francisco Earthquake of 1906 and the Great Chicago Fire of 1871.[1] In both cases, the disasters were reframed as opportunities for progress and positive change. Efforts at rebuilding in the aftermath of natural disasters in most cities have often exhibited two distinct tendencies: one with an emphasis on resiliency and the other emphasizing opportunity. Resiliency is usually immediate—a short-term vigorous attempt to reclaim a place as if the disastrous event were simply an inconvenience. Opportunity, on the other hand, usually covers a longer period and involves rethinking of social, political, and economic arrangements. While formulaic assertions of resiliency appeal to people's instinctive desire to bounce back to normalcy, descriptions of opportunities often focus on a long-standing regard for progress and growth in a wider context. Similar tendencies were well displayed in the arguments immediately following the disastrous date of August 29, 2005, when Hurricane Katrina struck the 120-mile Mississippi Gulf coast.

The Mississippi Gulf Coast and Katrina

The Mississippi Gulf Coast is a region that includes three counties (Hancock, Harrison, and Jackson) and eleven municipalities. The coastline of Mississippi has experienced varied cultural influences dating back to 1699, when Iberville landed at the bay of Biloxi and chose a site close to present-day Ocean Springs to build Fort Maurepas,[2] including control by Biloxi Indians; French, Spanish, and British armies; and later settlers, until the end of Spanish rule in 1819. Such diverse political and cultural influences can be traced to different communities that arose and developed over time. Current differences are manifested in casino-based progress in Biloxi, port-dominated activity in Gulfport, and art and tourism–based development in Ocean Springs. However, those differences do not hide the fact that collectively the Gulf Coast stands apart from the rest of Mississippi as a unique region in its own right.[3] The coastal areas are generally wealthier and more diverse than the rest of the state.

The coast had experienced population growth similar to that in many other parts of the South in the 1990s, which tailed off after 2000. In pre-Katrina projections for 2030 by the Gulf Regional Planning Commission, core areas of most municipalities were expected to decline while suburban areas grew.[4] At the time that Hurricane Katrina hit, most of the municipalities were facing somewhat similar planning challenges: urban sprawl, infrastructure deterioration, lack of affordable housing, weak economic driver industries, and downtown decay, to name a few. Immediately after the hurricane, recovery efforts focused on the region, so many local issues were sidestepped for a brief period. Quite logically, the immediate concern was to repair and rebuild critical infrastructure—such as police and fire stations, thoroughfares, and bridges—to facilitate the recovery process throughout the region.

To organize and coordinate the recovery efforts, the Governor's Commission on Recovery, Rebuilding, and Renewal enlisted the Congress for New Urbanism to lead a design charrette to produce comprehensive rebuilding plans. During the charrette, the impact of physical infrastructure design on future development and regional land use patterns was discussed extensively by the invited architects and planners (mostly from outside the region), but it took more than a year for most communities to begin developing plans for themselves, with clearly laid-out visions and objectives. The distinction between regional and local concerns is fundamentally important to understanding and explaining how the municipalities on the coast eventually embarked on divergent approaches to rebuilding.

Hurricane Katrina and Immediate Recovery

Most reports on the damage to the Gulf Coast used the term "pure devastation" to describe the aftermath of the hurricane. Figure 10-1 illustrates the damage assessment by Federal Emergency Management Agency (FEMA). The cities in Hancock County were directly under the eye of the hurricane, and the cities of Waveland and Bay St. Louis were almost entirely destroyed. The cities of Pass Christian, Long Beach, Gulfport, Biloxi, and D'Iberville in Harrison County were severely damaged from storm surge and high wind. The cities of Ocean Springs, Gautier, Moss Point, and Pascagoula in Jackson County, the easternmost part of the coast, were substantially damaged by the storm surge but escaped the devastation of the neighboring counties to the west.

As with most natural disasters, the recovery process began immediately. The most remarkable aspect of the recovery in Mississippi was not

FIGURE 10-1. FEMA Assessment of Katrina Damage on Mississippi Gulf Coast

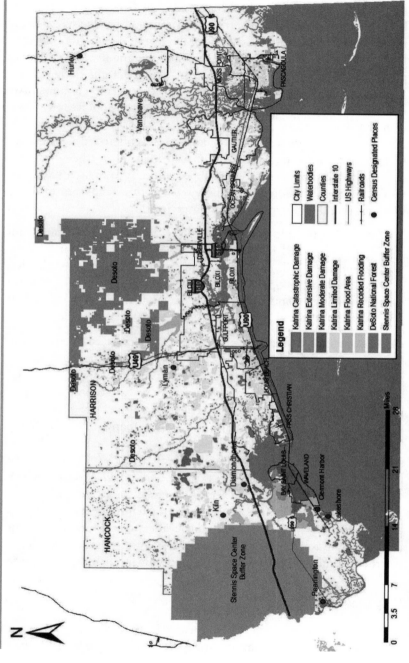

Source: Gulf Regional Planning Commission, "Hurricane Katrina: Three Years Out, Recovery on the Gulf Coast: Three-Year Report by Gulf Regional Planning Commission," September 2008 (www.grpc.com/PDF/FINAL11_2008Hurricane%20Katrina%20Three%20Years%20Out.pdf).

only the widely praised political leadership of Governor Haley Barbour but the formation of the Governor's Commission on Recovery, Rebuilding, and Renewal within two weeks of the storm. Led by Jim Barksdale (a leading philanthropist from Mississippi and the founder of Netscape) and guided by the Congress for New Urbanism (CNU), the design charrette was charged with preparing rebuilding plans for all eleven municipalities on the coast. During the charrette, called the Mississippi Renewal Forum, over 200 participants, including architects, engineers, traffic specialists, and FEMA workers, met for six days and nights, from October 11 to October 18, at the damaged Isle of Capri casino on the coast.[5] In his cover letter of the pre-charrette publication sent to invited participants, Governor Barbour noted the following, which he repeated in different ways in several other speeches and interviews:

> Out of this terrible tragedy, beyond all imagination, comes our opportunity, and I beg you not to let Mississippi miss it. . . . I'm determined we will not fail to seize this opportunity. . . . This is a once-in-a-lifetime opportunity to rebuild the right way and make the Coast bigger and better than ever. What we do now will decide what the Coast will look like in 10 years, 20 years and beyond.[6]

Most statements in a pre-charrette document titled "Rebuilding the Gulf Coast" similarly suggest a profound sense of pragmatic opportunism. While recognizing that immediate recovery was paramount, the authors and organizers of the Mississippi Renewal Forum clearly pushed for a rebuilding plan that was cognizant of the principles of traditional neighborhood development (TND). Andres Duany and John Norquist argued that the goal for the rebuilding phase was to undertake reconstruction that would lead to an outcome that was better than what was destroyed and that doing so was essential to the positive psychology of the state of Mississippi. How could such a tragedy be justified without a silver lining?[7] By suggesting the inferiority of what had been destroyed and the possibility of what could be built, leaders could satisfy the political need for optimism. Such narratives fit nicely into the argument of creative destruction and consequent growth that dominates in a capitalist society.[8]

Why New Urbanism?

An architectural movement that began in the 1970s, new urbanism is the dominant urban paradigm of our times; there is no legitimate competing idea of similar breadth and scope. Adjusting historic development patterns to our times, new urbanism essentially argues for a compact development pattern with an emphasis on physical design that promotes quality of life.[9] It seeks to promote mixed-use, mixed-income, walkable neighborhoods instead of sprawling, segmented development. New urbanists argue that their design principles also promote sustainable growth[10] and are economically efficient.[11] However, in the context of rebuilding efforts in Mississippi, Talen argues that the most important aspect of the new urbanist paradigm relates to the possibility of accommodating the ideals of social equity, not only in its design principles but also through the positive consequences of mixed-use and mixed-income development.[12] Talen further argues that even though social equity ideals can be accommodated in new urbanist plans, the actual realization of the ideals requires significant public investment.[13]

In the case of Mississippi, one can argue that there were at least two legitimate reasons that the Congress for New Urbanism seemed to fit well with the sense of pragmatic opportunism. First, there is simply no competing paradigm to new urbanism that could provide alternative visions for the coast. Although there are numerous criticisms of the sprawling urban pattern seen in almost all of urban America, most current planning models are either too narrow in scope or too small in geographic scale to make much of a difference in that pattern. Without a somewhat complete and elaborate vision, it would have been difficult to exhibit optimism for any set of piecemeal, disorganized ideas. Second, urban planning in general has been unable to find a practical way to realize big plans without compromising on the ideal of citizen participation. New urbanism, in contrast, at least offers some hope for making big plans with substantial possibility of citizen participation. Large-scale planning charrettes offer the possibility of citizen involvement from the visioning process to actual implementation. Hence the political necessity for spinning optimistic post-disaster narratives could legitimately lead to practical steps toward making regional plans.

Results from the Charrette

The design charrette yielded extensive plans for the entire Mississippi Gulf Coast along with specific plans for all eleven municipalities on the coast. The final reports were released in November 2005. The summary report included sections on the region, transportation, social impact,

FIGURE 10-2. Rendition of Integrated Casinos by Correa and Associates

Source: Mississippi Renewal Forum, "Summary Report," November 2005.

retail business, architecture, and flood hazards in addition to community reports on the eleven municipalities. In his introduction, Andres Duany expressed his sentiments: "These are the first steps of an epic journey. And it is our hope that, in the end, the people of the gulf coast will not forever be seen as victims of tragedy, but as a generation of those fortunate enough to have been there for the Mississippi renaissance."[14]

The regional analysis in the report identified two key issues: although 10 to 15 million tourists visit the Gulf Coast each year, they focus on casinos that are not integrated with the rest of the towns, and non-casino retail businesses are so suburban in character that few tourists visit them. The proposed solution (figure 10-2) recommended seamlessly integrating casinos into the overall city plan so that casinos do not appear as isolated structures largely removed from the rest of the town. That suggestion became especially important when the state changed its policy, which had permitted casinos to be sited only on water, to allow them to move inland.

In the area of transportation, the report recommended moving toward a more multimodal approach (figure 10-3) to relieve congestion, improve accessibility, and aim at place making rather than merely moving cars around. Some of the striking recommendations included realigning and revising US-90 to create a beachfront boulevard, moving the CSX rail line north of I-10, realigning the Biloxi Bridge connecting the cities of Biloxi and Ocean Springs, connecting east-west traffic using high-speed rail, and expanding public transit.

Recommendations in the area of social impact included strategies for greater citizen involvement and creation of a design institute to provide technical assistance to local government officials and promote cross-jurisdictional collaboration. The retail strategy emphasized integrating casinos with expanded downtown retail in mixed-use settings (figure 10-4) instead of building isolated, sprawling developments.

FIGURE 10-3. **Rendition of Multimodal Beachfront Boulevard after Realigning US-90**

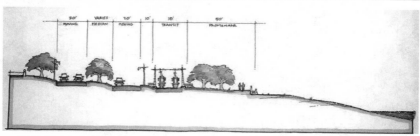

Source: Mississippi Renewal Forum, "Summary Report," November 2005.

The section on architecture argued for common design standards for the region outlined in the Gulf Coast Pattern Book[15] and adoption of smart codes aimed at mixed-use development. New FEMA standards were addressed in the section on flood hazards, with submersible housing suggested as an alternative to stilt houses.[16] Overall, the report was far more comprehensive than any earlier effort made at regional planning on the coast.

Social equity aspects of the ideas suggested in the report have been analyzed by Talen, who argues that social equity goals require further policy, institutional, programmatic, and process initiatives that go beyond physical design and that such initiatives have been largely absent in the coastal region.[17] Some of that lack is due simply to scant prior experience with planning, a point that is further emphasized by Evans-Cowley and Gough, who reported on the level of incorporation of new urbanist ideas in subsequent planning efforts in municipalities of Harrison County.[18] Moreover, the lack of planning experience was compounded by a few clear disconnects between the local residents and the outside planners. Vale and Campanella argue that a community's resilience is reinforced by maintaining continuity with previous conditions and that without regime change, the post-disaster era usually continues with the urban forms and planning practices of the pre-disaster era.[19] The immediate aftermath of disaster is generally not an appropriate moment for more radical changes. The continuation of the existing establishment gave a sense of continuity to communities on the coast, at least in terms of effective political leadership that exhibited future optimism, ably aided by the large-scale Mississippi Renewal Forum. Yet, on a more practical level,

FIGURE 10-4. Renewal Plan for Escatawpa Village in Moss Point

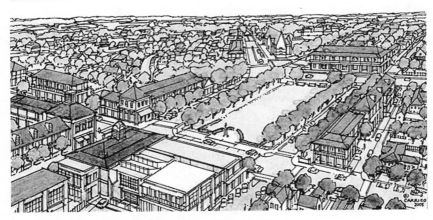

Source: Mississippi Renewal Forum, "Summary Report," November 2005.

local interests were far more influential in following years than were the radical departures envisioned at the forum.

Biloxi Bridge, Casinos, and Katrina Cottages

In his post-disaster statements, Governor Barbour referred to the coast as a single place, and the renewal forum began with a similar approach, in which the coast was viewed as being composed of smaller units that seamlessly contributed toward taking advantage of the pragmatic opportunities available to the region. Evacuation on the coast was far more complete than in New Orleans, and most residents had either not yet returned or were still too shocked to pay much attention to what was produced at the forum. In addition, although large infrastructure projects were funded by federal and state agencies, the implementation of more fundamental recommendations (Gulf Coast Pattern Book; smart codes; transect-based zoning; pedestrian-friendly, mixed-use, mixed-income developments; public transit; and cross-jurisdictional collaboration) had to be decided locally. In spite of the number of participants at the forum, most coastal residents were unable to participate in the charrette. Not surprisingly, the charrette has been lauded in many circles for its design elements, but there also has been persistent criticism that the recommendations are too "impractical," "costly," and "not what people

want." Moreover, planners were mistaken to assume that all municipalities envisioned their future in the same way. The differences were
nowhere more pronounced than in how the Mississippi Department of
Transportation (MDOT) dealt with the Biloxi Bridge, how larger and
more diverse municipalities viewed casinos, and the evolution of the so-
called Katrina cottages.

The bridge over Biloxi Bay, which connected quaint and smaller Ocean
Springs to larger and more diverse Biloxi, was completely destroyed
by the hurricane. While the MDOT proposed rebuilding the bridge as
a six-lane, 120-foot-wide, high-rise structure, the Mississippi Renewal
Forum had recommended rebuilding the bridge in two stages, with a very
different approach: four lanes for automobile traffic and another two
lanes for multimodal traffic, including pedestrians, bicycles, and public
transit. The MDOT proposal received support from the city of Biloxi
but strong opposition from the city of Ocean Springs.[20] Another design
issue concerned the height and aesthetics of the bridge. Two shipbuilding
operations (Trinity Yacht Shipyard and Northrop Grumman ship operations) voiced their opposition to a bridge without a draw span. MDOT
responded by proposing an 85-foot-high bridge with a 150-foot horizontal span. Mayor Connie Moran of Ocean Springs publicly advocated for
a more aesthetically pleasing "signature bridge."[21] The eventual compromise resulted in a 129-foot-wide bridge with six lanes of automobile
traffic and an additional 12-foot lane for bicycles and pedestrians with
adorned fascia girders and ornamental picket railings.[22] It was obvious
that while Biloxi saw casinos as its way to recovery, Ocean Springs saw
its future in mixed-use development based on the principles of traditional
neighborhood design.

Despite suffering extensive damage, casinos were some of the earliest
businesses to bounce back after the hurricane. The state passed a law
allowing casinos to be built on land within 800 feet of the shoreline, a
change that was expected to facilitate building new casinos all along the
coast. However, since the hurricane, most of the cities have not pursued
a one-dimensional strategy of casino-based economic development. With
the exception of the city of Biloxi, which has aggressively promoted itself
for casino development, most other municipalities, influenced to varying
degrees by new urbanist ideals, are at different stages of the community planning process needed to regulate and develop a downtown core.
Bay St. Louis has struggled to find a balance between permitting large-
scale condominium development and remaining a family-oriented town;

Gulfport is progressing toward adoption of smart codes; Ocean Springs has aggressively moved toward a comprehensive plan that incorporates mixed-use development.[23]

During the Mississippi Renewal Forum, one of the ideas offered as a response to the issue of affordable housing other than FEMA trailers was what became known as Katrina cottages. Attributed to Marianne Cusato, a New York architect, these are small (between 300 and 500 square feet) modular houses that can be moved as a kit. Once placed on the ground, they can be expanded and used as permanent homes. Immediately following the hurricane, most cities on the coast were lukewarm to the idea of the cottages and viewed them as unneeded. However, as frustrations with FEMA trailers grew and the Cusato design became popular for a variety of uses (from temporary housing to permanent multifamily dwellings), the cottages came to be accepted as an excellent opportunity to move out of trailers and into homes. Ocean Springs even has a neighborhood, aptly named Cottage Square, made up of the cottage homes and developed along the TND model.[24] Habitat for Humanity also decided to take up similar cottage-style development at several of its projects in Waveland and Bay St. Louis.[25] Within the first two to three years after the storm the practical results of recovery efforts on the coast seemed one-dimensional: casino-oriented, private automobile–dependent development. Now, with the passage of a few more years, it is quite possible that the results may vindicate Tiebout.[26] The municipalities appear to be recovering and progressing in different ways that may accommodate even wider sets of preferences for urban form, ranging from sprawling patterns to compact traditional neighborhood designs.

The municipalities that make up the Mississippi Gulf Coast are more dissimilar today than they were before Katrina. What is most interesting is that immediately after the hurricane, many suggested a radical departure from the sprawling urban pattern that had existed just before the disaster. That might have been because sometimes a loss is a bit easier to bear if one discounts what was lost and looks forward to an imagined future that promises comparatively superior replacements. Gradually, however, most of the communities have continued to move forward in directions similar to those that they were taking before the hurricane. The Mississippi Renewal Forum may have been organized too early and possibly with no large public commitment to its ideals, and many of the fundamental promises of the forum may never see the light of the day. Undeniably, however, although it may be years before the region is able to bring back most of what it had, cities within the region have diverged to create a variety of urban forms that did not exist there before.

Notes

1. For an interesting analysis of the narratives of recovery and rebuilding after the disasters in Chicago and San Francisco, see Kevin Rozario, "Making Progress: Disaster Narratives and the Art of Optimism in Modern America," in *The Resilient City: How Modern Cities Recover from Disaster,* edited by Lawrence J. Vale and Thomas J. Campanella (Oxford University Press, 2005), pp. 27–54.

2. "Pierre Le Moyne, Sieur D'Iberville," *Catholic Encyclopedia* (www.newadvent. org/cathen/07614b.htm).

3. "The historically rich, laid back, slightly tawdry Mississippi Coast has always stood apart from the otherwise largely provincial state. With its French Colonial history, the coast has carried few of the historical burdens wrought by cotton plantations, slaves and the civil rights movement." Quoted in Jennifer Steinhauer, "The Road to Rebirth Diverges on a Mississippi Bridge," *New York Times,* March 14, 2006.

4. Emily Talen, "New Urbanism, Social Equity, and the Challenge of Post-Katrina Rebuilding in Mississippi," *Journal of Planning, Education, and Research* 27 (Spring 2008): 277–93.

5. Jim Lewis, "Battle for Biloxi," *New York Times,* May 21, 2006.

6. Haley Barbour, "The Rebuilding Begins," in Mississippi Renewal Forum, *Rebuilding the Gulf Coast: Answering the Governor's Call for Rebuilding and Renewal on the Mississippi Gulf Coast* (Gaithersburg, Md.: Town Paper Publishing, 2005), p. 2.

7. Andres Duany and John Norquist. "One Step toward Recovery," in Mississippi Renewal Forum, *Rebuilding the Gulf Coast,* p. 3.

8. Kevin Rozario, "What Comes Down Must Go Up: Why Disasters Have Been Good for American Capitalism," in *American Disasters,* edited by Steven Biel (New York University Press, 2001), pp. 72–102.

9. Jennifer S. Evans-Cowley and Meghan Zimmerman Gough, "Evaluating New Urbanist Plans in Post-Katrina Mississippi," *Journal of Urban Design* 14 (November 2009): 439–61.

10. For detailed arguments, see James Howard Kunstler, *The Geography of Nowhere: The Rise and Decline of America's Man-Made Landscape* (New York: Simon and Schuster, 1993). See also William Fulton, *The New Urbanism: Hype or Hope for American Communities?* (Cambridge, Mass.: Lincoln Institute of Land Policy, 1996).

11. Calthorpe Associates with Leland Consulting Group and Tashman Associates, "East Sunnyside Village Plan, Clackamas County, Oregon" (Berkeley, Calif.: Calthorpe Associates, 1993).

12. Talen, "New Urbanism, Social Equity, and the Challenge of Post-Katrina Rebuilding in Mississippi."

13. New urbanism has also been criticized as social engineering designed to promote social homogeneity and a particular type of balanced community while maintaining exclusionary tendencies. For further analysis, see Christopher Silver, "Neighborhood Planning in Historical Perspective," *Journal of the American Planning Association* 51, no. 2 (Spring 1985): 161–74. Also see Tridib Banarjee and William C. Baer, *Beyond the*

Neighborhood Unit: Residential Environments and Public Policy (New York: Plenum Press, 1984).

14. See "Mississippi Renewal: Summary Report" (2005) (www.mississippirenewal. com/documents/Rep_SummaryReport.pdf).

15. See "A Pattern Book for Gulf Coast Neighborhoods" (2005) (www.mississippi renewal.com/documents/Rep_PatternBook.pdf).

16. In the summary report of the Mississippi Renewal Forum, these houses are offered as alternatives to stilt houses. The houses, which are constructed using hurricane-resistant and mold-resistant building technologies, feature raised porches on the ground floor, and they are expected to withstand infrequent deluge.

17. Talen, "New Urbanism, Social Equity, and the Challenge of Post-Katrina Rebuilding in Mississippi."

18. Evans-Cowley and Gough, "Evaluating New Urbanist Plans in Post-Katrina Mississippi."

19. Lawrence J. Vale and Thomas J. Campanella, "Axioms of Resilience," in *The Resilient City,* edited by Vale and Campanella, p. 345.

20. "Denyer: Megabridge not for O.S.," *Sun Herald,* November 16, 2005.

21. See "Ocean Springs–Biloxi Bay Bridge" (2008) (http://oceanspringsarchives. net/node/149).

22. See "U.S. 90 Bridge over Biloxi Bay" (2011) (www.parsons.com/projects/Pages/ us90-biloxi-bay-bridge.aspx).

23. "City Council Agenda: Gulfport" (September 22, 2009) (www.ci.gulfport.ms.us/ 2009Agenda/09222009.pdf); "City of Ocean Springs Comprehensive Plan" (2009) (www.ourplanningworks.com/os/Comp%20Plan%20Final%20reduced.pdf).

24. See "Cottage Square" (2007) (www.cnu.org/node/876).

25. Wally Northway, "First 'Eco-Cottage' Currently under Construction," *Mississippi Business Journal,* December 21, 2010.

26. Charles Tiebout, "A Pure Theory of Local Expenditures," *Journal of Political Economy* 64, no. 5 (October 1956): 416–24.

11

No More "Planning by Surprise": Post-Katrina Land Use Planning in New Orleans

Robert A. Collins

Planning for the rebuilding of New Orleans after Hurricane Katrina was the largest post-disaster urban planning effort undertaken in recent American history. The challenge was made more daunting by the fact that before the storm the city lacked a history of strong traditional urban planning practices. As a result, most processes had to be constructed from scratch. Despite few financial resources and a series of stops and starts, the overall planning process was successful in that as of August 2010 the city had a master plan with the force of law. The New Orleans experience can inform other communities about what to do and, perhaps more important, what not to do when planning to rebuild after a disaster.

Having a predictable, orderly land use plan is critical to post-disaster recovery in any city. It is necessary for informing and prioritizing spending as public and private money is invested in the city after the disaster. Limited resources mean that not every rebuilding project can be funded, and planning can help identify the projects most critical to rebuilding. A predictable land use plan assures citizens that their neighborhoods will remain neighborhoods. Also, real estate developers and private investors need a stable and predictable land use plan to guide their decisions.

Finally, a land use plan can ensure that buildings and infrastructure will be rebuilt in a stronger and environmentally sustainable manner.

The recovery process in New Orleans was extremely confusing in part because many different plans emerged simultaneously and most of those plans did not directly relate to each other. There was a short-term FEMA spending plan, called an emergency support function (ESF) plan; a school facilities master plan; and a plan from the Louisiana Recovery Authority (LRA) for infrastructure construction. (The LRA was the agency created by the state legislature for the purpose of distributing infrastructure construction funding from the federal government.) In addition, there were three different competing citywide plans and a large number of neighborhood plans.

In the absence of a decisive, popular mayor communicating a clear and concise vision of what the city should look like, the urban political process will tend to fragment into chaos, with various interest groups forming around neighborhood identity, ethnic identity, and socioeconomic status. That is what happened in the immediate aftermath of Katrina.

This chapter outlines the culture of planning in New Orleans before Hurricane Katrina and then summarizes the key developments in the planning process after the storm and floodwall failure. It then analyzes positive outcomes, identifies future potential pitfalls, and offers a concise argument of why the proposed land use and zoning reforms matter. Finally, it concludes by offering lessons learned in New Orleans that can be generalized to other cities recovering from disasters.

History of the Challenge

The post-Katrina planning process was not only challenged by the scale of the disaster but also by a social and political environment that had not been supportive of planning in the past. The city council heavily influenced the operation of the New Orleans City Planning Commission. The planning process was very politically charged in that many developers went directly to a city council member to discuss zoning changes rather than initiating the formal process of filing documents with the city planning staff.[1] In essence, the planning/zoning process in the past was not always an impartial administrative process adjudicated by credentialed professional city planners; quite often it was a political process adjudicated by politicians. New Orleans land use attorney Bill Borah describes a process of "planning by surprise" that is "totally discretionary and totally political," in which the advice of city planners is routinely ignored.[2]

Furthermore, in the past the city had very weak citizen engagement.[3] That was a function of both the lack of a formal city government process to engage citizens and a culture of disengagement—a laissez-faire attitude that tended to permeate all aspects of social life in New Orleans.

The city did not have a master plan with the force of law, and while it did have a comprehensive zoning ordinance, the zoning laws had no teeth. Any developer could get an exception (variance) to the zoning law at any time if he or she could get the votes on the city council.[4] Thus there was no way to predict whether a proposed use of land was permissible; zoning laws could be circumvented in an arbitrary and capricious manner.

Key Planning Developments Post Katrina

The planning for the rebuilding of New Orleans officially began on September 30, 2005, one month after the hurricane made landfall, when Mayor Ray Nagin announced the formation of the Bring New Orleans Back Commission (BNOBC). The stated purpose of the BNOBC was to oversee the development of a rebuilding plan for the city.[5] The BNOBC had seventeen commission members appointed by the mayor, and it was supported by hundreds of volunteer participants, including a team from the Urban Land Institute (ULI).

The BNOBC was funded by the Urban Land Institute as well as by individual donations from wealthy individuals and from real estate development corporations. In November 2005, the BNOBC issued the first draft of its report, which recommended that all officials make one unified request to Congress for support. The report was comprehensive and sophisticated, with recommendations on every major aspect of the city, including culture, tourism, transportation, and economic development.

However, the recommendations that attracted almost all of the attention of the media and the general public were the ones dealing with land use. The BNOBC recommended that the footprint of the city shrink in order to use resources and infrastructure more efficiently while the city was rebuilt. The BNOBC also recommended that those areas of the city that were not flooded or were only moderately flooded be rebuilt first to serve as anchors in the rebuilding process. The commission recommended that the areas with the highest level of flooding, such as New

Orleans East and the Lower Ninth Ward, not be rebuilt at the beginning of the process since they were long-term projects and their viability needed to be demonstrated first.[6]

The BNOBC's land use recommendations caused a public backlash because the areas where a rebuilding moratorium was recommended tended to be home to a large proportion of poor, working-class, and black residents. The credibility of the BNOBC was further harmed with the publication of a map depicting the areas where the building moratorium would be in effect, which became known as the Green Dot Map because of the way that it depicted areas for potential future parkland.[7]

Although the BNOBC process, which continued through March 2006, included public meetings and citizen input and culminated in the publication of a final report, the process was never decisively supported (or decisively opposed) by the mayor, even though he had appointed all of the commissioners. Many citizens were therefore left confused and wondering who was in charge.

In February 2006, while the BNOBC process was still going on, the New Orleans City Council initiated its own neighborhood planning process when it hired a different planning firm, Lambert Advisory. That move began the confusing, nonlinear process of competing plans. The city council's rationale was that the BNOBC effort intended to use neighborhood planning as a way to determine neighborhood viability, whereas the Lambert plan was designed to promote the survival of all neighborhoods. However, one of the criticisms of the Lambert plan was that it did not actually cover all of the neighborhoods in the city; it focused instead solely on flooded neighborhoods.[8]

In July 2006, responding to the need to present a unified recovery plan to the Louisiana Recovery Authority to receive infrastructure funding, the New Orleans City Planning Commission hired a team of planning consulting firms selected through a competitive bidding process to construct what would become the Unified New Orleans Plan (UNOP). The UNOP, which was funded by the Rockefeller Foundation, was intended to be comprehensive and to include all neighborhoods. The UNOP was to become the official plan for the city and to incorporate all of the previous planning efforts. Lambert Advisory publicly objected to the UNOP plan and the competition between plans continued.[9]

In September 2006, the Lambert team made final presentations to the city council,[10] and the council accepted its plans in October 2006.[11] By then, the Unified New Orleans Plan process was well under way. The

UNOP team held a series of citywide public meetings called community congresses. The UNOP team also held a series of neighborhood public meetings. The Lambert plan was merged with the UNOP plan, and they became one. The UNOP plan was approved by the city council in June 2007[12] and accepted by the Louisiana Recovery Authority later the same month.[13]

It took twenty-two months after Katrina for the city to complete an officially approved recovery plan. The LRA forwarded the plan to Washington, D.C., in order to receive additional federal infrastructure funding. While it is difficult to measure whether the city received adequate value from the plan from a cost-benefit standpoint, it certainly is true that if the city had not presented a plan to the state and federal governments it would have been impossible to acquire additional infrastructure funding.

In the next iteration of the planning process, in early 2008, the city council hired the Boston-based planning firm Goody Clancy to lead the effort to produce a comprehensive master plan. The Unified New Orleans Plan was primarily a recovery plan designed to guide rebuilding activities. A master plan is different from a recovery plan in that it is designed to guide the comprehensive design and physical development of the city over the long term. On November 4, 2008, the day of the U.S. presidential election, with huge voter turnouts, city voters approved an amendment to the city charter that would give the master plan the force of law for the first time in the city's history. The amendment also requires the city to draft a comprehensive zoning ordinance that conforms to the master plan.

Once again, the city began a long series of public meetings to allow citizens to express their concerns about their neighborhoods and to share their comments on draft versions of the plans. Goody Clancy, with the help of a large team of local planning firms working as partners, held both district meetings and citywide meetings. On January 25, 2010, the New Orleans City Planning Commission unanimously approved the draft of a 500-page master plan titled "Plan for the 21st Century: New Orleans 2030."[14] On April 22, 2010, the city council, by a vote of 6 to 0 with one council member absent, sent the proposed master plan back to the city planning commission with a list of proposed amendments, which the commission accepted. The draft then went back to the city council for a final vote. On August 12, 2010, by a vote of 6 to 0 with one council member absent, the final version of the master plan was approved.[15] It is now law.

House constructed under pre-Katrina land use regulations.

Goals of the Master Plan

Three key words govern the new master plan: "Livability, Opportunity, and Sustainability."

The first goal of the master plan is livability. It proposes to create compact, pedestrian-friendly, mixed-use neighborhoods that combine residential and light commercial uses such as grocery stores. Goals also include a blight eradication program to spur redevelopment and the construction of parks within walking distance of every resident.

The second goal is opportunity. The plan proposes to undertake market analysis to determine which industries are most likely to thrive within the unique New Orleans environment and to target those industries for infrastructure investment, which could include facilities for film, television, and music production. The plan also proposes a one-stop shop where businesses could go to receive all necessary city permits as well as to receive information about disadvantaged business grants and technical assistance with marketing and advertising.

The third goal is sustainability. The sustainability vision is broken down into three parts: resilience, transportation, and green initiatives. The plan proposes that the city become more resilient by coordinating flood control programs in order to learn to live with water. The central idea is to employ techniques that have been used successfully in the Netherlands (the Dutch model) to build a system of canals through which

House constructed under post-Katrina land use regulations in the new master plan.

flood water would flow through the city without inundating buildings during a storm.

In terms of transportation, the plan calls for more public transit lines, more bike paths, and a system of regular road maintenance. The public transportation plan is especially important because the city has never had a modern, comprehensive public transit system like those in the most economically vibrant cities in the United States.

Finally, the master plan emphasizes that New Orleans should become a green city by providing tax incentives for citizens to retrofit existing houses or to build new houses using green technology. Green technology includes the addition of solar panels as well as use of storm-resistant and energy-efficient materials.[16]

Positive Outcomes

Did the post-Katrina planning process make a positive difference in the lives of the citizens of New Orleans? The answer is yes. The federal government required an official recovery plan from the city in order for the city to receive certain types of infrastructure money from community development block grant funds through the Louisiana Recovery Authority. Not having a plan would have been devastating for the city. The UNOP plan, which incorporated parts of the BNOBC and Lambert plans initially, served to meet the requirements of the LRA and the federal government.

The second major positive outcome is the high quality of the master plan, which incorporates a best practices approach to rebuilding, using research and knowledge of what has worked and what has not worked in the past. That approach has never been used in the city of New Orleans in the past. In addition, it is holistic in the sense that besides dealing with zoning and land use issues, it focuses on figuring out how the city can live naturally with water and integrate itself with nature rather than trying to dominate, control, and suppress nature—the failed practices of the past. The inclusion of innovative Dutch flood control techniques is the most obvious example.

Third, the planning process organized the neighborhoods and the citizenry in general to a greater extent than they had been organized before. The result has been more citizens involved in the democratic process now than were before Katrina.[17] At the beginning of the post-Katrina planning process, most citizen participation was motivated by fear. Citizens felt that if they did not show up at public meetings and voice their opinions, their neighborhoods would be bulldozed and they would not be permitted to return. Many neighborhood residents also believed that the federal funding process was a zero-sum game. They felt that there were limited resources to distribute and that if they did not participate, other, more vocal, more organized neighborhoods would get the resources and the silent neighborhoods might get none. But residents were frustrated by the slow pace of the recovery, and many people were tired of attending meetings. They wanted to see tangible results of the recovery. They wanted to see streets repaved, buildings rebuilt, and public services totally restored to pre-Katrina levels.

As a result of the planning process, the city now has a large contingent of highly active neighborhood groups.[18] Some of the groups have as much, if not more, influence on the neighborhood planning process than any government entity. As a result of the long list of community meetings that took place before the master planning process, the community participation process has been institutionalized in the master plan, making it likely that these democratic impulses will continue. The approval of the charter amendment giving the master plan the force of law mandated that the city planning commission create a citizen participation program (CPP). As proposed in the master plan, the CPP will set up a standardized process to allow citizens to review proposed land use changes, and it will require district planners to meet with neighborhood groups on a regular basis. District planners will serve as liaisons between the city planning commission and the neighborhood organizations.

The fourth major positive outcome is that the city greatly improved what before Katrina had been a very weak planning tradition that put the city at a competitive disadvantage with other major cities in the United States, especially for business relocation decisions.[19] Most business owners look for order and predictability when it comes to zoning and land use, but New Orleans had little such predictability in the past. If the new comprehensive zoning ordinance follows the master plan as envisioned, for the first time the city should have a predictable zoning ordinance that will help to attract new industry to the city. That would not have been possible without the post-Katrina planning process.

However, there were some negative aspects of the planning process. First, it was a long, costly, and inefficient process. Because the process started and stopped several times, it took longer to deliver a final product to the LRA, delaying the release of necessary funds to the city. Because several different planning processes were competing with each other, the process ended up with a higher price tag than it would have had if it had been completed in one unified step at the beginning. The higher price was borne by the philanthropic organizations that funded the process, city taxpayers in terms of the work of the city planning staff, and the millions of volunteer hours from both residents and nonresidents that could have been focused more efficiently.

While it is certainly true that the size and complexity of the planning challenges were unprecedented, it is possible that if the mayor had provided more decisive and focused leadership at the beginning of the process, the process could have gone forward uninterrupted. There is no doubt that the process would still have been highly contentious and divisive because of the emotional nature of the conflicts involved; however, it could have been one process rather than three. A single recovery planning process would have been faster, less expensive, and more efficient than three separate processes.

Finally, residents have had to deal with the issue of "planning fatigue." More than five years after the storm, many citizens are tired and depressed and have no desire to attend any more meetings of any kind. They are discouraged because they do not see tangible projects being constructed after all of the work and time that they have put in. They feel the pace of recovery is too slow.

Cautions and Implications for Future Policy and Actions

Even with the proposed reforms, the success of the city planning process will still depend on politics. It is still highly dependent on the city council and the mayor working together and heading in the same direction. In order for the planning process to work efficiently, it will be necessary for the current mayor, Mitch Landrieu, to articulate a clear, concise vision of the city for the people to rally around. It will also be necessary for the new city council to proceed with completing the work of the comprehensive zoning ordinance with all deliberate speed. A master plan with the force of law is not enough. The real power to remake any city lies in the power of the zoning code. Until the comprehensive zoning ordinance is finished and implemented, the planning process will not be complete. Also, from a land use viewpoint, the completion and implementation of the zoning ordinance will officially mark the end the recovery planning process and the beginning of the growth process.

Furthermore, the city is still highly dependent on receiving federal government funding to complete infrastructure rebuilding. Because of falling tax revenues resulting from the national economic recession, both the city and the state governments are running large operating deficits and their ability to fund capital construction projects therefore continues to be severely limited. The best plan in the world cannot be implemented without money, and the needs of New Orleans continue to exceed the means of the city or state. Federal money must continue to flow in order for the recovery to proceed. The federal funds that would matter most to the plan are community development block grant funds, because they are usually earmarked for infrastructure construction.

The final concern is the effects on the city of the BP Gulf oil spill, which will be both indirect and direct. The indirect effects will be that the greater southern Louisiana economy will be damaged by the loss of jobs in the oil and gas, seafood, and tourism industries. That will further erode the tax base of New Orleans, which will result in less money to implement and maintain development and infrastructure. The direct effects will be that any future flood control measures in city and regional plans and developments will have to take into account the need for multiple lines of defense to keep oil and toxic chemicals—which will likely exist in measurable amounts in the water for years to come—out of the city.

Lessons Learned from the Post-Katrina Land Use Planning Process

There are several lessons that can be learned from the New Orleans case and applied to other cities that are planning their recovery from a disaster. The first lesson is that a strong chief executive with a clear vision is absolutely essential. Without a strong, decisive, popular mayor communicating a clear, concise vision of the future shape and appearance of the city, urban planning processes will always tend to devolve into chaos after a disaster.

Second, recovery plans cannot be perceived as negatively affecting poor or minority neighborhoods. The perception of discriminatory urban planning, even if it does not reflect reality, will instantly put city leaders on the defensive and they will waste valuable time and resources defending themselves against the charges. Indeed, in the case of the Bring New Orleans Back Commission, such charges derailed the commission altogether.

Third, efficient recovery planning should be a single, continuous, unified process performed by one agency. If the process stops and has to be restarted, or if, as in the case of New Orleans' competing plans, different planning entities are allowed to exist at the same time and directly compete with each other for attention and resources, time and money will be wasted and the completion of the recovery planning process will be delayed.

In the final analysis, the most important lesson to be learned is that all cities must have a master plan with the force of law and a comprehensive zoning ordinance. New Orleans had to create many of these processes from scratch, which made for a long, inefficient, and exhausting process. In many ways, the people of New Orleans suffered so badly after Katrina because of the failures of past elected leadership to conduct proper land use planning, including failing to conduct proper flood control planning. If a comprehensive plan had already been in place, along with a comprehensive process for citizen participation, the recovery process would have moved much faster, it would have cost less, citizens would have had more confidence that the process was fair and equitable, and a great deal of unnecessary pain could have been avoided. Having a master plan in place allows cities to attract people and jobs into the area and facilitates the building of a prosperous future.

Notes

1. Bruce Eggler, "New Orleans City Charter Amendment Would Give Master Plan the Force of Law," *Times-Picayune*, October 27, 2008.

2. Peter Reichard, "Chain Expansions Worry Neighbors, Preservationists," *New Orleans City Business*, January 31, 2000.

3. Frederick Weil, "The Rise of Community Engagement after Katrina," in *The New Orleans Index at Five* (Washington: Brookings Institution and Greater New Orleans Community Data Center, 2010).

4. Eggler, "New Orleans City Charter Amendment Would Give Master Plan the Force of Law."

5. For more information about the Bring New Orleans Back Commission, see www.bringneworleansback.org.

6. Bring New Orleans Back Commission, "Action Plan for New Orleans: The New American City" (2006).

7. "Plan for the Future," *Times-Picayune*, January 11, 2006 (www.nola.com/katrina/pdf/planmap.pdf).

8. Robert B. Olshansky and Laurie A. Johnson, *Clear as Mud: Planning for the Rebuilding of New Orleans* (Chicago: American Planning Association, 2010), p. 80.

9. Ibid., p. 103.

10. Gwen Filosa, "N.O. Neighborhood Plans Unveiled," *Times-Picayune*, September 24, 2006.

11. New Orleans City Council, Motion M 06-460, October 27, 2006.

12. New Orleans City Council, Motion M-07-271, "A Motion to Grant Acceptance and General Approval to the Citywide Strategic Recovery and Redevelopment Plan," June 21, 2007.

13. Olshansky and Johnson, *Clear as Mud,* pp. 212–14.

14. Bruce Eggler, "New Orleans Master Plan Wins Approval of City Planning Commission," *Times-Picayune*, January 26, 2010.

15. Bruce Eggler, "New Orleans Master Plan approved by City Council," *Times-Picayune*, August 12, 2010.

16. The full contents of the 500-page master plan can be found at www.nolamasterplan.org.

17. Weil, "The Rise of Community Engagement after Katrina."

18. John Pope, "Hurricane Katrina Forced Neighborhood Organizations to Collaborate," *Times-Picayune*, August 24, 2010. See also Neighborhood Partnerships Network Website (http://npnnola.com/).

19. Eggler, "New Orleans City Charter Amendment Would Give Master Plan the Force of Law."

12

Coastal Restoration and Protection and the Future of New Orleans

Mark S. Davis

New Orleans and coastal Louisiana are joined at the hip. It is impossible to understand New Orleans apart from the coast, and the fate and future of each is inextricably tied to that of the other. Those ties, often invisible to many—even to a generation or more of the city's own residents and leaders—have come into much clearer focus following the 2005 and 2008 hurricane seasons and the 2010 BP Deepwater Horizon blowout, an entirely man-made disaster. Those painfully acute catastrophes have combined with the chronic and largely induced collapse of coastal Louisiana, one of the continent's greatest estuarine and wetland regions, raising fundamental questions about the sustainability of both the coast and the city. They have also given rise to reborn awareness of the importance of both and to an emergent "civics of sustainability" movement that may represent the best hope for the future of these treasures and, by extension, for other parts of the nation that are facing their own struggles with survival and sustainability.

The blowout of BP's Deepwater Horizon well on the eve of the fifth anniversary of Hurricane Katrina, the storm that devastated New Orleans in August 2005, provoked eerily familiar feelings of uncontrolled vulnerability among the residents of the city and its adjacent coastal communities. There was no boarding up, no evacuation, and no stocking up on food and water, but there was deep and abiding fear about the effects that the spill would have on the wetlands, shorelines, and waters of the region and the cultures and economies that were dependent upon them. To be sure, the coast has been in a long and steep decline for decades, but it has never been stark enough to garner the attention necessary to do something about it—or to prompt an honest, open discussion about the human, economic, and environmental costs of letting it go.

Hurricane Katrina and its successors—Rita, Gustav, and Ike—raised the level of concern in some circles, but by and large they drew attention only to the fallibility of the levees around New Orleans and the need for storm protection elsewhere.[1] Somehow it got overlooked that due to Katrina and Rita, 217 square miles of land had been lost across south Louisiana, converted to open water, in a span of one month.[2]

The BP spill was different. It did not flood cities or strand people on roof tops. It coated marshes, reefs, and beaches. It threatened fish, birds, and wildlife. And it left adrift thousands of businesses, workers, and families who depend on the coast: fishers, boat operators, guides, inn keepers, restaurant workers, grocers, and more. The BP spill did what no hurricane had: it revealed the powerful but fragile connection between a functioning coast and a functioning culture and economy.

But whether the threat to the coast comes from nature or from human hands, it is now clear that a threat to the coast is a threat to a vital web of human society, exemplified by the connection between the coast and New Orleans. The future of the city is a work in progress, and it will turn on number of factors, not all of which are within its control. First and foremost, it hinges on the future that its residents and leaders are willing to shape for themselves. Second, it depends on the degree to which state, national, and private actions can be reconciled to achieve a meaningful and purposeful outcome. Finally, it will take a measure of luck, since even the best plans will not bear fruit if natural or political forces dictate a different outcome.

If we leave aside the things that cannot be controlled, the future of New Orleans depends fundamentally on whether the benefits of regrowing the city outweigh the risks. Put another way, do our collective hopes as a people for the future of New Orleans and the coast that it is part of outweigh our fears about dealing with—or even acknowledging—the challenges of creating conditions conducive to sustainability? Perhaps the best way of approaching that question is by considering the past.

History: A City Defined by Its Relationship with Water

Nowhere is the power of hope and fear to sculpt the history and development of New Orleans clearer than in the case of the city's relationship with the rivers, wetlands, and estuaries that surround it and the city's vulnerability to water-driven risk. The city always had a troubled relationship with its watery environs. On one hand, its proximity to the Mississippi River and the Gulf made the city's founding and rise to prominence inevitable. On the other hand, the risk of flooding from the river, torrential rains, and the Gulf made it a hard bargain with nature from the beginning.

Water also shaped the distinctive culture of the city and the region. The port of New Orleans made the city one of the great points of entry for immigrants coming to America from around the world, giving the city a cosmopolitan flavor that was apparent in only a handful of other American cities. In stark contrast to the metropolis of New Orleans, the meandering bayous, bays, lakes, swamps, and marshes of the surrounding delta gave isolating refuge to Native Americans, expatriate Acadians (today's Cajuns), runaway slaves, Vietnamese, and others forging a network of landscape-oriented cultures that remain to this day—for the time being, at least.

Coastal Louisiana is not so much a place as it is a process. It is the result of roughly 7,500 years of work by rivers, mostly the Mississippi, bringing freshwater, sediment, and nutrients to the shallow water shelf at the southern end of the North American continent. In time a system of swamps, marshes, and estuaries covering nearly 7,000 square miles, or 4.5 million acres, was built between the uplands of the Pleistocene Terrace and the Gulf of Mexico.[3] It was continually being shaped by the natural forces of rivers, the Gulf, soil subsidence, and erosion. It never stayed the same, but it was in functional equilibrium when Europeans colonized the delta in the early eighteenth century.

This is the coast that New Orleans was founded in. Its location was not a mistake. Its location was strategically chosen based on its proximity to the Gulf of Mexico and the Mississippi River (the mouth of the river was difficult to navigate at that time). Combine that with its modest but vital elevation (it was not below sea level then, and much of it is not today) and its distance from the Gulf, and you get, as geographer Peirce Lewis has called New Orleans, an "impossible but inevitable city."[4]

In settling the area, the Europeans—first the French, then the Spanish, followed by the English and the Americans—brought with them concepts and techniques that the coast had never seen. They were claiming property, building empires, and subduing a wilderness, and they had the tools, the capital, and the legal systems and theology to do it. The first levees on the Mississippi River were erected or raised (hence the term "levee," from the French "lever," "to raise") when the French established the settlement of New Orleans. New Orleans was never intended to be a mere outpost; because it was envisioned as a metropolis, the expansion of its flood protection and the settlement and leveeing of the banks of the Mississippi and its distributary channels followed in short order.[5] The walling off of the river from its flood plain had begun.

The first half of the twentieth century ushered in an unprecedented level of state, federal, and private actions that sent the coast into a steep decline. Navigational improvements such as the Gulf Intracoastal Waterway, oil and gas exploration and production, and the federalization of flood protection on the Mississippi River that followed the great flood of 1927 radically altered the hydrology of the coast. As early as the late 1920s, keen observers were already sounding an alarm, but by and large they were not being heard. Conservationist Percy Viosca, lamenting the loss of the state's wetlands, wrote in 1928:

> Reclamation and flood control as practiced in Louisiana have been more or less a failure, destroying valuable natural resources without producing the permanent compensating benefits originally desired. Reclamation experts and real estate promoters have been "killing the goose that laid the golden egg."[6]

Such sentiments were not shared by many, and the Flood Control Act of 1928 made the levees on the lower Mississippi River the nation's business and an overarching priority.[7] By the 1930s, Louisiana's coastal wetlands had shrunk to 3.2 million acres.[8] Today less than 2 million acres remain.

This is the coastal landscape that New Orleans finds itself in today as it tries to recover and create a viable future for itself. It is increasingly clear that any prospects that the city has to recover and prosper are tied to reestablishing some semblance of sustainability in the landscape that is collapsing around it. This is not a challenge covered by old school urban renewal, new urbanism, smart growth, or any other catchy planning approach. The future of New Orleans is dependent upon nothing less than a mutual survival pact with nature—starting with the wetland ecosystem of coastal Louisiana.

The fate and fortune of New Orleans and the communities around it is tied to that of the coast. That aspect of direct and immediate dependence on an ecosystem sets New Orleans apart from most other places, where the connections are less clear or at least less immediate. For over a century, the vulnerability of New Orleans to storms and rising seas has been growing as the buffering coast began to unravel. Since the causes of the collapse of the coast are mostly traceable to things that people did for economic reasons it was easy—indeed, it was policy[9]—to discount the growing risks. State and federal agencies feared the social and political costs of confronting the threats of an imploding coast more than they did the actual risks that coastal collapse posed to the viability of the entire economic, cultural, and ecologic web of the region. The riskiness of that approach was laid bare by a series of hurricanes that started with Katrina and by the BP spill. The lesson—that a new approach to living with nature and with risk was needed—had been cruelly taught and taught again, but was anyone learning? The answer to that question is a hopeful but uncertain maybe, and much will turn on the degree to which the Katrina/BP catastrophes force fundamental changes in policy and practice at the local, state, and federal levels.

Hurricane Katrina and Its Aftermath: A Moment of Uncertainty, a Moment of Possibility

Recovery from something like Hurricane Katrina is no simple matter. Unlike most natural disasters, which hit and leave fairly quickly and affect—however gravely—hundreds or thousands of people, the flood waters from Hurricane Katrina hit, destroyed, and stayed for nearly a month. Hundreds of thousands of people were displaced, and even homes and business that were high and dry had no utilities for months. There were no schools, hospitals, or grocery stores to come back to. Without people to serve, how could they reopen? Without basic services, how could people return? The fabric of the city was ripped apart. In such a situation the question isn't so much one of recovery but of rebirth—and as what?

It is no secret that New Orleans had a long and well-deserved reputation for civic indifference. It was an easy place to live well without much effort. No city in America was more loved by its residents, and none was more neglected. To be sure, people had hopes that things would improve, but for the most part the city's plans were not well-formed and they did not galvanize the community. Among the high-profile projects pursued by the city were quick fix ideas such as casinos, race tracks, and amusement parks. They may have been fine ideas, but they were rooted largely in enticing more visitors to visit the city and spend money rather than in building an educated, well-paid workforce or fostering any kind of sustainable relationship with the surrounding environment. In short, New Orleans was a city in love with itself but with almost no sense of its future. Its deep traditions made for an oddly cohesive and resilient city, but one that feared change. If there was one thing that Katrina and the BP oil spill delivered in spades, it was change.

New Orleans in the fall of 2005 and spring of 2006 was a city facing its own mortality. There were no guarantees; indeed, some observers pointedly suggested that New Orleans had been a mistake from the beginning and should not be rebuilt.[10] What was the point of rebuilding a wrecked city in a collapsing coast in an era of warming climates and rising seas? That was, and is, a fair question, and the answer lies in both the city's past and a new but growing realization that the city can rebound and prosper if it fundamentally changes the nature of its relationship with water.

For all of the attendant problems, the reasons for rebuilding New Orleans are largely the same as the reasons for its founding. It still occupies a strategically and commercially important location. While it has lost some of its stature as a port, it is still the place where shallow-draft vessels from the nation's heartland meet ocean-going deep-draft vessels. Perhaps most important, the city is not fatally vulnerable to storms and flooding. It was not the city's proximity to the Gulf that left it inundated; it was a poorly designed, built, and maintained set of flood walls, pumps, and levees that turned a bad storm into a catastrophe. If the city gets smart about how it manages and lives with water, it can sharply reduce its level of risk while enhancing the value of its abundant water resources—a luxury that few American cities have today. However, that won't just happen. The city will need to frame a vision of its future that is based on well-informed hopes and an honest assessment of the things that it should fear—like rising seas and a collapsing coast.

There is evidence that that is happening. Restoring wetlands and accommodating sea level rise are now broadly recognized as essential components of flood protection and the sustainability of the region.[11]

The state has recognized the need for smarter land use choices and has adopted a statewide building code.[12] Thanks to relentless civic and environmental activism, the Mississippi River–Gulf Outlet, a fifty-year-old monument to wishful economic development and disdain for the environment, has been deauthorized.[13] And the Army Corps of Engineers has shifted from providing a levee system with a high-protection target (against 1-in-300-year events) and a low-confidence level to a system with a lower level of protection (against 1-in-100-year events) and a higher confidence factor.[14] That may not sound like an improvement, but it is at least based on a more honest assessment of just how safe the city is, and in New Orleans today honesty counts when it comes to living with water.

In March 2010 the White House released a "road map" to guide the federal efforts to successfully restore the ecosystems of coastal Louisiana and coastal Mississippi.[15] That was the first comprehensive policy commitment concerning the restoration of coastal Louisiana ever to come from Washington. To be honest, it was not clear just where that road map would lead or who would be at the wheel. When the BP *Deepwater Horizon* well blew out, blew up, and sank, it was anything but clear whether there was anything left of that road map or if anyone was really looking beyond the spill to the fate and future of the coast.

But as the oil came in—closing fisheries; killing birds, endangered turtles, and dolphins; covering marshes, reefs, and barrier shorelines; and putting fishers, workers, and business owners at least temporarily out of work—the importance of the marshes, islands, and estuaries came into focus in a way that volumes of studies could not convey. Suddenly there was somebody—BP—at least partially on the hook for the damage to that system and for doing something to redress it. Finally the coast mattered. The federal road map now had a context for action and a driving urgency supplied by the duty of BP under the Oil Pollution Act to assess the natural resource damage that it had caused and to restore natural functioning or compensate for its loss. That point was driven home by President Obama in his Oval Office address on June 15, in which he committed not only to undoing the damage done by the spill but also to going further—to reversing the chronic decline the of the entire Gulf Coast.[16] Perhaps most important, the president appointed Ray Mabus, the secretary of the navy and a former governor of Mississippi, to lead the effort. For the first time, the viability of the coast was more than just one of the dozens of unreconciled federal interests in the area—it was a White House priority and it was someone's job to find a way to make it work.

The president's pledge has led to at least some encouraging interim actions. In September 2010 Ray Mabus issued a report with a set of wide-ranging recommendations, including most notably a recommendation that a new permanent federal/state/tribal task force be created to coordinate ecosystem restoration efforts in the Gulf.[17] Ultimately such a commission will require congressional authorization, but an ostensibly temporary version of the Gulf Coast Ecosystem Restoration Task Force has been created; it is chaired by the administrator of the U.S. Environmental Protection Agency.[18]

The task force was charged with developing by the end of October 2011 an implementation strategy for restoring the ecosystems of the Gulf. As bold as that charge is, the challenge of shaping a shared vision for the Gulf and an agreement on what needs to be done and how to do it will likely be difficult to surmount due to the competing and fractious nature of the various state, federal, and tribal interests involved. Those factors, plus the complicating reality of the necessity of congressional support, suggest that progress on the Gulf will come hard and only if nongovernmental stakeholders do much of the heavy lifting.

With respect to the state of Louisiana, its relationship with the coast was transformed by hurricanes Katrina, Rita, Gustav, and Ike. The drowning of New Orleans (and dozens of other communities that never reached the nation's attention) and the loss of 217 square miles of coastal land as a result of Katrina and Rita in the span of one month was a revelation. After years of plans, pronouncements, and ribbon cuttings it was clear that whatever Louisiana was doing to keep and restore its coast was failing. Indeed, it was apparent that balanced against the state's desire to spur economic development, not offend powerful interests, and avoid hard budget choices, saving the coast had never been a serious priority. It was not that the state was overtly cynical about its commitment to the coast (though at times it came awfully close); it was more a matter of finding it so much easier to issue platitudes about the environment than to take on the hard work of stewardship, which it inevitably put off until later. Katrina forced a reckoning.

In the space of six months, Louisiana fundamentally revamped its entire approach to dealing with the coast. In a dicey but essential move, storm protection, wetland conservation, and coastal restoration were integrated under a single state authority, the Coastal Protection and Restoration Authority. By the middle of 2007, the state had developed a master plan that took a more honest and urgent look at the coast and the state's future.[19] The master plan is to be updated every five years. In 2006, the state took what many had thought was an unimaginable step, filing suit against the federal Minerals Management Service (MMS) to block lease sales on the grounds that a fresh look at the environmental impacts of offshore oil and gas development was necessary after the savage impacts of Hurricanes Katrina and Rita revealed both a greater vulnerability and a deeper connection to the impacts of oil- and gas-related activity than had been widely acknowledged.[20] The disdainful response of MMS and the petroleum industry to the state's demand was a chilling portent of the profoundly dysfunctional approach to safety and environmental risk management that became clear after the *Deepwater Horizon* well blew out. That suit was ultimately settled, but not before so many of MMS's dysfunctional practices had been revealed that the political landscape shifted enough to allow the federal government to begin sharing the revenues that it received from outer continental shelf (OCS) oil energy development with states like Louisiana, which served as the support base for that activity. By law, Louisiana dedicated all of its share of those OCS revenues to coastal protection and restoration.[21]

None of the steps taken by Louisiana so far are enough to save the coast.[22] Furthermore, there have been unsettling signs that when push comes to shove, the state will settle for living behind levee walls instead of doing what will be necessary to strike a sustainable balance between environmental stewardship, economic development, and storm protection.[23] But in fairness, the state has at least put itself in a position in which it can make those choices if it can summon the will.

Even New Orleans, which has always viewed itself as being apart from the coast, has come to see that it is not. The recently adopted master plan for the city is predicated in substantial part on a new relationship with water, one that aspires to a minimum of a 1-in-500-year level of protection from flooding and that recognizes the importance of restoring the coast to the future well-being of the city.[24] That point was reemphasized in Mayor Mitch Landrieu's inaugural address on May 3, 2010, in which he stated that "we have a responsibility to not only shield and clean up our shoreline [referring to the BP spill], but to restore our coast once and for all."[25]

Much more will be needed, however. The real proof will come when the hard choices are made about which communities will get higher levels of protection—and when. It will come when the decisions are made on whether to fully commit to conserving and enhancing Louisiana's coastal wetlands. It will come when land use planning is made a priority, with the force of law. It will come when decisions are made about how to mitigate the impacts of the BP spill and to avoid such catastrophes in the future. And it will come when the state and the nation decide to develop and implement effective strategies for contending with climate change and rising seas.

None of this will be easy, but as the BP oil spill reminds us, there is no sustainability in standing pat. In Louisiana and elsewhere, a fundamental question must be answered: Are we as a people willing to make the laws, policies, investments, and commitments necessary to give ourselves a shot at a vibrant and sustainable future? Five years after Katrina there are hopeful signs in New Orleans and coastal Louisiana that we are finally on the verge of making the kinds of commitments and taking the actions that will be necessary. Will they be enough or taken in time to matter? Right now, we honestly do not and cannot know. But most other cities—which are, whether they admit it or not, facing their own version of a sustainability crisis—face the same question.

The fact that there are deep uncertainties is not itself cause for pessimism. Uncertainty is not destiny. At least in the case of New Orleans and the surrounding coast, it is a measure of opportunity to shape destiny. Prior to Katrina the future of New Orleans and the coast were far more certain—they were decidedly unsustainable. Today, because of the actions under way at the city, state, and federal levels—and perhaps most important, at the civic level—the city and the coast have a fighting chance. They cannot be what they were, but they can be made healthier, more resilient, and more sustainable. The window of opportunity is not large and the margin of error is slim, but concerted effort has given these remarkable natural, cultural, and economic resources another decisive turn at bat. The game is still on, and at stake is much more than just the parochial interests of a city and a region. Whatever the outcome, this is the place where the hardest lessons about stewardship and survival are being taught. If the wisdom, knowledge, and willingness needed to act can be assembled in time to make a difference in New Orleans and coastal Louisiana, then there is a better chance that we can do right by many of the nation's other threatened communities and natural treasures. This is the heart of the matter, and what happens here will echo across the country and for generations to come.

Notes

1. This point is perhaps best illustrated by contrasting the Lousiana Coastal Area (LCA) program and the Louisiana Coastal Protection and Restoration Authority (LACPR), both of which were authorized by Congress in the wake of Hurricane Katrina. The LCA program, which had been under development for years, is a coordinated and comprehensive program aimed at restoring the coastal ecosystems in southeast Louisiana to some state of functional sustainability. The program was authorized as part of the Water Resources Development Act of 2007 (Public Law 110-114, Sections 7001-7011) and contained nearly $2 billion in program and project authorizations. As of February 2011, none of those authorizations had been funded. By contrast the LACPR, which was authorized and funded through the Energy and Water Development Appropriation Act of 2006 (Public Law 109-103), was aimed at developing a comprehensive hurricane protection plan for South Louisiana that would provide protection against storm surges equivalent to those from a category 5 hurricane.

2. John A. Barras, "Land Area Changes in Coastal Louisiana after Hurricanes Katrina and Rita," in *Science of the Storms: The USGS Response to the Hurricanes of 2005,* U.S. Geological Survey Circular 1306, edited by G. S. Farris and others (2007), p. 98.

3. Louisiana Coastal Wetlands Conservation and Restoration Task Force and the Wetlands Conservation and Restoration Authority, "Coast 2050: Toward a Sustainable Coastal Louisiana" (1998), p. 22.

4. As quoted by Craig E. Colten, *An Unnatural Metropolis: Wresting New Orleans from Nature* (Louisiana State University Press, 2005), p. 2

5. Percy Viosca Jr., "Louisiana Wet Lands and Value of Their Wild Life and Fishery Resources," *Ecology 9*, no. 2 (1928): 216, 229

6. Ibid., p. 229.

7. Prior to the Flood Control Act of 1928, levees were primarily the responsibility of state and local governments. The existence of a larger federal interest had been recognized much earlier, such as in the 1879 creation of the Mississippi River Commission by Congress. But the federal interest had not yet been translated into the federalization of the flood control system on the lower Mississippi River, although through such pronouncements as the Army Corps of Engineers "Levees Only" policy in 1861 (A. A. Humphreys and H. L. Abbot, *Report upon the Physics and Hydraulics of the Mississippi River,* Professional Papers of the Corps of Topographical Engineers, United States Army, No. 4, page 417 (Washington: 1861, reprinted 1876), it did shape how flood control was practiced in the valley long before 1928. For a more complete discussion of the evolution of the federal role in Mississippi River valley flood protection, see John M. Barry, *Rising Tide: The Great Mississippi Flood of 1927 and How It Changed America* (Simon and Shuster, 1997).

8. Louisiana Coastal Wetlands Conservation and Restoration Task Force and the Wetlands Conservation and Restoration Authority, "Coast 2050," pp. 47–48.

9. See, for example, Viosca, "Louisiana Wet Lands and Value of Their Wild Life and Fishery Resources"; Louisiana Coastal Wetlands Conservation and Restoration Task Force and the Wetlands Conservation and Restoration Authority, "Coast 2050"; and Colton, *An Unnatural Metropolis.*

10. For example, see the August 2007 issue of *National Geographic,* the cover story of which was "New Orleans: Should It Rebuild?"

11. Coastal Protection and Restoration Authority, "Integrated Ecosystem Restoration and Hurricane Protection: Louisiana's Comprehensive Master Plan for a Sustainable Coast" (2007) (www.coastal.la.gov/index.cfm?md=pagebuilder&tmp=home& nid=82&pnid=76&pid=28&catid=0&elid=0)

12. Act 12 of the 2005 First Extraordinary Legislative Session (Louisiana).

13. The Mississippi River–Gulf Outlet was intended to be an economically beneficial shortcut from New Orleans to the Gulf of Mexico. The project was constructed before any environmental studies of the sort required by the National Environmental Policy Act were mandated. The channel never produced the hoped-for navigational benefits, but it did contribute to wetland degradation south of New Orleans and played a contributing role in conveying storm waters from Hurricane Katrina into the city. Congress passed legislation deauthorizing the channel in section 7013 of the Water Resources Act of 2007.

14. U.S. Government Accountability Office, statement of Anu Mittal, director, Natural Resources and Environment on Lake Pontchartrain and Vicinity Hurricane Protection Project, GAO-05-1050T, September 28, 2005 (www.gpo.gov/fdsys/pkg/GAOREPORTS-GAO-05-1050T/html/GAOREPORTS-GAO-05-1050T.htm); and *Elevations for Design of Hurricane Protection Levees and Structures,* U.S Army Corps of Engineers, New Orleans District, October 9, 2007 (www.mvn.usace.army.mil/ENG/ElevationsforDesignofHurricaneProtectionLeveesandStructures.pdf).

15. Louisiana-Mississippi Gulf Coast Ecosystem Restoration Working Group, "Roadmap for Restoring Ecosystem Resiliency and Sustainability" (2010) (www.whitehouse.gov/administration/eop/ceq/initiatives/gulfcoast/roadmap).

16. The White House, "Remarks by the President to the Nation on the BP Oil Spill," news release, June 15, 2010 (www.whitehouse.gov/the-press-office/remarks-president-nation-bp-oil-spill).

17. *America's Gulf Coast: A Long-Term Recovery Plan after the Deepwater Horizon Oil Spill* (September 2010) (www.restorethegulf.gov).

18. The Gulf Ecosystem Restoration Task Force was created by presidential executive order on October 5, 2010.

19. "Louisiana's Comprehensive Master Plan for a Sustainable Coast," April 2007.

20. *Blanco* v. *Burton,* 2006 U.S. Dist. LEXIS 56533.

21. Louisiana Constitution, article 7, section 10.2(E).

22. See, for example, Michael. D. Blum and Harry H. Roberts, "Drowning of the Mississippi Delta due to Insufficient Sediment Supply and Global Sea-Level Rise," *Nature Geoscience 2* (2009): 488–91.

23. For example, a proposed hurricane protection levee has been delayed by disagreements over its alignment. Local government officials and both of Louisiana's U.S. senators have advocated for an alignment that would protect more homes but also bisect a major estuary. U.S. EPA and others have cautioned against such an environmentally risky alternative. See Paul Rioux, "Donaldsonville-to-the-Gulf Levee Alignment Decision Is Postponed," *Times-Picayune,* April 20, 2010.

24. Adopted August 13 by New Orleans City Council, Ordinance Calendar No. 28.069. New Orleans Master Plan and Comprehensive Zoning Ordinance, "Plan for the 21st Century: New Orleans 2030," Executive Summary, pp. 96, 98 (http://nolamasterplan.org/documentsandrresources.asp#C12).

25. Inauguration speech of Mayor Mitch Landrieu, as published in the *Times-Picayune,* May 3, 2010.

PART 3

Building Resilience and Opportunity through Civil Society

13

Building Data Capacity to Foster Resilient Communities

Allison Plyer and Elaine Ortiz

Today data are an essential input to nearly every kind of decision made or action taken. To supply data that will inform a myriad of private sector activities as well as policy decisions, the federal government invests some $3 billion every year to support a dozen federal statistical agencies (and billions more every ten years to conduct the decennial census).[1] The volume of data publicly available from federal sources is so large that expertise is required to understand the totality of what is available, to identify the most appropriate data source for the decision at hand, and to know how to access the data and analyze it. State and local governments and private companies also invest untold billions in the collection and analysis of their own data to support operations and decisionmaking. In theory, most government administrative data are publicly available. But in practice, it is very difficult if not impossible for the public to access much government data. Many state and local governments do not have the workforce necessary to respond to data requests nor the capacity (or obligation) to provide data organized in formats that are useful to the public.[2] As a result, data critical for decisionmaking are truly accessible only to those who have the resources, skills, and infrastructure to compile and analyze it.

Following a disaster, the demand for data escalates as decisionmakers grasp for the certainty that numbers can provide in the midst of chaos and dramatically changed conditions. Because each disaster is unique (for example, Hurricane Katrina caused enormous residential destruction, while the Gulf oil spill caused immense environmental devastation), the data needed after a disaster will vary. Given the lack of data accessibility and the need for data to be "customized" for each disaster, it is no surprise that the National Research Council reports that leaders and managers in recovery situations often complain of a data vacuum that hinders decisionmaking on short-term priorities, resource allocation, and long-term recovery planning.[3] Having an established data intermediary with a sound technical platform and community-oriented mission in place before a disaster strikes enhances the resilience capacity of a region to meet the myriad and acute data needs that will arise after a disaster.

History and Values of the Greater New Orleans Community Data Center

Prior to Katrina, New Orleans may have had greater resilience capacity than other disaster-affected areas because the New Orleans philanthropic community had already invested in the skills and infrastructure to respond to significant demand for data.[4] The Greater New Orleans Community Data Center (the Data Center) was founded with philanthropic support in 1997 to help New Orleans civic leaders use data to work smarter and more strategically. The Data Center's operations were based on a set of principles articulated by the National Neighborhood Indicators Partnership (NNIP), namely to "democratize" data, that is, make data widely available rather than available only to those with the resources to access and analyze it.[5] The Data Center focused on helping nonprofit and government entities use data to improve community conditions through planning, grant writing, and advocacy. At the same time, the Data Center worked to ensure that the data that it presented were neutral. Data collection could not be sponsored by government entities lest it appear to be serving the interests of elected officials, and data had to be presented in a completely transparent manner, with all limitations acknowledged and implications examined from multiple perspectives. The Data Center's neutrality and high level of rigor gained the confidence of the general community, allowing disparate groups to work more productively on solving problems rather than quibbling over the validity of data.

In 2001, the Data Center published a highly usable, highly credible, and very responsive web-based data dissemination system. Its website (www.gnocdc.org) presented U.S. census 2000 data covering demographics, housing, poverty, employment, educational attainment, disabilities, and other information for all seventy-three New Orleans neighborhoods and nine surrounding parishes in easy-to-analyze tables and download-able spreadsheets. The indicators on the website were selected to answer 80 percent of the data questions that local organizations had. For the other 20 percent, the website included a feature called "Ask Allison," through which additional questions were received and responded to, typ-ically on the same day. All of the data met rigorous scientific standards, yet explanatory materials were written in clear, everyday language to ensure usability for a lay audience. The website's usability was credited with attracting significant traffic to the site. Before Hurricane Katrina, the website attracted an astounding 5,000 unique visits per month; in contrast, a counterpart data intermediary website in a much larger mar-ket—Washington, D.C.—attracted only 1,000 unique visits each month. Because this platform was in place, when Katrina struck, businesses and government decisionmakers were able to get timely and reliable answers to critical questions about who and what was affected in the New Orleans area, when, and where.

As Katrina approached, the five-person staff of the Data Center evac-uated. At the same time, traffic to the website skyrocketed, reaching 40,000 unique visits in August 2005 and 80,000 unique visits in Sep-tember 2005. From their evacuated positions in crowded hotel rooms or sleeping on the floor of friends' living rooms, Data Center staff ramped up their efforts to respond to the escalating requests for data. Effective web-based communication tools as well as strong organizational norms allowed the dispersed staff to continue functioning at a high level despite their displacement from homes and office.

As the rebuilding process began, the demand for data remained high, evidenced by average monthly traffic to the website of 15,000 unique visits. The Data Center's efforts to disseminate data to support rebuild-ing efforts accelerated. Questions submitted to "Ask Allison" came from a wide range of government entities, private companies, and nonprof-its and served as critical intelligence regarding the highest priority data needs following Katrina. The Data Center used this intelligence to priori-tize efforts for researching, compiling, and publishing data that would best support the recovery of the area.

Measuring Repopulation

As New Orleanians trickled back to rebuild their homes or find new homes, repopulation data for small geographies were frequently requested to inform the rational deployment of government and nonprofit resources as well as private sector investment decisions. Although demographic data describing age and gender were also needed to inform service provision, frequently updated basic population indicators emerged as the most needed data post-Katrina. The U.S. Census Bureau cannot currently meet that need because it has funding to produce only one annual population estimate for every county and that estimate has an associated nine-month lag time. Private data firms in the United States produce estimates at varying intervals but with a lag time of several months. In addition, the estimates typically lack the transparency needed to be considered neutral and are not always publicly available.

Understanding the need for frequent, small-area population data and the multiple investment decisions that the data would drive, the Data Center dedicated months of research to finding a sustainable public source of data that would indicate repopulation of the city and region. The Data Center investigated a large number of state and federal administrative data sets that had been used historically by demographers to generate population estimates, including, among others, utility accounts, U.S. Postal Service (USPS) counts of residences actively receiving mail, driver's license counts, registered passenger car data, and voter registration data. Assessing each data set's soundness, consistency, relevance, and timeliness, the Data Center concluded that the USPS data served as a reasonable and timely indicator of population resettlement (see figure 13-1).[6]

Tracking Facilities and Infrastructure

While individuals and developers rebuilt homes, government entities slowly began rebuilding the facilities and infrastructure that also were destroyed by the catastrophic flooding. Parents and businesses frequently requested information to find out what schools, hospitals, clinics, and child care facilities were reopened to help inform their decisions about returning. That information was rapidly changing, and data more than a few weeks old became essentially useless. The Data Center gathered and verified data on public schools, hospitals, clinics, and child care centers (in most cases, calling each individual facility to verify its status and address) and then mapped the data to provide context for recovery decisions. To ensure that the information would not circulate past its useful life, maps were published with a "Best Used By" stamp, as seen in figure 13-2.

FIGURE 13-1. Orleans Parish Active Residential Addresses per Square Mile, 2005, 2006, and 2007

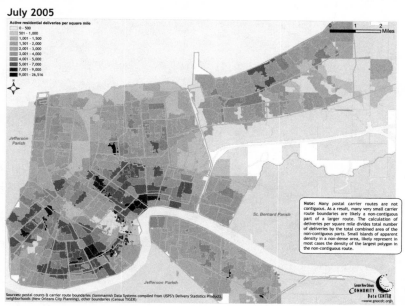

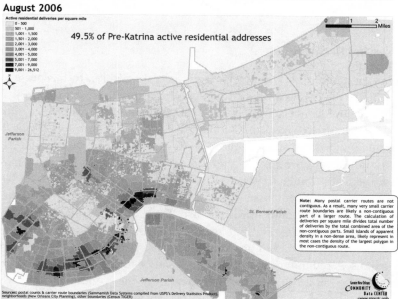

(continued)

FIGURE 13-1 *(continued)*

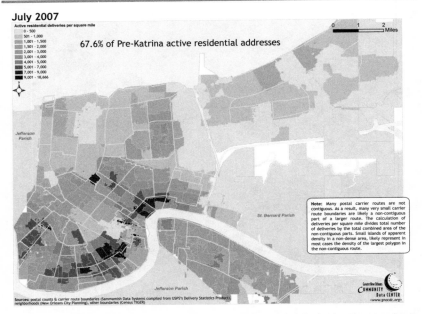

Sources: Sammamish Data Systems, data compiled from USPS's Delivery Statistics Product (postal counts and carrier route boundaries); New Orleans City Planning Office (neighborhoods); and Census TIGER (other boundaries).

Assessing Recovery

A large number of stakeholders, from federal agencies, to businesses, to U.S. taxpayers, were anxious to assess the region's overall recovery. To help stakeholders better understand the areas of greatest need for short- and long-term recovery, the Brookings Institution began publishing the Katrina Index (later renamed the New Orleans Index) in December 2005.[7] As data collection efforts became more intense, Brookings partnered with the Data Center to extend their data collection capacity. The New Orleans Index encompassed dozens of indicators covering population, housing, economy, and infrastructure. For example, longitudinal data on schools, hospitals, and public transportation systems were collected to demonstrate the speed at which they were being rebuilt and whether shortfalls were inhibiting recovery. Jobs, labor force, and unemployment data were compiled to measure the strength of the economy and whether there was a need for transitional support, such as temporary housing for

FIGURE 13-2. Open Public Schools in Orleans Parish as of November 30, 2006

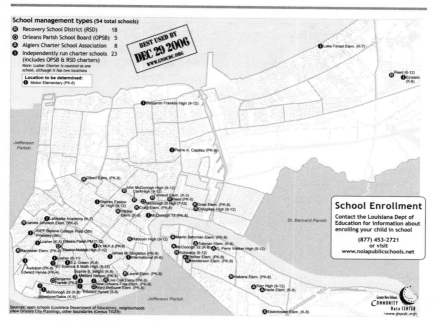

Sources: Louisiana Department of Education (open schools); New Orleans City Planning Office (neighborhoods), and Census TIGER (other boundaries).

workers. Trends in home sales and home sales prices were gathered to assess market confidence in the area. To ensure that data were actionable, the Data Center and Brookings accompanied them with analysis.

The identification of accurate and timely data was labor intensive. To get the most timely data at a small enough geographic level (for example, the parish rather than the state level), much of the data came from local rather than federal sources, as illustrated in table 13-1. To acquire the data, relationships had to be built with reliable local sources who themselves were experiencing post-disaster challenges of insufficient staff and increased demand. In some instances, individual data points had to be manually copied, cut, and pasted from hard copy reports or raw electronic data dumps had to be cleaned and tallied.

Initially the index was published monthly by the Brookings Institution. As the pace of change slowed, the frequency of publication shifted to quarterly in 2008, semiannually in 2009, and annually in 2010. Over

TABLE 13-1.   New Orleans Index Sample Indicators and Sources

Category	Indicator	Source
Housing	Average home sale price	New Orleans Metropolitan Association of Realtors
	Number of residential building permits	New Orleans Department of Safety and Permits
Services and infra-structure	Proportion of operational buses and streetcars	New Orleans Regional Transportation Authority
	Proportion of open hospitals	Louisiana Hospital Association and individual area hospitals
Workforce and economy	Unemployment rate	Bureau of Labor Statistics
	Proportion of open retail food establishments	Louisiana Restaurant Association
Emergency response	Number of households receiving FEMA housing assistance	Federal Emergency Management Agency (FEMA)
	Employment status of individuals who evacuated	Bureau of Labor Statistics

Source: *New Orleans Index* (Brookings Institution and Greater New Orleans Community Data Center, various years).

time, the Data Center sought out more granular data to provide neighborhood detail as decisionmaking and planning moved from the national to the local and neighborhood level. By the fifth anniversary of Katrina, data collection shifted from rebuilding measures to indicators of the overall well-being of the city and region, including entrepreneurship, size of the city's middle class, affordable housing, arts and culture, quality of public education, crime rates, and median household income by race and ethnicity (as a measure of equity and inclusion). Because the index was continually adapted to meet changing conditions and information needs, interest in the publication increased rather than waned. The number of downloads increased from 7,656 for the first anniversary edition to 23,622 downloads for the fifth anniversary edition.

Some critical questions could not be answered with readily available data. The Data Center made extensive efforts to find data that would indicate the strength of the levees as they were being rebuilt and measures of coastal wetland loss, for example. Although one-time studies were available, regularly updated indicators on this and other critical infrastructure were elusive. Similarly, accurate and timely data on small business recovery, real estate trends at the neighborhood level, number and location of evacuees, and federal spending were not available.

Supporting Equitable Community Development

In 2008, housing and community development emerged as an area in need of more detailed data analysis. In the first years of recovery, decisionmakers and developers had adopted a "build it and they will come" approach, based simply on the vast destruction to housing stock caused by the levee failures. But by 2008, the changing demographics and economy of the region combined with a large infusion of federal dollars to support home rebuilding resulted in uncertainty about what types of housing were still needed and how remaining federal funding designated for Katrina rebuilding should be spent. Much of the funding, a portion of which was designated for low- and moderate-income populations, came from the U.S. Department of Housing and Urban Development. Officials in Louisiana began to question the rebuilding of subsidized rental housing in particular and the remaining uses of the funding in general. The Data Center, in partnership with the Urban Institute, released a series of reports and briefs covering the demand for subsidized rental housing, the extent of blight, and housing affordability issues for homeowners and renters to help inform policy debates about remaining needs in the community.[8]

Impact

Since 2005, data and analyses published by the Data Center have been used in innumerable legislative committee meetings, city council meetings, public forums, hearings, and reports. The following is a small sampling of findings from a survey of Data Center data users, conducted by an independent evaluator, that illustrates some of the impact of the data and analysis disseminated by the Data Center:

—A state agency used data published on the Data Center website to position mobile health units and plan community outreach events, to calculate infectious disease prevalence rates, and to determine health professional shortage areas.

—The New Orleans Index and other data published on the Data Center website were used by nonprofits in Houston, Dallas, and elsewhere to make evacuees aware of services available in New Orleans as well as the strength of the economy so that the evacuees could make informed decisions about returning.

—The U.S. Army Corps of Engineers used data available at the Data Center website to prepare environmental impact reports in the development of their hurricane and storm risk reduction system.

—State officials used the New Orleans Index and other data available at the website to assess progress and to request funding from Congress.

—The Government Accountability Office used the New Orleans Index numerous times to update Congress on the progress of the recovery effort and to make recommendations about federal investment in the rebuilding effort.

—Block-level population data published by the Data Center were used to inform police, fire, and EMS staff deployment across the city.

—Data available at the Data Center website were used to inform philanthropic investments in school-based health care as the city's schools were rebuilt.

—The Data Center's housing data were used to assess demand for large housing developments funded by tax credits. Multiple private investors had to be confident of demand before they would invest.

—Data published on the website were used to demonstrate accurately the share of damage and the return rate to neighborhoods to counteract unfounded assertions such as that made to the city council by a particular neighborhood that it had sustained x percent of the damage and therefore should get x percent of the money.

—Data available at the website were used by a large nonprofit working to coordinate multiple service providers in a single neighborhood to create a set of facts so that the various partners could agree on a cohesive understanding of problems and priorities. In that way, the data acted as glue to support the partnership.

Ingredients for Success

A large number of research and nonprofit organizations have expressed interest in learning more about the Greater New Orleans Community Data Center as a model for guiding their own data collection and impact efforts. The key ingredients for success include dedicating sufficient staff for data assembly, maintenance, and analysis; building partnerships with multiple data sources; utilizing mainstream media as well as the Internet to disseminate information; and investing in mapping technology and training for more refined geographical analysis.

—*Dedicate significant staff.* The Data Center hired a full-time staff person to research, vet, and manage the data identified as highest priority for addressing pressing questions. This staffer investigated various data sources to identify the most reliable data for each question. She built and maintained relationships with local data providers, tracked revisions and updates to data sources, and monitored overall developments and changes in the availability of data. She conducted statistical tests to make comparisons between time periods and geographies. She continually added the most recent data points, and she archived and made revisions to historical data as they were released. The Data Center allocated another full-time staff person to analyze the data and respond to media requests, and a third full-time staffer to make graphic representations of the data and respond to data requests, which averaged sixty per month.

—*Build partnerships.* The Data Center built partnerships with a large number of local and state agencies and nonprofit associations to acquire, clean, and disseminate their data. The Data Center quickly became known for having a highly efficient system for disseminating data and responding to data requests. Many agencies without the staff to respond to a multitude of data requests—such as the New Orleans Department of Safety and Permits, New Orleans Regional Transportation Authority, and Louisiana Hospital Association—were willing to provide their data to the Data Center to relieve themselves of that burden. In addition, because the Data Center was impartial in its analysis of the data, the agencies were able to trust that the Data Center would not use the data against them (a common concern among government agencies about the release of their data).[9]

—*Use mainstream media.* The Data Center disseminated its data and analysis not only through its successful web-based platform but also through traditional broadcast media to optimize public awareness and increase the possibility of informing policy decisions. The Data Center developed extensive relationships with local and national media to get wide coverage of its data and analysis through television, radio, and newspaper and achieved more than 500 print media mentions each year.

—*Invest in technology and training.* The Data Center used powerful geographic information system (GIS) software to assign geographic coordinates to addresses and map the recovery status of key community facilities like police stations, health clinics, and schools. Data Center staff developed a robust system for incorporating local knowledge about the location of addresses and maintaining the information across data sets. The Data Center used GIS software to map the data available for small areas (for example, census tracts, neighborhoods, and planning districts), which allowed for more refined geographic analysis. Staff also employed sophisticated graphic software to refine and fortify the maps created in GIS. In that way, the Data Center created highly usable, easy-to-distribute maps that precisely and honestly conveyed the data.

Recommendations

Some communities have already recognized the value of a data intermediary that regularly gathers, vets, and widely disseminates data to measure progress in housing, schools, the local economy, and so forth. But in general, the need to amass the resources, skills, and infrastructure to effectively democratize data is undervalued, as evidenced by the fact that there are only three dozen NNIP data intermediaries nationwide. In the event of a disaster, resilience capacity is greater in communities that have a platform that pulls together and presents relevant and reliable data to support crucial decisions that can mitigate damage in the short term and enhance recovery in the long term. Having an established data intermediary in place before a disaster strikes is preferable. Obviously, it would be more difficult to set up a data intermediary in the days and weeks after a disaster has already struck.

After a disaster, high-level authorities (such as the Federal Coordinator for Gulf Coast Rebuilding) should work to break down barriers to access federal data that are critical to answering pressing questions identified by data intermediaries. As just one example, access to FEMA's Individuals and Households Program data at a granular level would have provided an indication of the number and location of evacuees post-Katrina. The census bureau was not able to acquire the data from FEMA until a full year had elapsed.[10] One year later, the data were no longer considered accurate because many evacuees made multiple moves following their initial displacement.[11] In addition, high priority should be placed on tracking federal spending for recovery and providing the data in a timely and transparent way for public access. High-level authorities could also work closely with the local data intermediary to request access to private data such as address-level real estate transactions.

In addition, custom data may be needed following a disaster, such as measurements of wetland loss or estimates of the long-term damage to the estuaries as a result of the Gulf oil spill. If a disaster causes massive population displacement, the census bureau could create custom estimates or conduct special surveys. The federal government should set aside appropriations to support such data collection and dissemination following any disaster.

But to be perceived as credible and independent, ideally data intermediaries would be sponsored by philanthropic organizations rather than government. The good news is that even under normal circumstances, independent data collection and analysis, if thoughtfully done as described in this case study, can provide a significant social return on the limited funds that philanthropies have to invest in the problems that they seek to solve.[12] And at the same time, by building resilience capacity, philanthropic investments in local data intermediaries may be one of the highest-yield disaster preparedness investments that a funder can make.

Notes

1. Council of Professional Associations on Federal Statistics, "Federal Statistics in the FY 2011 Budget," 2011 (www.copafs.org/UserFiles/file/reports/COPAFS2011 BudgetReport.pdf).

2. If localities provide anything, it is often data dumps, which may include duplicate or missing records, partial data, little documentation, and unintelligible fields and may require expertise to compile into meaningful formats.

3. National Research Council, *Tools and Methods for Estimating Populations at Risk from Natural Disasters and Complex Humanitarian Crises* (Washington: The National Academies Press, 2007)

4. According to Kathryn A. Foster, in chapter 2 of this volume, "Enhancing resilience capacity means amassing the resources, skills, infrastructure, processes, attitudes, and other factors that help you anticipate, mitigate, and cope with the next crisis, whatever it may be."

5. Thomas Kingsley and Kathryn L. S. Pettit, "Quality of Life at a Finer Grain: The National Neighborhood Indicators Partnership," in *Community Quality of Life Indicators: Best Cases V*, edited by M. Joseph Sirgy (New York: Springer, 2011).

6. Allison Plyer and Joy Bonaguro, "Using U.S. Postal Service Delivery Statistics to Track the Repopulation of New Orleans and the Metropolitan Area" (New Orleans: Greater New Orleans Community Data Center, May 2007) (https://gnocdc. s3.amazonaws.com/reports/GNOCDC_research_note_May07.pdf); Allison Plyer, Joy Bonaguro, and Ken Hodges, "Using Administrative Data to Estimate Population Displacement and Resettlement following a Catastrophic U.S. Disaster," *Population and Environment* 31 (2009): 150–75.

7. "New Orleans Index" (Brookings Institution and Greater New Orleans Community Data Center, various years).

8. For example, Allison Plyer and others, "Housing Production Needs: Three Scenarios for New Orleans" (GNOCDC and the Urban Institute, November 2009) (https://gnocdc.s3.amazonaws.com/reports/GNOCDCHousingProductionNeeds2009.pdf).

9. Kingsley and Pettit, "Quality of Life at a Finer Grain."

10. Victoria A. Velkoff, Jonathan Takeuchi, and Rodger V. Johnson, "Evaluation of the U.S. Census Bureau's Population Estimates for Counties Affected by Hurricanes Katrina and Rita" (U.S. Census Bureau, 2008).

11. According to American Housing Survey data, households displaced from the New Orleans Metro area moved a median of two times and fully 10 percent of displaced households moved five or more times. Bureau of the Census, *American Housing Survey for the New Orleans Metropolitan Area: 2009* (Department of Commerce, 2009), table 3.

12. M. Christine DeVita, "Power of Ideas: How Foundations Can Generate Knowledge to Spark Change," *Rand Review* (Winter 2010–11).

14

Rise of Community Organizations, Citizen Engagement, and New Institutions

Frederick Weil

Following Hurricane Katrina, observers worried that New Orleans might continue on the path of citizen passivity, inter-communal conflict, and corruption that was a long-standing part of its reputation. Instead, observers have been struck by the outpouring of citizen engagement, the rise of new or reinvigorated community organizations, and the calls for government responsiveness.

By many accounts, New Orleans had never developed a robust civil society in its long history before Hurricane Katrina.[1] Its elites were a closed group, its government was unresponsive, and most of its citizens swung between passivity and angry protest. As is typical of communities with closed and rigid elites, New Orleans had lost rank to more open, dynamic cities, in this case since the 1840s, when it was the third-largest American city.[2] In the half-century before Hurricane Katrina, New Orleans actually shrank in size, while a "New South" arose all around it.

In short, New Orleans had lost sight of what democratic theory, going back to Alexis de Tocqueville and John Stuart Mill in the mid-nineteenth century, identified as three important characteristics of a free society.[3] First, the initiative to address issues comes from free citizens working together in their communities. Second, government is responsive to citizens and partners with them, rather than commanding or excluding them. And third, civic engagement is open to all citizens, regardless of social standing or background, and leadership is open to merit. They argue that in an unfree society, by contrast, government discourages people from working together to solve their own problems and elites restrict participation on the basis of class, race/ethnicity, gender, or colonial status. Therefore, participation in a free society takes the form of interaction, reconciliation of opposing interests, and the formation of an idea (however imperfect) of a common good. Participation in an unfree society takes the form of resistance to oppression and petitioning of elites for benefits that people are prevented from working together to attain. Although these are ideal types, civic engagement in a free society seems to have much in common with the social "capacity" needed for "resilience" described by Kathryn Foster in chapter 2 in this volume.

The effort to recover from Hurricane Katrina seems to have spurred a new burst of civic engagement in New Orleans, giving the city an opportunity to regain lost ground. Sociologists suggest that communities respond to natural disasters by pulling together and cooperating in their attempt to recover because they feel that they all face a common challenge.[4] After Katrina, government assistance alone was never sufficient for recovery; therefore citizens and communities were motivated to work together to recover. Citizens had an incentive to cooperate and provide each other with assistance; communities had an incentive to partner with one another; elites had an incentive to accept leadership initiatives from outside their traditional ranks; and government had an incentive to accept offers of assistance and partnership from engaged citizens and communities. A virtuous circle of growing mutual trust and civic engagement began to displace the old vicious circle of distrust and disengagement.[5]

Summary of Post-Katrina Community Engagement

This chapter relies mostly on original data collected through the author's research project on community recovery in Greater New Orleans since Hurricane Katrina, especially on a survey of about 7,000 residents initiated in spring 2006 and continuing through spring 2011 that covered respondents' damage, recovery, social connections (social capital), and feelings; a survey of neighborhood association leaders conducted in partnership with the New Orleans Neighborhood Partnership Network (data collection is still under way, with about ninety leaders surveyed so far); and intensive ethnographic research, including videotaped interviews, conducted since shortly after the storm of neighborhood associations, churches, synagogues, and other faith-based groups, nonprofits, and other community organizations (more than 200 groups in total).

Overall Civic Engagement and Social Capital

Surveys of some 7,000 residents conducted by the author's research team reveal that New Orleanians since Katrina score below the national average on most measures of civic engagement and social capital included in the 2006 Social Capital Community Survey.[6] They express a good deal less social trust and are less likely to participate in various social activities. Yet at the same time, post-Katrina New Orleanians were substantially *more* likely to attend a public meeting at which town or school affairs were discussed, at least a few times a year. With the advent of frequent community and planning meetings focused on disaster recovery, perhaps we see "new" forms of civic engagement displacing an "old" style of civil distrust and disengagement in New Orleans.

Who Participates: Individual and Collective Resources

Research shows that participation requires resources, and resources are not distributed equally.[7] Citizens with greater individual resources, such as money, education, and time, participate more actively than citizens with fewer resources. Citizens with greater collective resources or social capital—cohesive communities, strong organizations, enthusiasm and mobilization, mutual trust—participate more effectively than those without collective resources. And higher-status citizens (who have more individual resources) usually have more collective resources as well. But collective resources can help lower-status citizens compensate for their lack of individual resources and thus help them participate at higher rates than they otherwise could. Lower-status citizens without compensating social capital are least able to participate.

Figure 14-1 suggests how these patterns seem to have played out in post-Katrina New Orleans. People with individual resources like money and education were less likely to receive storm damage because they lived in places that were less likely to flood; they were more likely to have adequate insurance; and they were more likely to be civically engaged. People with insufficient individual resources were more dependent on collective resources or, failing that, on government assistance to compensate and enable them to recover. People who had neither individual nor collective resources were least likely to recover.

FIGURE 14-1. **Storm Damage, Resources, and Recovery: Sequence and Effects of Different Types of Recovery[a]**

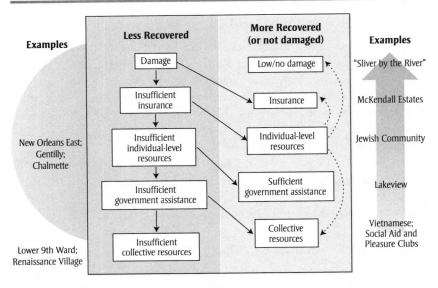

Source: Author's illustration.

a. The figure illustrates hypotheses about different paths to hurricane recovery. Solid-line arrows show an opportunity or decision tree, indicating different possible paths for moving out of the dark-shaded damage zone into the light-shaded recovery zone. (The arrows do not represent causation.) For instance, if a community suffers damage but has insurance, it has a path to recovery and moves into the light zone. Failing that ("insufficient insurance"), it might exit the damage area with individual-level resources, or some other means, further along the tree branches. Communities that have exhausted all potential resources or that have none are unable to move out of the dark zone into the light zone—that is, they are unable to recover. (Dotted-line arrows show a causal relationship, namely, that individual-level resources contribute to obtaining many other forms of resources as well.)

Well-to-do communities, therefore, were at an advantage: the "Sliver by the River" (Garden District, French Quarter, and others) received less damage; McKendall Estates residents were well insured; the Jewish community was well-off and had strong solidarity; Lakeview was upper-middle income and had a strong neighborhood organization. Less well-to-do communities like the Vietnamese and the Social Aid and Pleasure Clubs were able to compensate to some extent for inadequate individual resources by employing strong collective resources. Recovery in middle-income communities, like those in New Orleans East, Gentilly, and Chalmette, varied considerably according to whether the communities were able to organize themselves or receive sufficient government assistance. The low- to moderate-income communities that were most heavily damaged and were unable to draw sufficiently on collective resources, like the Lower Ninth Ward, have had a weak recovery. And individuals with little individual or collective resources, especially isolated poor people, lower-income elderly, those with disabilities, and those without strong networks of family and friends, have struggled most, often remaining in FEMA trailer parks like Renaissance Village in Baker, Louisiana, near Baton Rouge.

Civic Engagement and Recovery

Figure 14-2 reinforces that picture. Higher-status people and solidaristic communities participate more strongly. On a civic engagement index in the author's resident survey, better-educated and higher-income people are more engaged, as are Jews, church members, and members of Social Aid and Pleasure Clubs (SAPCs).[8] Residents of FEMA trailer parks are less engaged. The Vietnamese community, which has a reputation as a very tightly knit community that has only recently begun to abandon its traditional reluctance to engage in citywide affairs, remains less civically engaged than average. Perhaps that is due to its lesser integration into New Orleans society. The most striking finding in figure 14-2 is that Social Aid and Pleasure Club members score highest on civic engagement.[9] While SAPC members are mostly lower income and thus lack strong individual resources, they are nevertheless more civically active, service oriented, and trusting than even the rich or well educated. That finding is a powerful testament to the importance of social capital or collective resources in compensating for the lack of individual resources.

Figure 14-3 shows that higher levels of civic engagement and social capital in a census tract are associated with stronger community recovery. Specifically, greater associational involvement, civic leadership, service performance, attendance at club meetings, and social trust correlate significantly ($p < .01$) with stronger repopulation and less damage, blight, and violent crime in 180 census tracts.

Optimistic Developments: A New Form and Quality of Civic Engagement

A new style of activism has arisen in post-Katrina New Orleans. Civic engagement has evolved away from pressing for government assistance while government plays communities off against each other. New forms of engagement include

FIGURE 14-2. **Civic Engagement in Selected Social Groups**[a]

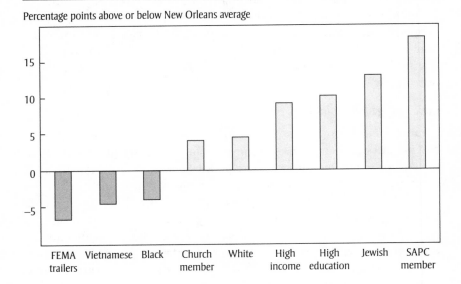

Percentage points above or below New Orleans average

Source: LSU Disaster Recovery Survey. *N* = ca. 7,000. Data collection began in spring 2006 and continued through spring 2011. More details are available at www.lsu.edu/fweil/KatrinaResearch.

a. Civic engagement scores are an average of scores on the following questions. Items in brackets are the answers included in the scale.

1. "Generally speaking, would you say that most people can be trusted or that you can't be too careful in dealing with people?" [Most people can be trusted.]

2. "About how often have you done the following?" Attended any public meeting in which there was discussion of town or school affairs. [Once a month or more.]

3. "Have you taken part in activities with the following groups and organizations in the past 12 months?" A neighborhood association like a block association; a homeowner or tenant association; or a crime watch group. [Yes.]

4. "Have you taken part in activities with the following groups and organizations in the past 12 months?" A charity or social welfare organization that provides services in such fields as health or service to the needy. [Yes.]

5. "In the past twelve months, have you served as an officer or served on a committee of any local club or organization?" [Yes.]

—increasing organizational capacity and autonomy

—greater strategic sophistication

—increasing citizen participation

—a new cooperative orientation and the emergence of new umbrella groups

—new recovery resources from "outside-inside" the community.

Moreover, government and established elites have perhaps become more open to citizen input than in the past. However, this is a recent development, and it remains to be seen how permanent it will be. Let's look at each of these factors in turn.

FIGURE 14-3. **Correlation of Civic Engagement and Social Capital with Community Recovery[a]**

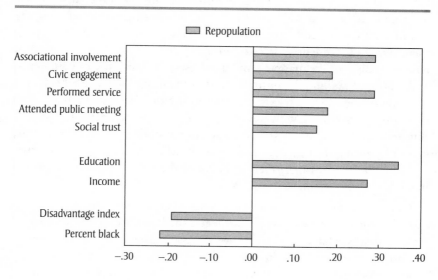

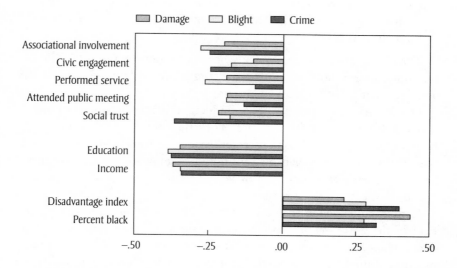

Sources: LSU Disaster Recovery Survey. Damage estimates are from the City of New Orleans; repopulation and blight estimates are based on postal delivery data from the U.S. Postal Service and HUD; data on violent crime are from the City of New Orleans Police Department.

a. Data are aggregated to the level of census tract (N = 180). Data are for Orleans and St. Bernard Parish census tracts; a few tracts are combined because of too few survey responses. Number of interviews per tract are: mean = 16; median = 12; maximum = 102; minimum = 3.

Increasing Organizational Capacity and Autonomy

Community leaders stress several important elements in increasing organizational capacity and autonomy: improved organization, including the
use of committees and block captains; data collection and developing
their own, independent sources of information; ongoing incorporation of
new technologies like mapping and databases; extensive use of volunteers;
and, above all, taking the initiative and not waiting for outside help.

Some of the older, preexisting community organizations already had
committee structures, which were quickly reactivated after the storm.
But one of the most innovative organizational initiatives, block captains,
grew organically out of the need to act quickly in the post-storm crisis
environment. Al Petrie, former president of the Lakeview Civic Improvement Association said,

> One of the first things we did was say, "Okay, we need to get in
> touch with people as best we can," and the best way we can do that
> is to see if we have people that we know and then that one of them
> knows on every block in Lakeview. . . . And we created a block
> captain network, where through everybody knowing somebody in
> Lakeview, we got somebody to volunteer to be the information offi-
> cer for a particular block. And by doing that, we started our whole
> surveying process.[10]

The block captain system quickly became an important tool for information gathering and dissemination, organizing, planning, and other
activities that helped to build community capacity.

Organizations became adept at conducting their own surveys of property conditions and infrastructure. They then input the data into GIS
mapping programs and computer databases and learned to analyze and
use their own data for their own purposes. Organizations also organized
and used their own workforce of volunteer labor, especially volunteer
groups that came to help rebuild.

Such initiatives enabled citizen organizations to become more independent of the government, especially when the government was slow and
overwhelmed in providing services during recovery. Indeed, when organizations found that the government was overwhelmed and unable to
perform its duties, citizens sometimes tried to bring their assembled data
to the government to help it organize its tasks more efficiently. Describing
how citizens can fight blight, Denise Thornton, founder and president of
the Beacon of Hope Resource Center, said,

[We've learned] the things to look for, how to fight blight, how to go to city hall and win in a constructive way. These blight teams have case files on every single blighted home, where they make phone calls, they do voluntary compliance. . . . You don't just sit around and wait for government to help you. You've got to do it yourself.[11]

A New Strategic Sophistication

A sense of urgency contributed also to the development of a new strategic sophistication among community leaders, who quickly realized that if residents thought that no one else was going to come back and rebuild, they would be discouraged, resulting in a self-fulfilling prophecy. If, conversely, residents thought that others were returning and rebuilding, that would give them the confidence to do the same. The question was how to manage impressions and create a critical mass.[12] Broadmoor put up banners and yard signs throughout the neighborhood that said "Broadmoor Lives," and people in New Orleans East put signs in their window and yards that read "We're Coming Back," well before they were able to return. That kind of signaling helped create a critical mass, or tipping point, to forge solidarity in the service of recovery.

On that basis, formal planning became much more productive. Residents came to planning meetings in large numbers and actively participated. In the neighborhoods that began the process earliest, such as Lakeview and Broadmoor, neighborhood meetings were large and had a buzz of anticipation, with neighbors eager to see each other.

Several ethnic/religious communities also engaged in their own community planning. The Vietnamese community around the Mary Queen of Vietnam (MQVN) Catholic Church and the Mary Queen of Vietnam Community Development Corporation had begun planning before the storm. MQVN had planned a retirement home in a park-like setting, accompanied by an urban farm and farmers' market, which it planned to make self-financing by serving not only New Orleans customers but also Asian produce markets throughout the United States. Hurricane Katrina interrupted development, but after the storm the community was able to quickly pick up where it had left off.[13] The Jewish Federation of Greater New Orleans (JFGNO) also engaged in extensive recovery planning, building on a long-standing tradition of community self-governance.[14] The JFGNO conducted a recovery survey in spring of 2006 and planning surveys in 2007 and 2010 and formed a set of planning committees that met and worked for a year.[15] The JFGNO also hired a new executive director, an Israeli urban planner from Jerusalem's city hall. Results of the surveys and conclusions from the planning committees were combined in a planning document at JFGNO's fall 2007 annual meeting. Among the most notable outcomes of these efforts was the creation of a successful "newcomers" program to attract young, dynamic new community members to relocate to New Orleans.

Increasing Citizen Participation

One of the most striking aspects of the post-Katrina period in New Orleans is how people who had never really taken part before have been drawn into civic affairs. People were galvanized by many things, including the "green dot" on a planning map that said that their community was slated for return to forest or park;[16] by anger at authorities who were viewed as unresponsive; or by feelings of love for and solidarity with fellow community members. A new civic leadership emerged from among people who had never been engaged before. Katherine Prevost, president of Bunny Friend Neighborhood Association in the Upper Ninth Ward, said,

> Before the storm, I was living my daily life. The storm changed me. . . . All I think about when I go to work is, "Let me hurry up and get these eight hours over with so I can do my community work." So when I leave my job, I put another eight hours in sometimes.[17]

A New Cooperative Orientation and the Emergence of New Umbrella Groups

Another centrally important feature of the new civic participation in post-Katrina New Orleans was its cooperative orientation. Community members pooled their efforts for the common cause of recovery and improvement. Communities partnered with each other to achieve common goals rather than competing with or confronting each other. Perhaps most surprisingly of all, many citizens reached out to government to act as a partner.

When Vietnamese community members began to return after the storm, those with building skills went house to house in teams, putting on new roofs, so that the owners could sleep in them, even while they worked on them. Others, without building skills, cooked communal meals for community members. Meanwhile, building supplies were warehoused in MQVN church buildings. Within about six months of the storm, most community members had returned and had usable housing, generally as a result of their own communal efforts.[18]

Communities also began to develop strongly cooperative relations with each other. Our survey of neighborhood association leaders asked about their relations with other neighborhood associations. As figure 14-4 shows, their assessment was that relations were good and overwhelmingly cooperative rather than competitive, and they identified specific areas and projects on which partnership was possible, including areas where one might predict competition.

Coordinating organizations also emerged that sought to reduce tensions or conflict among organizations in their community. Thus, the Social Aid and Pleasure Club Task Force and the Mardi Gras Indian Council worked to reduce tensions among their constituent groups and to address external difficulties that all their groups faced, especially concerning city regulations and relations with the police.

A similar phenomenon was the emergence of new umbrella groups formed to coordinate community groups and bring them together in addressing the challenges of disaster recovery. Some of the umbrella groups were formed *outside* the system of organizations that they sought to work with, and it is notable how well they have been accepted and embraced. Three important umbrella groups are the Neighborhoods Partnership Network, the Beacon of Hope Resource Center, and Sweet Home New Orleans. Despite differences among them, the groups share the mission of helping their member groups gain capacity and autonomy, find areas of common concern on which they can work together, find synergies on issues that would otherwise produce competition or conflict, and, perhaps most important, learn from each other. In this regard, they also differ from more traditional service-providing nonprofit organizations because they do not approach their task as expert professionals who seek to solve problems for their clients but rather as conveners who try to help organizations function together more effectively within their own ecosystem.

New Recovery Resources from "Outside-Inside" the Community

Intracommunity resources from outside the affected region, a sort of "outside-inside" resource, were critical. They were most prevalent in the faith-based and ethnic communities but were also important in the cultural community. The national and neighboring Jewish communities immediately mobilized to help the New Orleans Jewish community. Representatives from national Jewish organizations were on the ground in Baton Rouge, Houston, and the Mississippi Gulf Coast within twenty-four hours of the storm and immediately began providing monetary,

FIGURE 14-4. Relations among New Orleans Neighborhood Associations

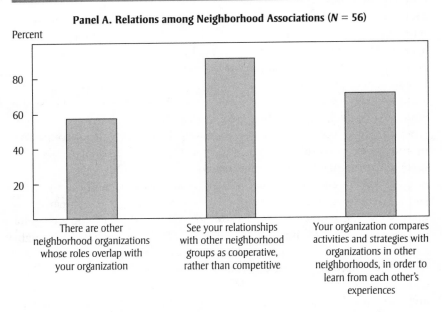

Panel A. Relations among Neighborhood Associations (*N* = 56)

Percent

The three bar categories:
- There are other neighborhood organizations whose roles overlap with your organization
- See your relationships with other neighborhood groups as cooperative, rather than competitive
- Your organization compares activities and strategies with organizations in other neighborhoods, in order to learn from each other's experiences

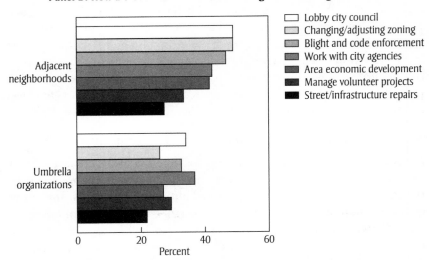

Panel B. How Do You Partner with other Neighborhood Organizations?

Legend:
- Lobby city council
- Changing/adjusting zoning
- Blight and code enforcement
- Work with city agencies
- Area economic development
- Manage volunteer projects
- Street/infrastructure repairs

Categories: Adjacent neighborhoods; Umbrella organizations

Percent

Sources: LSU/Neighborhoods Partnership Network survey of neighborhood association leaders; still in the field as of spring 2011.

logistical, and organizational assistance, aimed primarily at ensuring continuity of existing communal institutions so that the community could continue to function autonomously and provide for its members. At the same time, the neighboring Jewish community in Baton Rouge coordinated with New Orleans Jewish leaders to send boats into the flooded areas; within two or three days, they had picked up every single stranded community member as well as ferried anyone else that they could carry to dry land.

When the Vietnamese of New Orleans East decided to evacuate, they phoned ahead to their colleagues in Houston to tell them they were en route. As the convoy of cars arrived in Houston-area Vietnamese strip malls, local community members came running out, holding up fingers indicating the number of evacuees that they could take into their own homes. And when the MQVN community returned after the storm, its sister community on New Orleans' West Bank helped returning community members warehouse building materials and provided a local staging area for rebuilding. The cultural community also received massive assistance from musicians, artists, and others in cultural communities throughout the nation and around the world. Organizations like Musi-Cares (the Grammy nonprofit wing), Music Rising, Renew Our Music, and the American Federation of Musicians contributed money, organized fundraisers, and replaced instruments and equipment.

Outlook: Cautious Optimism

These developments are very helpful for New Orleans' prospects not only of recovering but also of actually growing out of some of its pre-storm problems. Yet while the new civic engagement can help drive progress, citizen participation must itself overcome several challenges if it is to help the city move forward:

Lower- and middle-class citizens must be able to overcome elite resistance to their participation. Perhaps the most striking finding of our large survey is the high level of civic engagement of Social Aid and Pleasure Club members. By the standards of the civic engagement literature, SAPC members are model citizens: they are community leaders; they perform service; they support each other in times of need.[19] When the hurricane hit, the Young Men Olympians mobilized its phone list and located all its members on their cell phones within days.[20] Asked to say a few words about what her club does, Sue Press, founder and president of the Ole and Nu Style Fellas SAPC, reeled off an unbroken, five-minute stream of accomplishments, from mentoring youth, to donating school uniforms to needy families, to holding a voter registration drive at her house.[21]

New Orleans elites were not accustomed to viewing SAPC members, who are mostly working-class African Americans, as community leaders, and generally questioned the clubs' value and excluded them from a seat at the table.[22] Yet the Social Aid and Pleasure Clubs perform the crucial leadership functions of drawing members of disadvantaged and excluded communities into the mainstream, providing opportunities and reducing the attraction of harmful activities. At his inauguration in 2010, Mayor Mitch Landrieu signaled that he would reverse the traditional elite view and reach out to SAPC leadership.[23]

Citizens must overcome government resistance to their participation. As discussed, community groups have grown increasingly capable and sophisticated, gathering their own data, generating their own development plans, and asking government to act as a partner in their efforts. Historically, the New Orleans government tended to resist citizens' bids to form partnerships or tried to co-opt groups that made the bids.

Since Katrina, communities sometimes employed hardball tactics to remind government to be open and responsive. But those tactics shared only the form—not the content or intent—of the more familiar protests demanding benefits from government. For instance, when the city called for neighborhoods to develop recovery plans in late 2006, the Broadmoor neighborhood had already developed its own, outside the city's framework. When it appeared that city hall might not accept Broadmoor's plans, which were widely acknowledged to have been well constructed with widespread citizen participation, community leaders organized a demonstration. Their protest was not intended to demand benefits but rather to assert the community's autonomy, keep Broadmoor's citizens engaged, and insist that government partner with the community rather than command it. Likewise, the traditionally quiescent Vietnamese community in eastern New Orleans organized a protest against the creation of a landfill garbage dump nearby. Again, while the form was similar to protests aimed at gaining benefits or avoiding disadvantages, this protest was intended mainly to keep its citizens engaged and to demand inclusion in decisionmaking that affected the community. That is to say, the Vietnamese community also demanded that government partner with them rather than make decisions for them.

These new "hardball" practices helped community organizations to act as partners with rather than petitioning clients of government, and by incorporating participation within a framework of active community organizations, they also helped to maintain and ensure higher levels of citizen participation after the euphoric period of immediate recovery.

Here, too, in its first few months in office, the Landrieu administration indicated that it intended to be more welcoming of civic participation and more transparent than its predecessors. The incoming Landrieu team invited several of the "new" community leaders to chair or serve on transition task forces and to join the administration.[24] Landrieu began to welcome citizen participation, including data collection, in his administration's fight against blight.[25] That openness may be starting to pay off. In our surveys, through the first five months of the Landrieu administration (until October 2010), satisfaction with New Orleans political leadership rose from 11 percent under Mayor Nagin to 16 percent under Landrieu, while dissatisfaction fell from 67 to 55 percent. Only time— and the administration's actions—will tell if those are honeymoon numbers or the beginning of a positive trend.[26]

Communities must find ways to extend participation beyond the euphoric early period of recovery into the period in which more mundane, less popular, and often technical tasks must be accomplished if progress is to continue. Most of the civic engagement described in this chapter seems oriented to the individual or neighborhood level. Yet many of the most central decisions New Orleans must make going forward take place at institutional, administrative, and technical levels. Some observers feel that, even under the best of circumstances, citizens cannot have much impact here because participation at this level requires such a high degree of expertise.[27] Therefore, there is a danger that if citizens are unable to compete at the expert level, their participation might ineluctably be pushed back to "old" forms like petitioning authorities rather than take "new" forms like partnering. Yet it is important to remind ourselves that experts do not actually govern. They implement decisions made by leaders, and the form that implementation takes reflects the character of leadership. If a city has a closed elite system, in which decisions are made behind closed doors, experts may appear to govern because elites prefer to obscure their own role. But when leadership is open and communities hammer out policies in public discourse, experts are required to implement decisions with a degree of transparency and accountability. If they do not, leaders hold them accountable, but more important, leaders hold each other accountable with checks and balances.

Conclusion

This account shows how civic engagement and participation helped drive recovery in New Orleans after Hurricane Katrina. Progress was fastest and most effective among communities that refused to wait for somebody else to help. The most successful communities did not take the law into their own hands or point the finger of blame. They mobilized their most valuable resource, their community members; they followed the most effective strategy, working with each other; and they took the view that government is not the problem: it belongs to citizens, and it can and must act as a partner to citizens. The Landrieu administration, in its first year in office, has shown signs of acting as such a partner. Therefore, the best policies going forward should encourage this civic orientation and include previously disadvantaged and excluded communities. Citizen and community organizations are asking to retain their autonomy and for government to partner with them. New Orleans has perhaps begun to seize the opportunity to change its narrative—even in the face of the 2010 oil spill—from that of pitiable victim to author of its own destiny and to serve as an advanced model of how civic engagement can drive a city's improvement.

Notes

1. Kent B. Germany, *New Orleans after the Promises: Poverty, Citizenship, and the Search for the Great Society* (University of Georgia Press, 2007); James Gill, *Lords of Misrule: Mardi Gras and the Politics of Race in New Orleans* (University Press of Mississippi, 1997); Ben Toledano, "New Orleans—An Autopsy," *Commentary*, September 2007, pp. 27–32.

2. Richard Campanella, *Bienville's Dilemma: A Historical Geography of New Orleans* (Lafayette: Center for Louisiana Studies, University of Louisiana at Lafayette, 2008).

3. Alexis de Tocqueville, *Democracy in America* (University of Chicago Press, 2000 [orig. 1835 and 1840]); Alexis de Tocqueville, *The Old Regime and the Revolution* (University of Chicago Press, 2001 [orig. 1856]); John Stuart Mill, "De Tocqueville on Democracy in America," vol. 1 and 2, in *Essays on Politics and Culture*, edited by Gertrude Himmelfarb (Gloucester, Mass.: Peter Smith, 1973 [orig. 1835 and 1840]); John Stuart Mill, *Three Essays: On Liberty* [orig. 1859], *Representative Government* [orig. 1861], and *The Subjection of Women* [orig. 1869] (Oxford University Press,

1975); Carole Pateman, *Participation and Democratic Theory* (Cambridge University Press, 1970).

4. By contrast, citizens recovering from a man-made disaster have an incentive to look for blame and fight each other for benefits to be gained from the responsible party that caused the disaster. See Allen H. Barton, *Communities in Disaster: A Sociological Analysis of Collective Stress Situations* (Garden City, N.J.: Doubleday, 1969); William R. Freudenburg, "Contamination, Corrosion, and the Social Order: An Overview." *Current Sociology* 45, no. 3 (1997):19–40; H. Paul Friesema, *Aftermath: Communities after Natural Disasters* (Beverly Hills: Sage, 1979); Duane A. Gill and others, "Technological Disaster and Chronic Community Stress," *Society and Natural Resources* 11, no.8 (1998): 795–816; J. Steven Picou, Brent K. Marshall, and Duane A. Gill, "Disaster, Litigation, and the Corrosive Community," *Social Forces* 82, no. 4 (2004): 1493–522; Russell R. Dynes and E. L. Quarantelli, "Community Conflict: Its Absence and Its Presence in Natural Disasters," *Mass Emergencies* 1 (1975): 139–52.

5. For further discussion and a literature review of vicious and virtuous circles of participation styles, see Frederick Weil, "Political Culture, Political Structure, and Democracy: The Case of Legitimation and Opposition Structure," in *Research on Democracy and Society*, vol. 2, *Political Culture and Political Structure: Theoretical and Empirical Studies* (Greenwich: JAI Press, 1994).

6. Robert D. Putnam, "The 2006 Social Capital Community Survey," Saguaro Seminar: Civic Engagement in America (www.hks.harvard.edu/saguaro/measurement/2006sccs.htm). Unfortunately, there seem to be no similar measurements for New Orleans before Katrina with which to compare measurements after the storm.

7. Sidney Verba and Norman Nie, *Participation in America* (New York: Harper and Rowman, 1972); Sidney Verba, Norman Nie, and Jae-On Kim, *Participation and Political Equality: A Seven-Nation Comparison* (Cambridge University Press, 1978); Sidney Verba, Kay Lehman Schlozman, and Henry E. Brady, *Voice and Equality: Civic Voluntarism in American Politics* (Harvard University Press, 1995).

8. The index includes the average scores on questions relating to whether most people can be trusted and whether the respondent had attended a public meeting, was a member of a neighborhood association, was an officer of local organization, or had engaged in service activity.

9. Social Aid and Pleasure Clubs are associations of mostly lower- to middle-income African Americans. They trace their heritage to nineteenth-century benevolent and burial societies created in response to racial discrimination and segregation. They developed the tradition of "jazz funerals," wherein a brass band would play a dirge on the way to the cemetery followed by jazz on the way out of the cemetery. The latter became known as a "second line" and today most SAPCs hold an annual second-line parade in which members and neighbors dance to brass band music on a long, circuitous route through the city. The clubs rightly regard themselves as keepers and innovators of the culture and proudly maintain and develop these living traditions. SAPCs continue to be service and fellowship organizations today.

10. Al Petrie, filmed interview with Wesley Shrum (professor of sociology, Louisiana State University), September 19, 2008, New Orleans. This and several other filmed interviews quoted in this chapter can be viewed at www.lsu.edu/fweil/KatrinaResearch.

11. Denise Thornton, filmed interview with the author, March 11, 2010, New Orleans.

12. Gerald Marwell and Pamela Oliver, *The Critical Mass in Collective Action: Studies in Rationality and Social Change* (Cambridge University Press, 2007).

13. Most information in this and later sections on the Vietnamese community is based on interviews by the author with Reverend Nguyen The Vien, pastor, Mary Queen of Vietnam Catholic Church, on April 22, May 14, June 6, September 9, and October 23, 2006; December 10, 2007; January 16 and April 22, 2008; and August 13, 2010 (videotaped); a videotaped interview with Mary Tran and Diem Nguyen, former and current executive directors, Mary Queen of Vietnam Community Development Corporation, August 12, 2010; and many informal discussions with community members since spring 2006. Also see Christine Hauser, "Sustained by Close Ties, Vietnamese Toil to Rebuild," *New York Times,* October 20, 2005; Sharon Cohen, "Vietnamese Priest Works to Rebuild His Flooded Parish," Associated Press, November 20, 2005; Patrick Strange, "Strength to Lead the Charge," *Times-Picayune,* August 29, 2006; John Pope, "East N.O. Priest Personifies Resilience; Vietnamese Leader Preaches Self-Reliance," *Times-Picayune,* September 03, 2006.

14. The Jewish community also provided extensive assistance to other communities. The Jewish Federations of North America (then called the United Jewish Communities) alone donated $11.4 million to other communities, and other Jewish organizations donated additional funds and goods; roughly 30,000 to 50,000 Jewish volunteers came to the Gulf Coast to help other communities rebuild through Hillel alternative spring breaks, synagogues, schools, and other mitzvah groups (e-mail to the author from Michael Weil, executive director of the Jewish Federation of Greater New Orleans, February 7, 2011). Assistance to others could be the subject of a separate chapter. It is not discussed in depth here not just for lack of space but also because this chapter focuses on communities' efforts to further their own recovery—that is, residents' own efforts within their own community.

15. The surveys mentioned in this paragraph were conducted by the author: April–December 2006 (N = 707); June–September 2007 (N = 791); 2010 (N = 144). See www.lsu.edu/fweil/KatrinaResearch and www.jewishnola.com/page.aspx?id=176820.

16. "4 Months to Decide," *Times-Picayune,* January 11, 2006.

17. Katherine Prevost, filmed interview with the author, March 3, 2010, New Orleans.

18. The U.S. Census reports that the Asian American population in Orleans Parish declined from 11,056 to 9,883 from 2000 to 2010 (http://factfinder2.census.gov). In other words, almost 90 percent returned (compared with 71 percent parish-wide), roughly what Father Vien told the author in multiple interviews. See footnote 13, which indicates that the return was rapid.

19. The Social Aid and Pleasure Clubs are highlighted here mainly because we have good survey data for them, yet they are just one of a number of organizations that provide support and assistance within lower-income African American communities. Others include churches, community cultural programs (for example, the Roots of Music after-school program for middle-school children; see www.therootsofmusic. com/), and extended families. The legacy of resistance to oppression is also strong, flowing not only from the civil rights movement (for example, Germany, *New Orleans after the Promises*) but also from older cultural roots (for example, Mardi Gras Indians, voodoo and spiritualism, Skeleton gangs). See, for example, Richard Brent Turner, *Jazz Religion, the Second Line, and Black New Orleans* (Indiana University Press, 2009); Michael E. Crutcher Jr., *Treme: Race and Place in a New Orleans Neighborhood* (University of Georgia Press, 2010); Al Kennedy, *Big Chief Harrison and the Mardi Gras Indians* (Pelican Publishing, 2010); Rachel Breunlin, Ronald W. Lewis,

and Helen Regis, *The House of Dance and Feathers: A Museum by Ronald W. Lewis* (UNO Press/Neighborhood Story Project, 2009); Ned Sublette, *The World That Made New Orleans: From Spanish Silver to Congo Square* (Lawrence Hill Books, 2009). Many of these organizations are more typical of lower- than middle-income black communities, whose forms of participation often resemble those of white middle-income communities more than those of black lower-income communities.

20. Waldorf J. Gipson III (vice president of the Young Men's Olympians SAPC), filmed interview with Wesley Shrum (professor of sociology, Louisiana State University), January 17, 2009, New Orleans.

21. Sue Press, filmed interview with the author, April 17, 2010, New Orleans.

22. "Witness: Second Line Shooting Victim Saved Kids," New Orleans Fox 8 Live, September 6, 2010 (www.fox8live.com/news/local/story/Witness-Second-line-shooting-victim-saved-kids/VciIa089Uk25oE75VMTTdA.cspx)

23. Landrieu had already established fairly good relations with these communities as lieutenant governor, a position whose mandate includes "culture," so the communities had some predisposition to optimism. Norm Dixon, president of the Young Men's Olympians, expressed such a feeling to the author in a Mardi Gras day interview, February 16, 2010. Landrieu invited Mardi Gras Indians and SAPCs to his May 3, 2010, inauguration celebrations and danced with them (see Deborah Cotton, "BigRed-Cotton," *YouTube,* May 03, 2010, "Mayor Mitch Landrieu and Mardi Gras Indians at Inauguration Gala" [www.youtube.com/watch?v=lUvQMX-imng]), and he made a point of publicly commiserating with the community following the tragic shooting death of a child at a second-line parade (see Ramon Antonio Vargas, "Mayor, Congressman among Those Mourning 2-year-old Jeremy Galmon," *Times-Picayune,* October 4, 2010.)

24. Transition chairs included LaToya Cantrell, president of the Broadmoor Improvement Association; Denise Thornton, founder and president of Beacon of Hope; and Timolynn Sams, executive director of the Neighborhood Partnership Network. Hires include Lucas Diaz, formerly the executive director of the Hispanic organization, Puentes, as director of the city's new Office of Neighborhood Engagement; Charles Allen, past president of the Holy Cross Neighborhood Association; and Denice Warren Ross, deputy director of the Greater New Orleans Community Data Center.

25. "The strategies outlined in the Mayor's plan came out of a collaboration between City officials and staff, non-profit organizations, community members and urban blight experts from across the country. Beacon of Hope is especially excited to see included in the comprehensive strategy the importance of resident-collected blight data to help inform city agencies of conditions in each community." Beacon of Hope Resource Center, "Mayor Landrieu's New Plan to Fight Blight Includes Resident Data Collection," *October News,* October 20, 2010. See also Frank Donze, "Mayor Mitch Landrieu Sets Goal of Clearing 10,000 Blighted Eyesores," *Times-Picayune,* October 1, 2010, and "Mayor Unveils Comprehensive Blight Eradication Strategy," City of New Orleans, September 30, 2010 (www.nola.gov/PRESS/City-Of-New-Orleans/All-Articles/MAYOR-UNVEILS-COMPREHENSIVE-BLIGHT-ERADICATION-STRATEGY).

26. For instance, this trend masks race differences: satisfaction rose among whites by 18 points, but changed very little among blacks. This very early trend, based on only a few respondents, will bear watching.

27. Jürgen Habermas, *Toward a Rational Society* (Boston: Beacon, 1970).

15

Plugging into the Power of Community: How Social Networks Energize Recovery

Ann Carpenter and Nancy Montoya

In times of conflict, what qualities do residents value most in their communities? What qualities do they rely on for survival? The increasing magnitude of recent disasters has challenged the limits of resilience in communities along the Gulf Coast and elsewhere in the United States, resulting in dispiriting obstacles to recovery. However, despite the extreme physical damage inflicted by Hurricanes Katrina and Rita, a surprising number of Gulf Coast residents remained connected to their communities. By nurturing those connections, residents were able to use them to help determine whether or not to return and, in most cases, to recommit to rebuilding their community. That was due in part to strong preexisting social ties, which facilitated the restoration of basic services and other functions.

Frederick Weil's research suggests that the post-Katrina period of Gulf Coast recovery has produced an increase in citizen participation,[1] which has had the effect of improving the adaptive capacity of communities through powerful social networks. Formal and informal community-based groups embodying strong social networks have organized or strengthened in the wake of the 2005 hurricane season, with transformative effects. Resilience factors—such as resources, skills, governance, and economic characteristics[2]—may vary by community and even within communities.

However, it is important for stakeholders to build strong social networks before, during, and after damaging events in order to increase the resilience capacity, performance, and self-government of the local population, particularly among those who are most vulnerable or most at risk of being marginalized.

Why Social Networks?

Social networks are assemblies of individuals or groups related to one another through connections such as familial ties, friendship, similar interests, similar beliefs, or other types of common circumstances. Such networks can exist independent of physical space; however, networks often are organized or based geographically. Social networks are the foundation of social capital, which is defined as "investment in social relations with expected returns."[3] It should be noted that while a social network may provide economic benefits, that is not the primary motivation for adopting ties with others.[4] Rather, the interactions themselves provide an intrinsic benefit in addition to any economic profit.

Robust social networks are associated with myriad benefits to individuals, households, and organizations, such as increased community mobilization; better physical, psychological, and social well-being; improved employment opportunities; better access to financial resources; and an increase in those seeking and using social services.[5] Social networks allow social capital to be transferred and accumulated in a community. Isolation or lack of social network support is associated with the inverse of those conditions, and yet a significant population remains on the margins, unable or unwilling to participate in supportive networks. As revealed by Robert Putnam in *Bowling Alone,* the percentage of the U.S. population participating in formal networks such as church groups, unions, and parent-teacher associations has been declining for years,[6] creating a society with fewer formal ties through organizations, if not through other types of social interactions.

Strong social networks are also important for reducing social vulnerability in preparing for and responding to a disaster.[7] Social networks have been shown to facilitate emergency response (such as evacuation) and disaster mitigation from the bottom up, which is more effective in fostering social and cultural change than a command-and-control approach.[8] In addition, the existence of social networks serves as a predictor for household-level disaster preparedness by increasing the perception of the availability of resources.[9] However, social networks may fall prey to pre-existing conflicts and dissolve even while recovery is under way.[10] Many networks, such as faith-based organizations or citizen volunteer groups, operate in response to a disaster or emergency but are not part of disaster planning and management. Other networks may not have been part of original disaster planning and management plans but may become formalized and incorporated in them in preparation for future emergencies. Social networks are also subject to stress resulting from disasters. Correspondingly, if networks deteriorate, decisionmaking and response times are jeopardized.[11] Furthermore, without resilient networks in place, communities are more vulnerable to future disasters.

An Analysis of Two Communities

In order to further explore the relationship between social networks and resilience, the Federal Reserve Bank of Atlanta selected two communities that were severely impacted by Hurricane Katrina for a case study and quantitative analysis, conducted in fall 2010. While demographically similar, the areas themselves are physically different. Bay St. Louis is located in Hancock County, Mississippi, on the coast of the Gulf of Mexico. The city is a small beach town, albeit one with an eclectic, historic atmosphere. Surrounded by cottages and bungalows painted in ice-cream pastels, its Main Street features art galleries, specialty shops, and institutions. Farther along the coast are perched stately bayside homes as well as a few vacant lots, still awaiting reconstruction in 2010. Other pockets of retail and residential development farther away from the coast are struggling to return. Bay St. Louis was located very close to the eye of Hurricane Katrina. Damage was caused by wind and a thirty-foot storm tide. The storm toppled the bridge to Pass Christian, and the area was effectively isolated for more than two years, necessitating a forty-five-minute detour to reach other Mississippi communities and a broader range of services.

The Broadmoor neighborhood, located in the heart of the New Orleans crescent in a lower-lying area of the city northeast of Tulane and Loyola universities, is much denser and more urban than Bay St. Louis. Although the neighborhood is registered with the National Register of Historic Places, it exhibits a different kind of New Orleans architecture, including Craftsman, Colonial, and Mediterranean-revival style homes. Recent planning documents state that the residents "view themselves as a

A restored residential streetscape in Bay St Louis, 2010.

residential enclave amidst many of the City's amenities and service areas" and that the "working class" community is "racially, economically and religiously diverse."[12] While Bay St. Louis's businesses are woven into the heart of the community, the core of Broadmoor is primarily residential and the majority of businesses are clustered along major transportation corridors, such as South Claiborne and Washington avenues, consistent with the first wave of New Orleans' middle-class, suburban-style development. Because of environmental risks, Broadmoor was one of the neighborhoods identified for further study and evaluation in the recommendations of the Urban Land Institute (ULI) recovery plan commissioned by Bring New Orleans Back (BNOB).[13] Neighborhood residents and leaders interpreted that to mean that the neighborhood was not considered suitable for repopulation, and they harnessed existing social capital to challenge that perception. Residents have begun to rebuild the historic neighborhood, focusing on grassroots efforts forged by residents through associations and bolstered by philanthropic support. As reported by Latoya Cantrell, president of the Broadmoor Improvement Association (BIA), rebuilding efforts in Broadmoor have been brisk. The BIA concluded a survey using volunteers in June 2010 that found that 83 percent of 2,400 properties surveyed "had been returned to productive use," a term used by the association in its site reviews to indicate substantial completion of renovations.[14]

While both areas sustained injury due to Hurricane Katrina, the primary causes of destruction were very different in nature. Unlike Bay St. Louis, whose destruction was directly related to tidal surges from the Gulf of Mexico, Broadmoor was affected by a man-made disaster, the result of flooding from breached levees as water traveled to lower ground due to substandard construction. Relatively little damage was directly caused by hurricane-force winds and no damage was caused by a direct storm surge in New Orleans. Rather, after the storm had passed, the levees broke in surrounding areas and water seeped into the bowl of New Orleans. It was estimated that homes in Broadmoor received from four to eight feet of water and some flooding remained for upward of three weeks.

In the 2000 census, the communities of Bay St. Louis and Broadmoor shared similar demographic characteristics, such as population size and household income levels. They were selected for this study in order to provide both individual case study information and a comparison of how populations are networked in communities with similar demographics. Recent demographic estimates are shown in table 15-1.

Federal Reserve researchers used dual analysis techniques to understand the levels of resilience in each community. They first conducted a quantitative analysis of the numbers and types of establishments that foster social networks that existed before and after Katrina in both communities. In addition, focus groups were held with community leaders and residents to determine how social networks survived, reconstituted, and adapted in the response and rebuilding stages of disaster recovery. Each approach yielded distinct findings, with several cross-cutting themes.

TABLE 15-1. Demographic Profiles of Bay St. Louis and Broadmoor

Measure	Bay St. Louis		Broadmoor	
	2000	2009	2000	2009
Total population (ZIP code)	8,209	4,939	8,848	6,444
Median household income	$31,303	$31,777	$34,106	$29,375
Land area	6.7 square miles		0.56 square miles	

Sources: U.S. Census Bureau, 2000, and Esri Updated Demographics, 2009.

Role of Businesses and Institutions in Facilitating Networks

In order to measure the potential for social networking activities, using data available before and after the 2005 hurricane season, researchers compared businesses and organizations that constituted social gathering places and formal social networks in the two case study communities. According to an earlier study of five flood-impacted communities by Sherraden and Fox, social networks such as community organizations were found to contribute significantly to day-to-day recovery activities and those organizations were most effective when they had a physical address at which activities could be centralized and staged.[15] The types of establishments selected for this analysis were derived from a measurement of social capital focused on engagement in formal associations[16] and from the literature on social gathering places known to facilitate richer social networks.[17] The businesses and organizations analyzed were aggregated to general categories determined by industry sector. Categories included membership organizations (professional, civic, and social); religious organizations; educational services; social services (child and family services, job training); beauty salons and barbershops; recreation and entertainment venues (bowling alleys, golf courses, movie theaters, gyms); and restaurants, cafés, and bars.

Overall, from 2004 to 2009, Bay St. Louis experienced a larger decrease in social networking places than did Broadmoor, by 21 percent rather than 18 percent, respectively. That was due in large part to a decrease in the net numbers of restaurants, cafés, and bars and social services. Despite the overall net loss of those types of establishments, Bay St. Louis experienced an increase in religious organizations. The numbers of membership organizations and education services in Broadmoor were stable, as they were in Bay St. Louis. Broadmoor experienced the largest

FIGURE 15-1. Social Networking Places, Bay St. Louis, 2004 and 2009

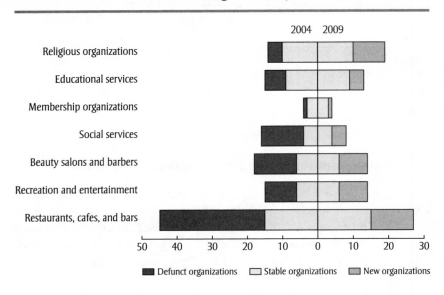

Source: ReferenceUSA, U.S. Businesses Databases, 2004 and 2009 (Omaha, Nebraska).

net losses in restaurants, cafés, bars, and social services. The impact of those losses may have been cushioned by Broadmoor's proximity to the city center and to universities, where residents may have had more service options than residents of Bay St. Louis had. Many of the businesses that disappeared were very small and lacked the resources to return.

After researchers examined the net numbers of establishments by sector, before and after Katrina, they isolated individual establishments to determine where turnover occurred and what types of establishments had not regenerated. For each community, entries in the 2004 and 2009 directories were assessed as stable (existing on both the 2004 and 2009 listings); new (existing in 2009 but not in 2004); or defunct (existing in 2004 but not 2009). As seen in figures 15-1 and 15-2, stable organizations account for less than half of social networking places in 2004 and 2009 for both Bay St. Louis and Broadmoor. The level of turnover in established sectors such as religious organizations and educational services is unsettling. In focus groups in both communities, residents referred to schools and places of worship as cornerstones of the community and often saw them as sources of reliable information in emergencies. Such institutions could

FIGURE 15-2. Social Networking Places, Broadmoor, 2004 and 2009

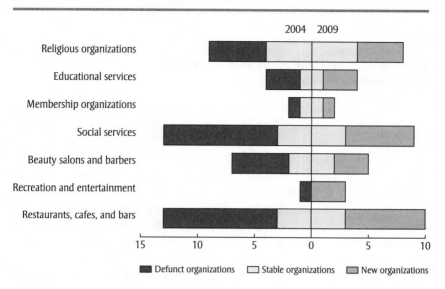

Source: ReferenceUSA, U.S. Businesses Databases, 2004 and 2009 (Omaha, Nebraska).

be strengthened to continue to be a source of resiliency and to signal renewed investment and more convincing community assets, although it is difficult to do so without a base population to support them. In places, resources shifted to markets supported by a broader population base, given the population decreases after Katrina. While many of the institutions in Bay St. Louis were absorbed by others due to a lack of capacity, others, like the First Baptist Church, deliberately engaged in expansion of their physical facilities to better serve the needs of the community.

Geographic plotting of the businesses and organizations highlighted in this analysis revealed an interesting pattern in both communities. In each community, commercial establishments generally fall along neighborhood boundaries or main corridors, while social services, educational services, and places of worship fall in the interior of the neighborhood. Essentially, businesses seem to act as elements that stitch together different neighborhoods or parts of town. In contrast, churches and temples, schools, senior citizens' centers, and public health services are centrally located, embedded in the fabric of a residential area. Given the importance of these types of organizations in anchoring social networks, their central location within the case study communities is potentially important. These findings were vetted and expanded on by the focus groups with residents.

Focus Groups on the Role of Social Networks in Community Resilience

In addition to the analysis of businesses and organizations, in fall 2010 Federal Reserve researchers held separate focus groups with residents and community leaders of Bay St. Louis and Broadmoor. Focus group attendees were selected for their role as leaders in specific segments of the community. In Bay St. Louis, many in the focus group had lifelong ties to the community, but their periods of full-time residency ranged from ten years to their entire life. The Broadmoor focus group included a formal community leader, a pre-Katrina transplant to the area, and a thirty-year resident with strong ties to the faith community and experience in offering professional support to disaster victims. Very few of the focus group members in either group evacuated ahead of the storm, and all reported remarkable survival stories.

Bay St. Louis offers noteworthy lessons based on the information volunteered by the participants in how a community can step in to fill the role of other strong social networks, such as family. One example of the community's strength was provided by the local senior center. Like many coastal communities, Bay St. Louis had been a magnet for retirees seeking a warmer climate and a lower cost of living. At the time of the storm, the city had a senior center but no shelters. As Katrina approached the city, the director of the senior center ignored protocol and made the deliberate decision to stay behind, knowing that the center was on high ground and anticipating the need for senior emergency housing in the aftermath of the storm.

A common theme among residents affected by Katrina was that they did not expect to be displaced from their homes for more than three or four days; most were anticipating returning home once the storm had passed. Many seniors stayed behind, either because they anticipated a similar scenario or had no family to go to or resources with which to evacuate. After it became clear that the devastation was substantial and that they would be unable to survive on their own, many began migrating to the senior center. Others were shuttled in after being rescued from more perilous conditions by firefighters, police officers, or neighbors. First responders and staff at St. Rose of Lima Catholic Church also referred vulnerable residents to the center for shelter. At the height of its operation, the shelter housed 165 individuals, including infants as well as elderly and infirm individuals. Although the center was not an officially sanctioned emergency shelter and residents were given no formal notice that the facility was being used as a shelter, residents were referred through word of mouth and relied on their personal trust in the center as a resource.

Before Katrina, Broadmoor's community assets included a library and school, which did not provide viable shelter. While the evacuation rate for Broadmoor was estimated at 90 percent, those left behind had few options: they could shelter in the upper floors of flooded homes, wait for water rescue or air evacuation by helicopter (an uneven and slow process), or swim through flood waters to higher ground or to the compromised shelters at the Superdome and Convention Center. As mentioned before, many were unprepared for an extended stay and lacked potable water, nonperishable food, and basic medical supplies. The oppressive heat also presented a medical challenge for many, contributing to dehydration and infection. Local places of worship in Bay St. Louis and Broadmoor were the first to provide space for returning residents to gather and get information once conditions improved. In Broadmoor, the Church of the Annunciation later provided fellowship and office space for the BIA, which was then fighting to keep Broadmoor viable. The BIA was incorporated in 1970, with a goal of keeping its multi-racial, multi-ethnic community living in harmony during "blockbusting" efforts at segregation. After Katrina, it became a powerhouse for community collaboration in revitalization efforts.

Several other examples demonstrate how residents used their personal ties to reconstitute their community. For seventeen years, business owners and leaders in Bay St. Louis promoted Second Saturday, a monthly art and gallery walk in the historic district that showcased the work of local artists and provided an opportunity for residents to enjoy conversation and refreshments. The focus group fondly recalled those events as more than just a way to bring commerce to downtown; the events also functioned as an opportunity for fellowship with neighbors. On a Saturday shortly after the storm, with limited power and water, thirteen residents gathered at the foot of Main Street to restore Second Saturday. The movement grew to be so popular that by December the events were being held every Saturday. Residents explained that the historic district and certain anchor businesses constitute the iconic heart of Bay St. Louis.

Both communities eventually obtained support through external social ties as well. Broadmoor was able to garner national support when the president of the BIA, through a series of introductions, met Walter Issacson, president and CEO of the Aspen Institute and former CEO of CNN. Issacson had been raised in Broadmoor, and their meeting led to a variety of high-powered resources, including Harvard University's Kennedy School of Government's participation in redevelopment efforts. In Bay St. Louis, non-native volunteers invested not only their labor and time but also their money in cafés, bookstores, and galleries. Members of the focus group pointed out that nonlocal volunteers were critical financial supporters of local businesses. Along the way they were embraced by the residents and made permanent friends: several stayed or returned to make Bay St. Louis their home.

Findings and Recommendations

Given the literature as well as the evidence discussed earlier, it is apparent that social networks are vital in ensuring that communities and their members have access to the resources and information necessary to rebound after a disaster. In the case of Katrina and Rita, the case study communities came together to overcome the lack of state and federal support and the relatively slow response times. They also understand the power of social networks for brokering relevant and reliable information and for providing the spiritual and emotional support and resources necessary for survival and recovery. Those resources include volunteer labor; financial contributions and access to loans, grants, and other tangibles that speed recovery; and community rituals that nurture social and business capital. Businesses and organizations, particularly places of worship and schools, provide the spaces and conditions that social networks need to thrive and to help residents make a healthy transition from depending on low- or no-cost support services to developing a sustainable retail and service sector.

Several strategies may help harness social networks for community resilience. These strategies fall into two categories: people based and place based. One relatively easy people-based strategy would be to incorporate informal networks into formal emergency planning and management activities, such as engaging members of the community to serve as block captains. For example, the role of the Broadmoor block captains has evolved from taking a census of their neighbors and contributing location and contact information to BIA to providing detailed information on recovery. Most recently, they have been ensuring that evacuation information for contacting residents is complete and up-to-date. This strategy increases access to resources and reliable and trustworthy information for residents in existing networks.

Improving associational activity, or inclusion in formal organizations, can also improve network participation. Education and income are the chief indicators of involvement in associations.[18] Therefore, economic development strategies that improve educational attainment and workforce development are potential strategies to increase participation in formal networks. Broadmoor's experience with tapping into the professional expertise of its residents seems to reinforce this finding. Efforts should also be made to incorporate vulnerable populations—elderly people, children, those living in poverty, minorities, and others who may be disenfranchised—into formal social networks. One effective post-Katrina strategy that the city of New Orleans has adopted is to register housebound residents such as the elderly and disabled and residents who do not own a car. Registration allows people to request transportation in the event of an evacuation or emergency, and the city has engaged volunteers to provide transportation to these at-risk citizens. Broadmoor used this and its block captain strategy to ensure the safe evacuation and return of its residents during Hurricane Gustav in 2008, when almost 100 percent of the neighborhood evacuated.

Purely place-based strategies may seem less relevant than people-based strategies given the present focus on social networks rather than the physical properties of communities. However, data from the focus groups indicate that the physical spaces that draw residents together and evoke a sense of community matter a great deal. In Bay St. Louis, the heart of the community was clearly the historic downtown. Residents fought to preserve the downtown area from large-scale development prior to the storm, and their efforts intensified after the storm. In the end, Bay St. Louis and Broadmoor used their collective strengths to reject development deemed harmful to their way of life. The communities chose to capitalize on their historic and architectural assets to anchor and regenerate their human connections. Both communities now have a redevelopment philosophy and strategy in place that affirms their values. In the case of Bay St. Louis, the community has adopted a historic district to preserve its built environment. Although the spirit of community and other intangible qualities of Bay St. Louis were important to residents, it was clear that their landmarks and institutions supported and were supported by the social relationships that they valued most.

The award-winning U.S. Highway 90 bridge spans Henderson Point and Bay St. Louis.

One strategy that involves both people and place is the use of public participation in planning. Meetings incorporating residents in municipal decisionmaking are essential mechanisms for informing citizens, identifying key values, calming fears, resolving conflicts, and building consensus for recovery efforts. As citizens juggled stabilizing their families with earning a living, they were also struggling with insurance companies, re-creating financial documents, and physically rebuilding their homes and businesses. Yet, in both of the communities, formal citizen engagement remained strong and in many instances exceeded the pre-disaster level of commitment.

The first BIA meeting took place in January 2006, with over 600 residents meeting on a front lawn under tents. It can be surmised that this extraordinary activity was a response to perceived external threats or to the opportunity to make a positive contribution to a fragile ecosystem. In Broadmoor's case the threat was extinction: city leaders required a community to demonstrate a 51 percent return rate in order to be deemed viable. Five years later, civic engagement in both communities remained elevated, but a common concern was the fear of "Katrina fatigue" and "planning fatigue" as well as of individual burnout. In each community, flagging energy can be reinvigorated by place-based, infrastructure improvements: in Bay St. Louis, the newly rebuilt bridge was both a practical necessity and a symbol of the community's endurance, and Broadmoor has capitalized on two reimagined, LEED-certified architectural and institutional jewels.

Another suggestion for how residents can better engage in social networks is to adopt technology more broadly. Many residents who were unfamiliar with technology as a means of connecting with family, community, or businesses quickly learned how to use high-tech communications to manage their personal relationships, obtain real-time information, and fact-find and filter incorrect and often unconstructive messages after the disaster. New Orleans's local newspaper, the *Times-Picayune,* set up neighborhood forums where residents could locate each other and connect with a virtual community. Across the Gulf Coast, forums, blogs, and other social connectors sprang up. Technologically enhanced social networks expanded to include supportive citizens in other states, opportunities to make online donations, and links to technical expertise in development and environmental preservation. Residents continue to actively look to technology, particularly social networking resources and mobile phone technology, to keep informed and to manage real-time threats.

Two lingering questions remain: Can new, organically nurtured leaders progress in their leadership skills? Will local organizations continue to thrive if funding and technical assistance shrinks five years after Katrina? Since 2005, the Gulf Coast has been forced to recover from a number of disasters. While other communities faced with multiple upheavals in such a short time have continued to erode (for example, parts of the Rust Belt), the Gulf Coast has, in many ways, increased its resilience to outside forces. These revitalized communities are better poised to respond to future disasters and to rebuild sustainably and equitably. As seen in Broadmoor and Bay St. Louis, the fostering of strong social networks has been a crucial component of recovery. Ideally, these networks can continue to thrive and facilitate the long-term survival of the cultural and environmental treasure that is the Gulf Coast.

Notes

1. Frederick Weil, chapter 14 in this volume.
2. Kathryn A. Foster, chapter 2 in this volume.
3. Nan Lin, Karen Cook, and Ronald Burt, *Social Capital: Theory and Research* (New York: Aldine de Gruyter, 2001).

4. Kenneth Arrow, "Observations on Social Capital," in *Social Capital: A Multifaceted Perspective,* edited by Partha Dasgupta and Ismail Serageld (Washington: World Bank, 2001).

5. See David A. Snow Jr., Louis A. Zurcher, and Sheldon Ekland-Olson, "Social Networks and Social Movements: A Microstructural Approach to Differential Recruitment," *American Sociological Review* 45, no. 5 (1980): 787–801; Lisa F. Berkman and others, "From Social Integration to Health: Durkheim in the New Millennium," *Social Science and Medicine* 51 (2000): 843–57; Lu Ann Aday, "Health Status of Vulnerable Populations," *Annual Review of Public Health* 15 (1994): 487–509; Mark S. Granovetter, "The Strength of Weak Ties," *American Journal of Sociology* 78, no. 6 (1973): 1360–80; James D. Montgomery, "Social Networks and Labor-Market Outcomes: Toward an Economic Analysis," *American Economic Review* 81, no. 5 (1991): 1408–18; Yoram Ben-Porath, "The F-Connection: Families, Friends, and Firms and the Organization of Exchange," *Population and Development Review* 6, no. 1 (1980): 1–30; and Richard C. Birkel and N. Dickon Reppucci, "Social Networks, Information-Seeking, and the Utilization of Services," *American Journal of Community Psychology* 11, no. 2 (1983): 185–205.

6. Robert D. Putnam, *Bowling Alone: The Collapse and Revival of American Community* (New York: Simon and Schuster, 2000).

7. Susan L. Cutter, Bryan J. Boruff, and W. Lynn Shirley, "Social Vulnerability to Environmental Hazards," *Social Science Quarterly* 84, no. 2 (2003): 242–61.

8. B. E. Aguirre, "On the Concept of Resilience," Preliminary Paper 356 (University of Delaware Disaster Research Center, 2006).

9. Douglas Paton, "Disaster Preparedness: A Social-Cognitive Perspective," *Disaster Prevention and Management* 12, no. 3 (2003): 210–16.

10. Graham A. Tobin, "Sustainability and Community Resilience: The Holy Grail of Hazards Planning?" *Environmental Hazards* 1 (1999): 13–25.

11. David R. Godschalk, "Urban Hazard Mitigation: Creating Resilient Cities," *Natural Hazards Review* 4, no. 3 (2003): 136–43.

12. "Broadmoor Plans" (www.broadmoorproject.com/Broadmoor_Plans.html).

13. "New Orleans, Louisiana: A Strategy for Rebuilding" (www.uli.org/Community Building/AdvisoryService/~/media/Documents/ResearchAndPublications/Reports/AdvisoryServicePanelReports/NewOrleans05.ashx.

14. Latoya Cantrell, in discussion with the author, November 2010.

15. Margaret Sherrard Sherraden and Ellen Fox, "The Great Flood of 1993: Response and Recovery in Five Communities," *Journal of Community Practice* 4, no. 3 (1997): 23–45.

16. Andrew M. Isserman, Edward Feser, and Drake Warren, "Why Some Rural Communities Prosper While Others Do Not" (Washington: Office of the Under Secretary for Rural Development, U.S. Department of Agriculture, 2007).

17. Anil Rupasingha, Stephan J. Goetz, and David Freshwater, "Social Capital and Economic Growth: A County-Level Analysis," *Journal of Agricultural and Applied Economics* 32, no. 3 (2000): 565–72.

18. Putnam, *Bowling Alone.*

16

Interracial Alliance Building in a Resilient New Orleans

Jasmine Waddell, Silas Lee, and Breonne DeDecker

The rebuilding and recovery process after hurricanes Katrina and Rita was a catalyst for conceptual changes in the discussion and analysis of planning for resilient communities in the context of place, race, and class.[1] Factors that improve resiliency capacity include low poverty rates, income equality, civic engagement, and social trust, to name a few.[2] The 2005 disasters illuminated the need for the Gulf Coast region to develop an agenda that reflects its demographic diversity and entrenched poverty. In this chapter we make a case for interracial alliances, in particular between African Americans and Hispanics, as a key ingredient for creating a resilient and economically sustainable New Orleans.

In 2007, Oxfam America contracted Elizabeth Fussell to prepare an internal report on the demographics of Latin American populations migrating to the city of New Orleans after the hurricanes. The report's findings on Mexican and Brazilian immigrants revealed that the new immigrants suffered many of the same labor abuses that African American low-wage workers sustained in the hospitality sector. Fussell's report and body of work on post-2005 immigration motivated Oxfam America to fund further research

The authors would like to acknowledge the editorial support of Sara Chaganti, a Ph.D. candidate at the Heller School for Social Policy and Management, Brandeis University. The authors would like to thank the Domestic Office of Oxfam America under the leadership of Ajulo Othow for funding this research.

into the integration of post-Katrina Hispanic immigrants in the low-wage labor force in the city of New Orleans. In 2008, Oxfam America contracted Silas Lee and Associates to conduct an opinion poll of racial attitudes of African American and Hispanic workers in New Orleans.

Background

On August 29, 2005, Hurricanes Katrina and Rita exposed the race and class stratification that has historically eroded the roots of trust and equality between groups in the community.[3] Before the hurricanes, New Orleans was a bustling port city with a variety of industries, including tourism and the oil and gas industry, but it also had a high rate of poverty.[4] In a sobering 1986 study, economist Gordon Saussy noted the following about race and class stratification in New Orleans: "When racial—particularly white-black—differences are considered, our social and economic class distinctions more closely resemble caste distinctions."[5] These racial distinctions have made it extremely difficult to forge class-based alliances, despite the existence of an extensive low-wage work sector, including the tourism and hospitality industry, that employs workers of different racial and ethnic backgrounds. The lack of class-based alliances has left the labor abuses in the region largely unchecked, with a few notable exceptions, such as the Indian workers' march to Washington in 2010, which was organized by the New Orleans Worker Center for Justice.[6]

In 2003, Silas Lee released a demographic analysis of New Orleans in which he compared the social and economic status of African Americans and whites in New Orleans from 1983 to 2004.[7] Lee described the romanticized perception of New Orleans and the paradoxical realities faced by African Americans in their quest to fulfill their aspirations in New Orleans. Lee surmised: "Our celebratory culture and accepting nature conceals a city with a troubled soul. After reviewing some of the social and economic data from the 2000 census for New Orleans, it is apparent that we are a city confronted by the challenges of the future, yet haunted by the problems of our past."[8] The problems of the past included widespread poverty, social exclusion, and government corruption. The challenges of the future in 2003 were exposed internationally and exponentially compounded in 2005 by hurricanes Katrina and Rita. During the storms, dysfunctional and disaffected government institutions left the city under water, and the recovery pitted low-wage workers against one another as they competed for jobs and affordable housing.

Hurricane Katrina laid bare tensions between different racial and soioeconomic groups and among low-wage workers, especially African Americans and Hispanics.[9] By 2010, New Orleans had 140,000 fewer people than before the storms.[10] Between the 2000 and 2010 censuses, the Hispanic population in New Orleans grew by over 3,000 people while the African American, white, and Asian populations all shrank.[11] The African American community lost the most—more than 100,000 African Americans did not return to New Orleans after the storms.[12] For those with resources, returning was less daunting than for those who were inadequately insured and could not afford the increased cost of rental housing. At the same time, Hispanic workers were being attracted to the city to take jobs in debris removal, home reconstruction, the hospitality sector, and other economically vulnerable jobs, while African American workers and their families struggled to recover their homes and find work. To exacerbate this bifurcation of experience, Hispanics experienced an epidemic of theft of earned wages by employers, which increased distrust and inhibited building relationships across racial lines.[13] In a city not categorized as a "twenty-first century gateway," the arrival of Hispanics forced recalibration of the dialogue on the relationship between race, class, and opportunity.[14]

The tension between African Americans and Hispanics was exacerbated by the federal government's use of the disasters to adopt neoliberal economic policies that citizens had otherwise resisted.[15] In the immediate aftermath of Katrina, President George W. Bush issued a proclamation to suspend the Davis-Bacon Act, which provides for prevailing wage standards for federal government construction contracts. The president defined the devastation of hurricanes Katrina and Rita as a "national emergency," which justified relaxing the requirements on employers to pay "prevailing wages" to workers under the federal construction contracts issued to rebuild the city. Louisiana has been a "right to work" state for decades. In the right-to-work context, labor protection refers to regulations designed to protect domestic workers and national boundaries from "illegal aliens," and its impact on workers has been chronicled by local and national labor relations scholars as well as political analysts.[16] Suspending the Davis-Bacon Act privileged employers and enabled them to exploit low-wage labor. Furthermore, the Department of Homeland Security removed the requirement that employers prove that their employees were legally allowed to work in the United States. These two policy shifts meant many local laborers could not afford to work at the wages being offered, while an influx of migrant workers filled the labor gaps.[17] Even though Davis-Bacon was reinstated, it did not apply to contracts that were already signed, thus perpetuating low wages for certain projects. This pattern of controlling the availability of decent wages further weakened workers' rights in a state that was already strongly pro-business.[18]

The political economy of labor in New Orleans following Katrina has disadvantaged both the Hispanic and African American communities, both of which have suffered the privatization of risk supported by post-disaster public policies. Both groups have experienced insecure and dangerous living environments. However, the arrival of a wave of immigrant workers in New Orleans after Katrina also yielded new opportunities for class-based alliances.[19]

From a Shoulder Hug to a Full Embrace

Our review of the theoretical literature on cross-racial alliance building reveals both facilitating and inhibiting factors and a typology of strategies. The factors that encourage successful cross-racial coalitions include public leadership; intraracial solidarity, such as pan-Hispanic alliances; and an examination of existing race, class, and gender hegemonies.[20] For example, public leadership can provide incentives for coalition building through funding and public education. One of the factors inhibiting formation of cross-racial coalitions is the movement for a color-blind or post-racial society. Priestly argues that the discourse on building color-blind society colludes with capitalist race, class, and gender hegemonies by inhibiting a real examination of those hegemonies and the impact that they have on communities.[21] Transformation of the problems that cross-racial alliances seek to redress is impossible without first conducting a deep analysis of those problems. The typology that emerges has two poles: "response and support," or the "shoulder hug" approach; and the "full embrace" approach, which follows from an honest, self-reflective dialogue about the differences to be reconciled. This typology categorizes alliance building strategies, which are neither linear nor mutually exclusive.

Our research demonstrates that New Orleans, which took the shoulder hug approach to interracial alliances before the storms, has taken the same approach since then. The shoulder hug approach is characterized by acknowledgment of common interests but only tentative engagement—a "response and support" approach that is characteristically devoid of sustained action. Examples include co-authoring of public documents, attending meetings but not actively participating, and making public statements of solidarity for the media without following up with action. The study that underlies this chapter was designed to facilitate the full embrace approach, which has the potential to be a cornerstone of a resilient New Orleans.

One illustration of an effective and mutually beneficial full embrace coalition existed between the Black Panther Party and the United Farm Workers in the late 1960s. The alliance was engineered by Bobby Seale, Huey Newton, and Cesar Chavez to advance the Safeway boycott.[22] Both organizations had an explicit consciousness-raising mission, which meant that a thorough examination of power hegemonies was at the core of both organizations. The significance of the alliance was that it demonstrated that class-based solidarity can facilitate inter-minority coalitions. The coalition also facilitated opportunities for interracial learning and support through a common struggle.

Hispanic support for President Obama's candidacy was another opportunity for interracial alliance building. According to Pew Hispanic Center polls in 2008, Hispanics overwhelmingly supported the Democrats and President Obama. According to Pew's nationwide survey of 2,015 Hispanics conducted from June 9 through July 13, 2008, Hispanic registered voters supported Obama for president over Republican John McCain by a 66 percent to 23 percent margin.[23] The significance of Hispanic support for Obama's presidency is a positive indicator of the potential of interracial alliance building nationally and at the local level in New Orleans. The Catholic Church also presents a significant opportunity for New Orleans. The Gulf Coast has the largest African American Catholic community in the United States, which can provide a common foundation for African Americans and Hispanics in New Orleans that transcends job competition and affirms a social justice agenda.[24]

Methodology

The purpose of this study was to assess race relations between African Americans and Hispanics and to gather information about the similarities and differences between the two groups' experiences of discrimination and opportunity. The methodological approach was action oriented. That is, the activity of conducting the study was intended to facilitate interracial learning—a crucial foundation for the development of a full embrace cross-racial alliance. The research was developed and implemented through an advisory group that included the funder, the research consultant, and community representatives from the target populations of African American and Hispanic residents.

We conducted a total of four focus groups in 2008. All focus group participants were recruited through Silas Lee and Associates, and the final participants were selected through a screening interview. Each focus group had approximately ten participants, all of whom were compensated for their participation. The two focus groups of African American residents of New Orleans were segmented by home ownership, as an indicator of social class. In addition, the homeowners were more likely to have had direct experience hiring low-wage Hispanic workers.[25] The two focus groups of Hispanics were segmented by pre- and post-Katrina migration. All four groups were facilitated by a local media celebrity from the target ethnic group to establish comfort by providing a well-known voice and to show the importance of the topic by having a person of importance facilitating. The Hispanic focus group was conducted bilingually; the Spanish feedback was translated for analysis.

The findings from the focus groups were used to develop a questionnaire to be distributed in a public opinion poll. We collected new data instead of using existing opinion poll data because the process of collecting the data was an important part of the participatory action-oriented research. The members of the advisory group worked together to develop poll questions based on the focus group results. The questionnaire was administered to a random sample of 450 African Americans and an opportunistic sample of 160 Hispanics. There was a different data collection strategy for the Hispanics because the sampling frame generated by randomly generated telephone numbers would not effectively target the Hispanic population, in which many new immigrant families relied on cell phones with area codes outside New Orleans. The margin of error for African American poll results was 3 percent; the margin of error for the Hispanic poll results was 5 percent.

Findings

The results of the focus groups and opinion poll reinforced the theme of tentative support. Overall, both groups were supportive of developing interracial alliances based on common concerns such as health care, public safety, and discrimination. Both groups identified the church as an institution to lead the efforts. Despite optimism, prevailing stereotypes were expressed, and it was evident that the large social distance between the two groups must be bridged if interracial alliances are to be successful.

Focus Group Findings

The focus groups yielded important information about intraracial and interracial perceptions, barriers, and opportunities for the African American and Hispanic populations in New Orleans. The bond of common experience as victims of discrimination was weakened by a pervasive lack of trust between the two groups. The main factors were perceived to be job competition, social isolation, and language differences. Indicators of opportunity for a shared social justice agenda revealed stronger potential among post-Katrina Hispanic immigrants and the non-homeowner African American group. That may be a consequence of history and strong working relationships between non-homeowner African Americans and post-Katrina Hispanic immigrants in the low-wage labor sector. Common complaints in all four groups included a lack of services and resources for health care and public safety.[26] Those deficits could serve as a foundation for interracial coalitions to advocate for government and civil society provision and support of such essential services for New Orleanians.

The African American groups expressed a range of reactions to the issue of interracial relations. The homeowner group viewed new Hispanic immigrants through the lens of employer. They described the relationship as friendly, but not trusting. Non-homeowner African Americans were at the other end of the spectrum; they extolled the "commonality of experiences as a uniting force between the races." After candid discussions in both groups about the barriers of language and social isolation, one respondent summed up the ethos of the African American groups as one of trepidation and hope. After contemplation, a focus group participant observed, "This [focus group] is a beginning. One step makes a big difference, and we will be the difference." Many participants had not considered the potential benefits of a cross-racial alliance before joining a focus group. That quote represents the attitude change that occurred when open dialogue was facilitated and strategic questions were asked within the groups.

The gulf between the pre- and post-Katrina Hispanic groups was larger than the gulf between the two African American groups because it spanned history, social class, and local and national politics. A sentiment common in the two Hispanic groups was that language differences and racism contributed to exploitation and increased tensions between them and the non-Hispanic community.

The two Hispanic groups had different, but similarly limited perceptions of the African American community. While the pre-Katrina Hispanics described African Americans as prominent in music and sports, the post-Katrina Hispanics expanded the description to include pathologies such as drug use, sexual perversion, and other deviant behaviors. Some pre-Katrina Hispanics celebrated African American New Orleanians as "overcomers." Consistent with those perceptions, pre-Katrina Hispanics felt comfortable living in racially mixed neighborhoods while post-Katrina immigrants were more comfortable living around whites because of safety concerns. Conversely, pre-Katrina Hispanics, despite living and working with African Americans for decades, felt pessimistic about building an African American–Hispanic alliance because of the lack of trust and the absence of a broader constituency including whites and others in the process. New Hispanic immigrants felt optimistic about the potential for a partnership with African Americans, describing it as natural for the two groups to address social justice issues jointly. One of the Hispanic focus group participants captured the themes raised in the Hispanic focus groups when she said, "We have to be here, and we [African Americans and Hispanics] have to get along. How can we start the dialogue?" All four groups talked about generational differences and the role that their children will play in carrying the conversation forward. Through the dialogue that this study facilitated, there was an appreciation of the need to continue and see where it might lead.

Opinion Poll Results

The opinion poll reinforced themes identified in the focus groups. The prevailing responses indicated significant differences in attitudes based on social class, social distance, and age. The poll results indicated that while inter-group comfort has been tenuous, there were commonalities in perceptions and experiences of discrimination. Both groups shared an interest in breaking common ground and building a cross-racial coalition based on a common vision of social justice for New Orleans. Questions about the potential of cross-racial alliance building revealed support overall from both groups.

Both groups expressed confidence with respect to their capacity to put aside their differences to work together on redressing discrimination. Among African Americans, the lower middle class (household incomes between $21,000 and $30,000) was the most pessimistic (only 58 percent of lower-middle-income respondents felt that the groups could work together on discrimination while 71 percent of African American respondents overall felt that they could). Hispanics also had high levels of confidence overall about working together. Here the participants with household incomes of more than $45,000 were among the most optimistic Hispanic sub-groups (67 percent felt that the groups could work together on discrimination while only 58 percent of the 160 Hispanic respondents overall agreed).

When asked about working together on jobs, the African American group with $21,000 to $30,000 in household income was the most pessimistic while the group with $31,000 to $45,000 in income was more optimistic. Similarly, Hispanics with household incomes of $21,000 to $30,000 were more pessimistic than the overall Hispanic population polled. These results reflect perceived job competition: the upper-middle-class groups perceived less job competition than the lower-middle-class groups. There was very little evidence of preconceived ideas about Hispanics and African Americans working together to achieve social and economic equality in New Orleans, but Hispanics who were renters and those who made less than $20,000 as a household were the most likely to have considered the possibility a lot (43 percent and 44 percent respectively, compared with 38 percent of the overall Hispanic population polled).

Both groups had a strong belief in the importance of establishing alliances. Respondents with household incomes under $20,000 and those over sixty years of age were most likely to find it important. Answers to a question comparing the ability of the church to lead an alliance-building effort to that of other institutions—such the respondent's child's school, a community group, and family—and to a question about the potential effectiveness of the church in improving African American and Hispanic relations indicated that both Hispanics and African Americans trusted the church more than other institutions to lead a coalition effort.

The main barriers to alliance building identified by both groups were trust and perceptions of the other group. There were significant age and class differences in both groups. Of African Americans under forty years of age, 68 percent thought that trust was a major barrier while only 60 percent of the general polled population of African Americans agreed. Among Hispanics, 72 percent of lower-middle-class respondents (people with household incomes between $21,000 and $30,000) thought trust was a major barrier while only 63 percent of the general Hispanic population thought so. These findings likely reflect perceived job competition.

Looking into the future, African American renters, households with incomes under $20,000, and those under the age of forty were most pessimistic that relations between African Americans and Hispanics would improve; that finding also likely reflects perceived job competition because these are the groups on the front lines of low-wage work.

The theme of social distance raised in the focus groups also played out in the opinion poll findings. Social distance within the Hispanic community was evidenced by the finding that Hispanics overall viewed Mexicans less favorably than Hispanics from Central and South America, a result that could be explained by Howard Becker's "labeling theory" regarding the human implications of perceptions of pathologies such as drug trafficking and social depravity perpetuated by the media and by rumor.[27] The poll findings showed that Hispanic respondents with household incomes of less than $20,000 were least likely and that those under forty and over sixty years of age were most likely to have an African American friend. Households with incomes of less than $20,000 were more likely to be post-Katrina newcomers and those over sixty years of age were more likely to be pre-Katrina immigrants and to have a longer history in the city.

Overall, the findings point to the promising potential of coalition building between African Americans and Hispanics in New Orleans. The coalition is most likely to be successful if led by the church and if internal class and ethnic tensions with each group are tackled head on. More dialogue rather than less will support the development of cross-racial and class-based alliances, thereby nurturing resiliency and socioeconomic sustainability.

Implications for Resilience in the Region

This study of racial attitudes, race-specific experiences of discrimination and prejudice, and the potential for putting aside differences and building coalitions for social justice delivers hope that such alliances are possible in New Orleans. As the region copes with the BP oil spill and other disasters, the strength and resiliency of the region will depend on community-based strategies for developing social trust, civic engagement, and ultimately social change. This study is a beginning for African American and Hispanic coalition building and for interracial alliance building in the region. A longitudinal study of African American and Hispanic racial attitudes and a project including the Vietnamese population would further explore the potential for the full embrace approach to coalition building.

The literature on interracial alliance building posits that leadership plays an important role in creating and sustaining interracial alliances. As a trusted institution, the church shows tremendous potential to lead a coalitional effort. In New Orleans, building resilience also requires residents to navigate the cross-currents of race and class evidenced by the social chasm between African American and Hispanic low-wage workers that appeared in the aftermath of the storms. Resilience becomes sustainable when institutions transition from market-based disaster management to community-centered recovery and development of resilience.

The history of any community is always remembered for those signature events that leave an indelible mark on the souls of those who survived them and forever stoke the spirit of those who come afterward. Hurricane Katrina was one of those events, whereby the city's history will be forever identified as pre- or post-Katrina. Interracial coalitions between the changing African American and Hispanic populations in metro New Orleans can anchor the renewal of New Orleans and build resilience in the region, led by a civil society locked in a full embrace.

Notes

1. Thomas F. Gieryn, "A Space for Place in Sociology," *Annual Review of Sociology* 26 (2000): 463–96.

2. See Kathryn A. Foster, "Professing Regional Resilience," chapter 2 in this volume.

3. University of New Orleans Survey Research Center, "Annual Quality of Life Polls" (1986–2010) (www.poli.uno.edu/unopoll/studies/).

4. Amy Liu and Allison Plyer, "The New Orleans Index at Five" (Brookings Institution and Greater New Orleans Community Data Center, 2010) (https://gnocdc.s3.amazonaws.com/NOIat5/Overview.pdf).

5. Gordon Saussy, "Unscrambling the Egg of Metro New Orleans' Economy" (1986), Homer L. Hitt Collection, University of New Orleans Library, Subseries IV.1, Box 41 (http://library.uno.edu/specialcollections/inventories/348.htm).

6. Julia Preston, "Suit Points to Guest Worker Program Flaws," *New York Times,* Feburary 1, 2010.

7. Silas Lee, "A Haunted City? The Social and Economic Status of African Americans and Whites in New Orleans: A Comparison of the 1983 and 2003 Census Data" (2003) (www.silaslee.com/).

8. Ibid.

9. Oxfam America, "Mirror on America: How the State of Gulf Coast Recovery Reflects on Us All" (2008).

10. Allison Plyer, "What Census 2010 Reveals about Population and Housing in New Orleans and the Metro Area" (Greater New Orleans Community Data Center, 2011).

11. Ibid.

12. Ibid.

13. Desiree Evans, "New Orleans Day Laborers Want Wage Theft Criminalized" (Institute for Southern Studies, 2009) (http://www.southernstudies.org/2009/07/post-48.html).

14. Audrey Singer, Susan W. Hardwick, and Caroline B. Brettell, *Twenty-First-Century Gateways: Immigrant Incorporation in Suburban America* (Brookings, 2008).

15. Naomi Klein, *Shock Doctrine: The Rise of Disaster Capitalism* (New York: Metropolitan Books/Henry Holt, 2007).

16. William Canak and Berkeley Miller, "Gumbo Politics: Unions, Business, and Louisiana Right-to-Work Legislation," *Industrial and Labor Relations Review* 42, no. 2 (1990): 258–271.

17. Haley E. Olam and Erin S. Stamper, "The Suspension of the Davis-Bacon Act and the Exploitation of Migrant Workers in the Wake of Hurricane Katrina," *Hofstra Labor and Employment Law Journal* 24, no. 1 (2006): 145 – 180.

18. Pia M. Orrenius and Madeline Zavodny, "Do Immigrants Work in Riskier Jobs?" *Demography* 46, no. 3 (2009): 535–51; Kevin Fox Gotham and Miriam Greenberg, "From 9/11 to 8/29: Post-Disaster Recovery and Rebuilding in New York and New Orleans," *Social Forces* 87, no. 2 (2008): 1037–68.

19. Leo B. Gorman, "Latino Migrant Labor Strife and Solidarity in Post-Katrina New Orleans, 2005–2007," *Latin Americanist* 54, no. 1 (2010): 1–33.

20. Karen Kaufmann, "Cracks in the Rainbow: Group Commonality as a Basis for Latino and African-American Political Coalitions," *Political Research Quarterly* 56, no. 2 (2003): 199–210; Rene Rocha, "Black-Brown Coalitions in Local School Board Elections," *Political Research Quarterly* 60, no. 2 (2007): 315–27; Paula McClain, "Coalition and Competition: Patterns of Black-Latino Relations in Urban Politics," in *From Politics to Practice: Forging Coalitions among Racial and Ethnic Minorities,* edited by Wilbur Rich (New York: Praeger, 1996), pp. 52–63.

21. George Priestly, "Ethnicity, Class, and Race in the United States: Prospects for African-American/Latino Alliances," *Latin American Perspectives* 34, no. 1 (2007): 53–63.

22. Lauren Araiza,"In Common Struggle against a Common Oppression: The United Farm Workers and the Black Panther Party, 1968–1973," *Journal of African American History* 94, no. 2 (2009): 200–23.

23. Mark Hugo Lopez and Susan Minushkin, "2008 National Survey of Latinos: Hispanic Voter Attitudes" (Pew Hispanic Center, 2008) (http://pewhispanic.org/reports/report.php?ReportID=90).

24. According to a March 1, 2006, NPR broadcast, Hurricane Katrina devastated the historically African American Catholic churches in metro New Orleans, but the history of the church permeates the culture of the city: Karen Grigsby Bates, "Venerable New Orleans Parish Merged in Katrina's Wake," National Public Radio, March 1, 2008 (www.npr.org/templates/story/story.php?storyId=5239705).

25. Karin Kurz and Hans-Peter Blossfeld, *Home Ownership and Social Inequality in Comparative Perspective* (Palo Alto, Calif.: Stanford University Press, 2004).

26. These complaints confirm that the reforms documented by Karen DeSalvo in chapter 4 of this volume and by Nadiene Van Dyke, Jon Wool, and Luceia LeDoux in chapter 5 are sorely needed, are emerging, and must be sustained.

27. Howard Becker, *Outsiders: Studies in the Sociology of Deviance* (Mankato, Minn.: Free Press, 1963).

17

Leadership for a More Equitable Louisiana

James A. Joseph, Lance C. Buhl, Richard L. McCline,
and Leslie Williams

L ouisiana's great challenge is to overcome the enormous physical and psychic problems created by hurricanes Katrina and Rita in ways that serve all its people over the long run. To succeed, Louisiana—indeed, any jurisdiction aiming to increase the effectiveness and scope of its service to constituents—urgently requires leaders who emulate consistently the qualities that Nelson Mandela exhibited in leading the anti-apartheid struggle and in serving as first president of the new South Africa (1994–99). He led both during the "storm" of protracted battle over starkly opposing definitions of justice—and did so twenty-seven years of that time from prison—and during the subsequent, equally challenging time, which involved quite different demands. He not only made the transition from the first to the second without a hitch, he was effective in both roles. He succeeded because he possessed the vision and the habits of heart and action that elevated the whole nation to a more just path.

Mandela's are the qualities that Robert Greenleaf sees in "servant leaders," those whom we call effective leaders. Being an effective leader has traditionally been understood by citizens as something that only heroes can master (the man or woman on a white horse phenomenon), usually by hoarding influence and power within hierarchic organizations. The projection of state power beyond national borders has been viewed as the domain of the "warrior caste." In stark contrast, Mandela's influence at home and his standing abroad went far beyond what might be suggested by the size of the military or the gross domestic product of South Africa, because for Mandela leading was a way of being. His attractiveness and influence came from the power of his personality, the elegance of his humanity, the wisdom of his judgment, the loftiness of his ideals, the calmness of his temperament, the depth of his commitment to forgiveness and reconciliation, and his willingness to share power with others and to use it to lift and serve the entire nation.

As we see it, Mandela cultivated and employed the four elements of integrated intelligence that characterize leadership as a way of being: emotional, moral, social, and spiritual intelligence. Mastering and employing these capacities defines the true discipline of any leader who wishes to be effective over time. Mandela also exemplified in his thoughts and actions a belief that there is an instinct for servant leadership in all of us, highborn or low. The authors also insist that this instinct can and should be discovered and nurtured throughout the citizenry. Indeed, this chapter's underlying message is that for societies to work properly, efficiently, and justly across the spectrum of economic, political and social life, effective leadership and effective citizenship are inseparable and interchangeable.

On these ideas and with Mandela in mind, we built the Louisiana Effective Leadership Program (LaELP), in its third year as of this writing. A joint venture of the United States–Southern Africa Center for Leadership and Public Values at Duke University and the Center for Entrepreneurial and Leadership Development at Southern University (Baton Rouge), its fellows are primarily but not exclusively African American, mid-career, fast-track professionals in business, government, and the nonprofit sector. The program, in part, stands as a response to the embarrassing question that the Gulf region's seemingly unending natural and man-made disasters over the last several years have raised once again. "Isn't it true," people almost everywhere ask, "that Louisiana lacks a sufficient supply of leaders who can move the state toward a promising future—better, less corrupt, more encompassing, more inclusive?"

These questions can and should be raised about any state—indeed, about the nation as a whole. However, we are not naïve: Louisiana's reputation for leadership has not been exemplary, tarnished as it has been from time to time as another politician or executive is indicted, convicted, or fired for some crime or failure of duty. Public expectations in Louisiana historically have been low and cynical.

We understand, too, that the idea that the natural talent for leadership is broad based stands against the typically more persuasive thesis that only a few can lead well. This chapter is a refutation of conventional wisdom. Abandoning the leadership scarcity theory in favor of the leadership promise theory is one of the nation's most pressing requirements. Every person has the capacity to lead—to contribute to strengthening his or her family, organization, community, state, and nation. We were not surprised, in recruiting and training mid-career leaders in Louisiana over the past three years, that the state has a deep and broad supply of leadership talent across sectors.

A singular (though not the only) "failure of leadership" in Louisiana is that its institutions have not developed a reliable system for discovering and nurturing leadership capacity in those who already occupy positions of authority. That is especially the case with respect to persons of color.

Three goals have steered our program. First, we expect each LaELP fellow to leave the program as a leader who consistently bases his or her decisions on universal moral principles. Second, we want to build a large cadre of such leaders across the business, government, and nonprofit sectors. Last, we expect that over time such a cadre will change the nature, understanding, and expectations of leadership in the state.

Rethinking the Culture of Leadership

Our aim is to change the culture of leadership in Louisiana. Its institutions should become places where reflective thought about the effective and ineffective uses of power is nurtured. That requires that we broaden the context of leadership to include transformative ends and means—those directed at securing greater measures of justice for all citizens. Of course, transactional objectives and behaviors—those related to getting important things done and moving ahead by coming to terms with particular interest groups (those who oppose as well as those who support our objectives)—are necessary too. However, it is essential to create a synthesis of what is desirable and what is doable. Leaders of the civil rights movement spoke often of the need for the movement to avoid becoming a clash between conscienceless power and powerless conscience. It was a transforming nonviolent movement that appealed to people's better nature. It was also transactional in that it made compromises, built coalitions, and negotiated deals—but always within morally defensible parameters. The servant leader seeks to increase and optimize transformational ends and ensure that transactional means are consistent with the values and the realization of those ends.

Assessing Whether a New Culture of Leadership Is at Work

There are three questions that Louisianans can ask in order to certify that a new culture of leadership in Louisiana exists. First, are leaders with formal authority consistently using a broader, more inclusive definition of those whom they seek to serve? Are they taking into full account especially the needs and talents of those heretofore considered "the other"—children and families living in or at the edges of poverty, persons of color, people of different (or no) religious traditions? Such consciousness builds on humankind's innate sense of fairness and embraces the common good as central features and measures of a leader's and a society's worth. We should not expect the perfect leader, but we should evaluate leaders through an elevated definition of sufficiency. Do they advance the well-being of all of us?

Second, are leaders seeking to discover, develop, reward, and apply the personal talents and capacity for leadership in all of those for whom they are responsible? It is this dependence on the capacity of the citizen to contribute to the common good that the nation's founders relied on in laying out the constitutional rules that have guided the development of the United States. This belief also drives the most productive business and nonprofit organizations.

Third, do leaders build on the indwelling capacity for responsible action in all citizens? Do they seek to engage them often and openly in an ongoing dialogue about values, goals, and means? The political theorist James McGregor Burns has described this as a kind of moral conversation through which, over time, leaders and followers raise public moral discourse and expectations of one another to higher, transformative levels.[1]

Our contention is that those who meet these tests will be what Robert Greenleaf called servant leaders:

> The servant leader is servant first. . . . It begins with the natural feeling that one wants to serve, to serve first. Then conscious choice brings one to aspire to lead. That person is sharply different from one who is leader first, perhaps because of the need to assuage an unusual power drive or to acquire material possessions.[2]

Leadership in Different Contexts of Power

How are leaders' decisions affected by the way that power is defined? Let's examine five types of organizations through this lens, noting in each the degree of freedom that leaders with transformational goals actually have.

Consider first the "authoritarian" organizations, which use the military model of leadership. Leadership positions exist within a clearly delineated hierarchy—the chain of command—that defines how power, responsibility, and accountability are distributed. Traditionally, the capacity of superior officers to coerce those below them in the chain of command was critical in determining motivation and activity throughout the ranks. Authority was maintained as much by disincentives—threats of punishment—as by incentives. The modern military, while still requiring strong leadership within a command-and-control structure in which leaders must be able to act quickly and decisively, no longer trains leaders simply for heading a hierarchy. Leaders with transformational values and goals understand the importance of dispersed leadership. They think of leadership more as "leading other leaders" and less as "leading followers." For example, within the U.S. Army, one of the best-run organizations in the world, every uniformed member is taught that he or she must be prepared to fill in for a fallen comrade. Leadership is everyone's job.

A second model, still essentially authoritarian, is the business corporation in which the senior executives' power to lead is strengthened by their use of incentives to reward subordinates who meet corporate goals and objectives that executives deem important. Despite well-written statements of values and codes of conduct, these organizations are what they reward. The transformative leader must understand that and tie organizational values closely to the performance review process and the compensation system, as is often the case in marketing and manufacturing, for example. Moreover, it is equally important to ask "what" and "why" as well as "how" questions, thinking in terms of doing the right things more than just doing things right.

Third are bureaucratic systems, most of which we identify (probably unfairly) entirely with governments. Here, perseverance is power. The appointed leader may be high on the organizational chart, but position alone does not command authority or influence, because permanent civil servants can resist by stalling, losing, or ignoring an order from the top as it moves down the bureaucracy. The transformational leader therefore must work persistently to win the respect of the system's permanent employees, demonstrating a commitment to their well-being and placing policies in the larger context of serving public rather than partisan or parochial ends. Gaining trust and respect trumps resistance.

Fourth, numerous organizations have moved away from strictly hierarchical models for distributing power. Today, many large enterprises in the business, nonprofit, and government sectors are flatter and less bureaucratic. And there has been an explosion in all three sectors of membership organizations that are flat indeed. Collegiality is the prized form of decisionmaking. Transformative leaders in these organizations seek to build honest, sincere relationships. They work to build a sense of belonging, involving others (regardless of formal position) in making decisions that affect them and in determining how they will do their work and what they must achieve. They shape consensus.

The fifth example of how context affects the ability to use power effectively—that is, transformatively—relates to social movements, in particular those that seek to extend social justice. Movement leaders discover their effectiveness in persuading and in sustaining commitment and momentum and in exhibiting authentic interest in listening to, caring about, and identifying with the needs of others. These leaders demonstrate their own passion for change by helping members discover their own capacity for moving from victimhood to active participation in creating new circumstances.

In reality, leaders often encounter a shifting medley of structural influences. Effective leaders learn how to read the tea leaves and master a corresponding array of leadership styles to fit the circumstances, all while maintaining their commitment to transformational means and ends.

Louisianans have experienced the failure of leaders to do that. In normal circumstances, most of the states' citizens would reject the idea that things should be governed by a strong authoritarian leader with centralized power; however, that style was absolutely required in responding effectively and immediately to Hurricane Katrina. It was the failure to concentrate and use power to save people, homes, and communities for so long that deepened the immediate (and for many the long-term) consequences of that storm. While authoritarian leadership was necessary in the relief stage of the disaster, the recovery and reform stages that followed called for other forms of leadership, which were not always found in the same person who had been effective in the first stage.

Leadership styles and strategies are shaped as much by culture as by context. Louisiana has its own distinct culture, highlighted most often by its food, music, and the resiliency of its people in coping with adversity, but culture does more than shape identity and provide a sense of belonging. It influences who is chosen to lead and how followers respond to those whom they choose to lead. Effective leaders must be able to cope with diversity within their own communities as well as work across the cultural boundaries of other communities.

Rethinking Structure Itself: The "Flat Table" Concept as a Corollary of Servant Leadership

What often gets in the way of transformative action is organizational structure itself. As we have described, multilayered, hierarchical organizations historically have concentrated formal decisionmaking power increasingly up the chain of command, often discouraging creative energy and autonomy at lower levels. But the problem often is as much a product of habit as of institutional design. Even when layers of hierarchy are removed, patterns of control persist.

Our program offers a different organizational premise: that the more power is dispersed within organizations and among its members up and down formal chains of command (indeed, within society as a whole), the more powerful those organizations and the nation become. They are more likely to achieve their goals and objectives precisely because their members actively commit to and are empowered to achieve them. We counsel fellows to create what coauthor Richard McCline calls "flat table" organizations and productive ways of thinking about them.

Ancient Greek leaders had warriors sit in circles so that each was protected but could see and hear who was talking and could be heard by all. The flat table concept envisions a circle of organizational equals, acknowledging that all organizations have both a social and a business dimension. Flat tables suggest assemblies of equals and promote active, reflective listening; they are places where each participant can be seen and heard, providing each with emotional safety. Because servant leaders seek to promote the self-actualization of all members of their organizations, flat table designs are powerful means for promoting that goal. Not everyone at the table has equal authority or skills, but, more important, each—whatever his or her particular responsibilities and position in the organization—is equal in terms of respect and encouragement to think creatively and contribute to the organization's success.

We train our fellows to consider whether and how to flatten the organizations in which they serve in order to help members of the organizations to think constructively about power and its uses. Structure and formal roles and responsibilities are important, but, as so many organizational theorists and practitioners suggest, they need to be simplified, made less hierarchical and layered, so that power and responsibility are much more broadly spread. Leadership under any circumstances depends for its vitality, effectiveness, and direction on all those engaged in an enterprise. Acknowledging and tapping the capacity to exercise leadership in each member of the organization is the challenge. Members of effective teams complete rather than compete with each other.

Finally, we suggest that three aspects of social justice are at play in flat table designs. The first is interpersonal justice: truth telling; making it known to all that "other people matter"; according respect to all regardless of title and location in the organization chart (if one actually exists); making sure that input is sought from all members of the group or organization. Second is informational justice—the broad sharing of facts, important thoughts, and key assumptions up, down, and across the organization. Informational justice gives everyone equal access to nonconfidential information, banning favored groups and secret agendas, and it honors transparency in decisionmaking. Reciprocal communication, a form of procedural justice, is the process of engaging in substantive two-way conversations, regardless of title and position, so that members will express themselves in an unrehearsed and original fashion. Honoring these principles enables leaders to lead by sharing and placing their goals and means under general scrutiny instead of by merely exercising formal mandates and the authority to punish.

Archbishop Desmond Tutu (1999) captured the team-building effect of the flat table when he invoked the concept of ubuntu, which he summarized as meaning that "we are people through other people":

> A person with ubuntu [our assumed servant leader] is open and available to others, affirming of others, does not feel threatened that others are able and good, for he or she has a proper self-assurance that comes from knowing that he or she belongs in a greater whole and is diminished when others are humiliated or diminished, when others are tortured or oppressed.[3]

Rethinking Self in Order to Be a Servant Leader

With a virtual leadership industry emphasizing what the leader needs to know and do, the Louisiana Effective Leadership Program helps its fellows examine themselves through the lenses of transformative values and actions and to adjust and develop their individual ways of being accordingly. Our subsidiary point is the truism that who you are in the office with respect to the uses and responses to power is very likely to be who you are at home with your family, on the road with strangers, and in meetings with friends and colleagues.

To succeed, first we must rid ourselves of certain ways of thinking and responding that get in the way of seeing others clearly. By way of illustration, many leaders exercise power in a haze of what we call "delusions of adequacy." Whether they exhibit raging self-confidence, a debilitating sense of unworthiness, or a simple lack of self-awareness, such leaders behave in dysfunctional ways. For example, they act as if they are fully competent to understand, train, and advise others; to formulate fitting policy; to make the right decisions and implement and monitor them; and to lead everyone else to truth, profit, and a better life—all by themselves. Often, of course, the delusion inflicts itself in more subtle forms, most commonly in resisting the admission that one's competencies have their limits. However it strikes, the delusion of adequacy is insidious and hard to detect and confront. It gets in the way of the ability of others in the unit to use their talents to best effect and, in all, undermines the ability of the organization to optimize its resources for best effect. Delusions of grandeur—really only the most extreme version of delusions of adequacy—are less widespread, though much more obvious. Delusions of adequacy corrode the generative premises of effective leadership. They get in the way of acknowledging, encouraging, and working to develop and rely on others' competencies. The southern African notion of ubuntu, Western democratic theory, and the sheer growing complexity of contemporary economics and technology make that clear. To serve effectively, the leader must understand his or her limits, share power, seek others' knowledge and insights, and involve others meaningfully in decisionmaking.

Second, we must develop new habits—"habits of the heart." This insight is an ancient one. Aristotle in the fourth century B.C. argued that "we become just by the practice of just actions, self-controlled by exercising self-control, and courageous by performing acts of courage." In the

Louisiana Effective Leadership Program, we provide support for testing and strengthening existing positive habits and for building others.

We begin by asking fellows how they relate to others, both those whom they've known a long time and strangers. We suggest that they practice four key skills for stimulating productive dialogue with others: to refrain from making premature judgments about the other, because such judgments block our ability to acknowledge the humanity of the other as she or he is; to identify one's own assumptions about the other, which block our ability to find common ground and build consensus; to listen to the other so as to understand what she or he is actually saying; and to sharpen skills in collaboration, because, as Hurricane Katrina so fully demonstrated, often the problems that we face are too complex to address without integrating all possible voices and sources of wisdom. Servant leaders understand that those voices and sources are much more broadly distributed in society than is traditionally recognized.

Fellows often tell us that these skills are among the most difficult to acquire but the most rewarding of the skills that they acquire through the program. To assist them along this path, we provide opportunities in the three retreats that we hold across the year for them to practice these and related skills, particularly through two- or three-person "discernment groups," a secular melding of Quaker and Roman Catholic practices.

We focus in plenary sessions and group case studies on ethics and accountability, examining why ethics is not simply a moral or civic imperative but a part of enlightened self-interest. These sessions include practice in designing ethical and effective organizational communications. We also devote time to the importance of building supportive networks—partnerships across the old boundaries of the private, public, and voluntary sectors. Such alliances increase the likelihood of success in tackling critical social issues and solving pressing social problems. Nowhere has this been more evident or important than in the aftermath of Katrina. While some national organizations still have a tendency to parachute into the state without touching base with local counterparts, the significant new growth of social justice networking within Louisiana in the past five years would not have been possible without national foundations working closely with local nonprofits. Even local community organizations that in the past would have been unlikely allies have now learned how much they increase the impact of limited resources by working collaboratively.

For their part, our fellows recognize the importance of working together on behalf of social justice. They constitute a potent and budding alliance of rising leaders committed to transforming Louisiana. Specifically, as part of LaELP's curriculum, they practice the skills and discipline of "leaders leading leaders" in defining public policy advocacy projects, each of which has (and in some cases has realized) potential for making Louisiana a more equitable place for lower-income families and children.

Most critically, for those who commit themselves to the demanding work of transformation, we emphasize developing habits of personal renewal. Our fellows know many colleagues who have burned themselves out in addressing critical needs. They come to acknowledge the difficulty in accessing moral and ethical wisdom from a place of fatigue, depletion, and stagnation. They begin to grasp the imperative of attending to their own fitness at every level—intellectual, spiritual, emotional, and physical—as a necessary means of serving others. The imperative of servant leadership, in all, requires fellows to change not only what they do, but who, through thought and action, they are.

Having challenged them to take a more thoughtful and demanding course throughout life and appreciating the personal demands of their respective leadership journeys, the program puts structures in place to support their decisions. A day and a half of the opening retreat is devoted to a collective examination of personal renewal's role in effective leadership. And we provide each fellow with an executive coach, requiring that she or he complete fifteen one-hour sessions across the year.

Executive coaching is by far the most resource-intensive aspect of the program. In times of economic pressure, it would a natural first target for trimming costs. Yet over the history of the program, coaching has proven to be among the most significant levers to effect real change in fellows. Over 95 percent of all fellows tell us that coaching is the glue that holds the program together, the crucible within which they examine who they are as leaders and make choices about how they want to change to become more effective. The coaching element is a key to making a difference through our fellows in the culture of leadership in Louisiana.

Coaching's effectiveness arises from several facts. It is the one aspect of the program that lasts across the fellowship year, so is a cohesive learning experience. It is undoubtedly the program's most potent self-awareness tool, as coaches help fellows look unflinchingly at both their strengths and their shortcomings as people and as leaders. Such self-knowledge is an essential foundation for leadership as a way of being. And coaching provides the critical bridge between theory and practice. Profound personal change rarely happens solely as the result of a new idea or a self-improvement resolution. To have real impact, these impulses must be translated into consistent, sustained action. That translation process, from mental construct to behavioral habit, requires iterative cycles of experimentation, reflection, and adoption into practice in the real world of decisionmaking. Our coaches understand how to work with their respective fellows in building customized learning experiences that enable each to manage the cycles successfully in their daily realities.

End Note

Are leadership development programs—especially ours and any organized around similar principles and goals—effective? We cannot offer sufficient data to assist Louisiana's citizens in answering, hopefully in the positive, the three questions that we posed above about whether a new culture of leadership is taking root in the state. For one thing, the sixty or so fellows that we've trained in servant leadership over the past three years are too small a number to have such an impact—yet. But like the 164 fellows in the international program (2002–08) upon which LaELP is based, Louisiana fellows consistently report after their year-long fellowship experiences that the program has been "transformative." That is, they now understand and practice leadership in ways that mark servant leaders. They assess and react to others without relying on premature judgments about them but with a clearer sense of their leadership potential and of the need to work collaboratively. Many fellows report that others say that they see changes in their behavior, changes that they appreciate. Fellows describe thinking in different ways about more productive, affirmative uses of power. Hard-core empiricists are likely to be skeptical, but we think that the cumulative feedback is quite promising. For a series of quotes about the program from fellows in both the international and the Louisiana programs—and for more descriptive material about both programs—please see http://clpv.sanford.duke.edu/. Finally, we would note that at least three of the six public policy advocacy projects completed by the first two classes have been pursued after completion of the program: creating a permanently funded state Affordable Housing Trust Fund; seeking state authorization of a system of "community benefit agreements" in publicly funded commercial developments;

and creating an adult and family literacy demonstration project. And we are quite optimistic that fellows in the class that graduated in April 2011 will refine and implement the three projects that they developed: decreasing the incidence of HIV/AIDS among Louisiana's most vulnerable populations, increasing the skills of citizens to engage effectively in public discourse, and successfully marrying the "going green" movement to workforce development among low-income populations.

Notes

1. James MacGregor Burns, *Leadership* (New York: Harper Colophon, 1979), pp. 18–23, 460.

2. Robert K. Greenleaf, *Servant Leadership: A Journey into the Nature of Legitimate Power and Greatness* (New York: Paulist Press, 1977), pp. 13–14.

3. Desmond Tutu, *No Future without Forgiveness* (New York: Random House, 1999), p. 31.

18

The Role of Philanthropy in Reducing Vulnerability and Promoting Opportunity in the Gulf South

Ivye Allen, Linetta Gilbert, and Alandra Washington

The philanthropic sector responded in the aftermath of hurricanes Katrina and Rita in ways that government and the private sector were not well-equipped to respond. In less than one month, 90,000 square miles from Texas to Alabama had become ground zero for what would be the largest and costliest natural disaster in the United States.[1] Faced with this catastrophe, the philanthropic sector, defined in many different forms, responded with financial support, in-kind help, and personal involvement. At the time, organized philanthropy at all levels faced the difficult question of where to begin. How could philanthropic groups use their resources strategically to supplement the much more considerable federal support that was to flow into the region?

This chapter addresses the philanthropic sector's response during the rebuilding and recovery of the Gulf South. While the process is still incomplete, we believe it is important to reflect on some of what has occurred, what is working, and what can be done better in the future. We believe that our reflections, although framed in the Katrina and Rita experience, have broader relevance and

The authors wish to thank Roland Anglin, Julie Burak, and Allsion Harris for their comments and suggestions on various drafts of this chapter.

can inform funders who take action in future disasters—from tornadoes in the Midwest to coastal oil spills such as the recent BP spill in the Gulf of Mexico and now the tragedy in Japan.

Philanthropy in the Gulf Coast before Katrina and Rita

In the twenty years before hurricanes Katrina and Rita hit, the number and assets of foundations in the Gulf South showed steady growth, although at a slower rate than in other regions. As wealth increased in the region, so did philanthropic leadership and programmatic development. Unfortunately, that growth was not on a scale that reduced the economic and social gaps between the Gulf South and the rest of the nation; in fact, the gaps continued to widen. Essentially, the region's young and underdeveloped philanthropic sector had not yet achieved a critical mass of expertise and resources.[2]

The support that nonprofits were receiving from philanthropy was insufficient, sporadic, and—to some degree—ineffective in increasing their institutional capacity to better serve their communities.[3] Nonprofits were often called on to do too much and therefore stretched themselves too thin, thereby hindering their advancement to the next level of leadership, service provision, and influence. Many organizations devoted a large amount of staff and board time to organizational survival in the face of insufficient resources, leaving less time for programmatic work, networking, and collaboration.[4]

That is not to say that philanthropy's ability to build civil society and the nonprofit sector in the Gulf South was totally deficient. Although organized philanthropy has an extensive tradition in the agrarian South, it has been limited as a change agent because of the lack of regional wealth relative to that of the industrialized North.[5] In addition, philanthropy derived from wealth generated in the South—specifically the Gulf South—and the choices made in investing that wealth were closely aligned with historic racial and ethnic exclusionary practices.[6]

It is not a stretch to say that the civic, public, and wealth infrastructure of the Gulf Coast remains significantly underdeveloped relative to that in other regions in the United States.[7] The restricted capacity of regional philanthropic institutions to address grinding poverty and racial exclusion and their tepid interest in doing so limited Southern social and economic development throughout the twentieth century.

That underdevelopment contributed not only to inequalities in wealth and power but also to chronic underinvestment in public infrastructure and degradation of the environment that left communities vulnerable to natural disasters. As public, private, and philanthropic resources flowed to the region after Katrina and Rita, the central question was whether those resources would be used to rebuild destroyed communities in ways that were equitable or in ways that re-created the uneven development that had been so clearly revealed to the world.

Resilience and Opportunity

When the disasters struck in 2005, the Gulf South was already saddled with very real and significant challenges, including high poverty rates, poor health status, inadequate education systems, and lack of leadership with a long-term vision of how to promote progress in addressing the region's challenges. The effects of the storms made a bad situation even worse, as the thin safety net woven by government and the charitable/philanthropic sector was stripped away. The intense pressure felt by nonprofits and regional philanthropic organizations to meet preexisting needs became even more intense when systems were strained under the weight of even more people requiring assistance.

Organized philanthropy in the region took time to analyze the situation and amass resources, while grassroots philanthropy in the form of faith institutions, ethnic support organizations, and other civil society groups delivered goods and services to those in immediate need.[8] The tremendous effort of these civil society groups to help their neighbors is in danger of receding into history. The resilience of the groups, which grew and functioned over time with little or no operating or management support, deserves a level of documentation and analysis that it has not yet received.[9]

The damage to the region was evident to the world, but the scope of need was almost too vast for funders to identify where grant making should begin. Some funders reported feeling overwhelmed by the gravity of the disaster and unsure of how to respond.[10] The nonprofit community lacked a unified front to present to funders. Many of the large and well-established local nonprofits were unable to locate their leadership, which had been dispersed throughout the United States for the first three to six months following the storms.

Anxious Gulf Coast residents often developed new nonprofits (more than 100 between October 2005 and January 2006) headed by passionate, previously unengaged leaders. The new groups and others formed the newly emerging nonprofit sector, which benefited largely from national and regional philanthropic investment. This sector continues to engage with business, government, and the philanthropic sector in redeveloping the region.[11]

Philanthropic Response

Because of the unique institutional structure of foundations, they can serve in several roles—partner, convener, and funder—and provide critical and timely investments in money, expertise, and human capital, helping nonprofits and communities marshal resources and develop strategies to create a more civil society.[12] In the aftermath of Katrina and Rita, philanthropic groups were a steady, influential voice, calling for efficient use of the resources available and ensuring equitable outcomes for all affected. Foundations reminded the various players that the situation presented a once-in-a-lifetime opportunity to ensure that the Gulf South region came back better and stronger—more resilient—than it was before the storms. The stated message was that community buy-in, along with good planning, would improve the long-term chances of success in moving the region forward.

Although a huge amount of capital and expertise was made available in the region, fundamental roadblocks made the philanthropic sector's job even more difficult. The most obvious were the technical and logistical challenges in applying for and distributing funds. Communications infrastructure was disrupted for weeks, limiting the ability to begin opening the funding dialogue in many areas for up to two months. More difficult to see from a distance were the deeply entrenched barriers—including issues of race, trust, and power—that existed before the storm and threatened to hinder or handicap recovery efforts. Not only was the physical devastation unimaginable and daunting, the gravity of the situation was compounded by the reduction—and in some cases complete absence—of human and financial resources immediately after the storms.

Significant amounts of philanthropic resources went to the Gulf Coast. Three months after Hurricane Katrina, donations already were hovering near the $3 billion mark. Corporations, foundations, and other institutional donors contributed $490 million, or 16 percent of total donations received. As of mid-November 2005, however, approximately 35 percent of institutional funding had yet to be assigned to a recipient. That represented $170 million in relief funding that remained in limbo during a period of pressing need.[13] National foundations tried to direct resources to local foundations to the extent possible, but they were not always able to do so. The system was pushed far beyond its capacity as it struggled to process and deploy resources.

To its credit, the philanthropic sector at both the national and local levels recognized the need to collaborate to build capacity and to get the recovery process started. Professional networks built through collaborative grant making and participation in national philanthropic networks had, over the years, produced a regional set of philanthropic leaders known to their national colleagues. The result was that national philanthropic leaders knew their counterparts in the affected states and were able to begin a conversation without having to build brand-new relationships.

Community foundations in Baton Rouge, New Orleans, Shreveport, Alexandria, Biloxi, Jackson, Mobile, and other Gulf Coast cities received an outpouring of contributions. National and international giving for the disaster in Louisiana was so significant that it was not possible to task any existing community foundation with the responsibility of receiving the resources and implementing a statewide giving program. The governors of Louisiana and Mississippi responded by creating new entities to receive and distribute disaster funds. The Louisiana Disaster Recovery Foundation (LDRF) has shown tremendous innovation in its ability to expand its initial role.[14]

Regional foundations, such as the Mary Reynolds Babcock Foundation and Southern Partners Fund, increased their support for local organizations assisting in recovery and rebuilding. These institutions and others have a history and mission focused on supporting community-based social justice organizations in the region to transform the culture and structure of power in the Gulf Coast. Some national foundations, such as the Twenty-First Century Foundation and the Ms. Foundation for Women, established funds or made investments to deliver resources specifically to progressive and community-based organizations in the affected region that had a social justice and equity agenda.[15]

Other national foundations, such as the Bill and Melinda Gates Foundation, the Ford Foundation, the Rockefeller Foundation, the Open Society Foundation, the Bush-Clinton Foundation, and the J. Paul Getty Foundation, supported artists, faith leaders, and cultural workers in acting as key forces in rebuilding and recovery.[16] As a result, some of these groups led the way, promoting collaboration and helping residents in the region adjust to the psychic devastation that was so prevalent in the wake of the disaster. However, even with the investments of these national foundations and the creation of new philanthropic institutions, the assets of foundations in the region were and still are limited.

Seizing Opportunity

Foundations drew on ingenuity and resourcefulness to overcome the preliminary hurdles presented by a weak and fragmented nonprofit realm, a lack of familiarity with the local environment, and a scarcity of basic information. Many national foundations sent consultants and program staff to assess the damage first hand, but the large number of foundations involved led to inefficiencies in the initial recovery phase. Time was lost; but the time spent by foundation professionals talking to new groups, emerging leaders, and existing groups and leaders was a necessary step in developing a full picture of the region's needs.

In the interim, national foundations supported existing national and local groups working in key areas such as housing and community economic development. The key lesson from that strategy was the necessity of doing something immediately, but it also recognized the importance of building a thoughtful set of strategies through a process of advice and consent. As discussions among foundation presidents and program officers continued, they gave rise to the idea of using philanthropy to promote an "equitable recovery" with a core focus on the advancement of marginalized racial and ethnic minorities. As one report framed the issue:

> The major recommendations contained in these pages suggest that the hurricanes that devastated the Gulf region require a significant and concerted institutional response. To be clear, the institutional response is not necessarily a huge influx of resources; rather, the response must be that of a philanthropic leader who can devise effective internal mechanisms for cooperation and collegial focus on the Gulf, coupled with leadership in getting the wider philanthropic community involved. An adjacent, but no less important, recommendation is that any institutional response must grapple with race and poverty as separate and linked realities of life in the region. They are separate in that not all of the poverty is race based, but they are linked in that many problems of race are still linked to poverty and exclusion, both social and political. This perspective

allows a grounded look at many traditional concerns . . . but with a unique opportunity to shape transformation without many of the entrenched barriers that conditioned past grant making.[17]

The philanthropic sector used several key strategies in its attempt to promote an equitable recovery in the Gulf:

—willingness to partner with local communities affected by the disaster in order to inform and guide recovery operations

—formation of strategic alliances and networks among philanthropic organizations to allow for greater flexibility in grant-making activities

—increased willingness to fund advocacy and public policy work, coupled with efforts to increase the capacity of nonprofits to perform that and other challenging work

—continuous support of efforts focused on increasing the capacity of local nonprofits in order to leave them with stronger leadership, more effective programs, and better communications than they had before

—connecting and strengthening philanthropy at all levels to support resilience in future disasters.

Many foundations attempted to inform their actions through direct collaboration with the affected communities. The Rockefeller Foundation made a unique investment in citywide citizen engagement to enable a significant transformation of power in New Orleans. Its early assessment of proposed plans for the redevelopment of New Orleans noted that ordinary citizens, many of whom were still living outside New Orleans three to six months after the storms, had no concrete voice in planning the city's redesign.

The foundation negotiated a grant with the mayor, governor, and the Greater New Orleans Foundation to establish funds to support a citywide planning process that would create the Unified New Orleans Plan (UNOP). The process required organized, open input from city residents about neighborhood redevelopment, infrastructure design, and location of schools and other public facilities.[18] The UNOP concept legitimized community engagement as a critical democratic practice in the rebuilding of the region.[19] Other foundations, such as the Ford, Gates, Surdna, and Kellogg foundations, subsequently invested in the community-organizing efforts necessary to sustain engagement of community-based nonprofits and individuals in the redevelopment process.

Corporate philanthropy's investment in New Orleans presented another unique, sustained commitment to support community engagement in the redevelopment process. Building on pre-Katrina investments in a neighborhood that remained intact after the storms, New Orleans–based JPMorgan Chase organized national, regional, and local philanthropy to collaborate with residents and neighborhood organizations in the Central City neighborhood. Using resources from the combined assets of the bank and foundation, JPMorgan Chase leaders led a collaborative of twenty funders to invest in three resident-identified projects that if stabilized, developed, or restored would catalyze economic, social, and health opportunities for low-wealth families.[20]

By 2010, 70 percent of the residents had returned to the Central City neighborhood, and all three projects were well under way and had begun to catalyze other projects in the neighborhood. Significant numbers of families at various income levels have returned, and city policies regarding affordable housing, education, and health have been positively affected by the vision of the residents and their funder partners.

In another instance of collaborative philanthropic investment, the Gulf Coast Fund for Community Renewal and Ecological Health of Rockefeller Philanthropy Advisors organized an advisory board made up of community and nonprofit leaders from the affected communities to direct its efforts. The board had significant influence in its advisory role at crucial moments in the foundation's grant-making process. Several other prominent foundations, including the Babcock Foundation, the Foundation for the Mid South, and the Bedsole Foundation, funded similar community-driven convening and planning efforts in Mississippi and Alabama.[21] Through the process of meeting with and consulting local community members, philanthropic organizations overcame some of the issues arising from post-disaster gaps in information by directly involving local citizens.

Collaborations, affinity groups, and intermediaries emerged as the philanthropic response began to unify into a coherent force. The new organizations experimented with a range of communication techniques (with varying levels of success) and often used pooled resources to streamline and expedite their grant-making procedures. In addition, national foundations without strong ties to the region used intermediary organizations to obtain a fundamental understanding of the issues in order to better inform their regional grant-making strategies.[22]

Building Philanthropic Networks and Coordination

Many new networks and coalitions were born in the early days of disaster relief as organizations with shared goals attempted to maximize their efficiency and impact. One such coalition, the Gulf Coast Funders for Equity (GCFE), was organized immediately after Katrina by funders including the Twenty-First Century Foundation and the Southern Partners Fund to serve as a regional information-sharing network. GCFE kept funders connected through regular conference calls and created a direct connection with nonprofits through its website. Those forums evolved into a vital community-building tool for the region's nonprofits and potential funders, and by sharing information member organizations were able to distribute funding effectively through a system of expedited applications, referrals, and common grant documents.[23]

Another barrier to progress had been a lack of coordination that stretched from the federal government down to the volunteers who were coming in large numbers to the Gulf Coast. The Foundation for the Mid South was the first organization to bring together regional nonprofit leaders and funders; within two weeks of the disaster, it began to gather information, develop principles, and identify the work ahead. The initial meeting in Memphis, Tennessee, resulted in a memorandum that was instantly adopted by national philanthropic organizations and federal and state lawmakers.

Along with embracing the potential value of collaborative strategies, several organizations employed other innovative techniques in the attempt to accelerate grant-making activities to address the urgency of the situation. The Ms. Foundation for Women, for example, conducted phone interviews with representatives from potential grantee organizations and then used the information obtained to draft formal grant applications on behalf of the organizations. This process alleviated pressure on local organizations that lacked the time or the resources to complete formal grant applications in the aftermath of the storms. The Ms. Foundation's initiative benefited such organizations as the Mississippi Conference of the National Association for the Advancement of Colored People and the Southern Rural Black Women's Initiative.[24] The capacity of regional nonprofits was limited before the storms and even more so afterward. Their resilience hinged on their ability to secure the capital necessary to allow them to begin resuscitating both themselves and their communities. Without the expedited grant process that was developed through the use of collaborative communication networks and innovative information-gathering techniques, many organizations would not have succeeded in rebuilding their organizations.

Increasing Advocacy and Shaping Public Policy

Once foundations had a better understanding of the complex issues affecting recovery and the limited resources and capacity of the charitable sector, they recognized that new approaches to funding and support were required. Funding programmatic work was simply not going to be enough. To resolve the disparities and issues that had plagued the region for decades, the philanthropic sector acknowledged the need to focus on systems change and building leadership and capacity within the charitable sector.

It became clear that the foundations needed to develop the nonprofit sector's ability to promote progress and transformation in the Gulf through advocacy, and increasing the sector's effectiveness in advocating for public policy improvements was a focus for many foundation program officers. Only through systems and policy change could the resources coming into the region be used to ensure an equitable and inclusive recovery. Otherwise, the expected outcomes would be the reestablishment of communities of exclusion and the disenfranchisement of vulnerable populations, a waste of a rare opportunity to effect real change.

Advocacy efforts would play a crucial role in guiding the distribution and use of funds to ensure just and equitable redevelopment.[25] In attempting to fund advocacy work in Louisiana and Mississippi, several grant makers lamented the limited capacity of local advocacy groups to conduct advocacy campaigns. Some grant makers even said that in terms of their level of competence, the region's advocacy groups were approximately ten to fifteen years behind similar groups in the rest of the nation.[26]

By increasing nonprofits' advocacy skills, the philanthropic sector's efforts to convene and network organizations working on similar issues were simultaneously enhanced. Baptist Community Ministries, for example, orchestrated a great effort after Katrina to convene groups working under the broad umbrella of criminal justice transformation.[27] By pooling their resources, the groups could focus on shared goals and have greater influence with policymakers.

Other groups, such as the Louisiana Disaster Recovery Foundation, have worked to ensure that displaced residents are able to advocate for themselves in their neighborhood's organizing and planning process. Direct support was provided in community-organizing training sessions on policy, advocacy, and fundraising. The Equity and Inclusion

Campaign launched a regional effort to streamline the recovery response, convening representatives from over fifty foundations, nonprofits, and think tanks at the national, regional, and local levels. Local and national government took notice, and the Equity and Inclusion Campaign became a strong voice in shaping rebuilding and rebuilding policy at all levels.[28]

When organizations have needed more direct support to carry out advocacy work effectively, philanthropy has supported their efforts with both financial and human capital. In addition to providing monetary support to struggling grassroots and advocacy organizations, Oxfam, an internationally known development intermediary, also hired several full-time staff members to assist local groups directly—much of their work focused on Mississippi.[29]

Embracing Community Philanthropy

In an attempt to strengthen Gulf Coast communities, many national and regional philanthropic organizations encouraged the use of community philanthropy to further augment rebuilding efforts. Drawing on insights from the Gulf Coast, the Foundation for the Mid South suggests that the fundamental definition of "philanthropist" ought to be broadened to include all citizens and institutions donating their money, time, or services in an attempt to produce a beneficial transformation in their communities.[30] The community philanthropy movement can take many forms—for example, monetary donations to a community foundation; charity through giving circles; and the donation of in-kind goods and services from local businesses and professionals.

The power of the movement lies not only in the financial resources available to its members but also in the networks that they represent, which can build relationships capable of fueling, guiding, and expediting an equitable recovery process. The potential influence of the community philanthropy movement is powerful.[31]

By merit of their close connection and dedication to the populations that they serve, community philanthropy organizations are uniquely positioned to assist in disaster recovery efforts. Many of the issues faced by national philanthropic organizations in the wake of disaster stemmed from a lack of familiarity with the region and its complex social structure. Community philanthropy can avoid many of those issues by anticipating the nuances of the needs of the affected populations. After the storms, it often was the smaller community foundations that were able to identify and serve the difficult-to-reach areas that were receiving inadequate disaster relief. Community philanthropy organizations, such as area churches and local giving circles, also acted as aggregators of local knowledge in post-disaster recovery.[32]

Conclusion

The organized philanthropic responses to hurricanes Katrina and Rita were significant and varied. In addition to giving time, talent, money, and physical space to aid families and communities devastated by the hurricanes, faith institutions and other community groups played key roles as conveners and information clearinghouses during the months immediately following the storms. National foundations, after an initial period of analysis and learning, built productive relationships to support local groups in their goal not only to rebuild, but to rebuild in a way that promotes social and economic equity.

We as a nation must not forget that the job is not done. In fact, we are just beginning a twenty-year or longer project to build a more equitable and resilient Gulf South. The philanthropic sector especially has a continuing role to play. As a field, philanthropy must

—*continue investing in the development of philanthropic institutions* with the capacity and leadership to play a key role in building civic capacity in the Gulf Coast primarily through building nonprofit capacity to hold public institutions accountable and playing a community and economic development role in vulnerable communities.

—*continue building the capacity of existing community foundations* in the region to become more equipped and better prepared to address racial, social, and economic inequities.

—*continue building a network of philanthropic organizations,* including those working in community philanthropy, that focus on equity as a central component of community and regional development. This network should be composed of community and private foundations in Alabama, Louisiana, and Mississippi and should provide a venue for organizations to address common challenges and to network with colleague institutions in the region.

—*continue supporting and expanding advocacy efforts* that promote equitable public policies, ensuring that all people have the opportunity to participate in our economy and society.

—support a diverse set of young leaders in the private, public, and nonprofit sectors whose vision encompasses economic growth in the region coupled with concern for social equity and the environment.

Notes

1. Normand Forgues-Roy, "Was Katrina the Biggest, the Worst Natural Disaster in U.S. History?" *History News Network* (2005) (http://hnn.us/articles/17193.html).

2. Marcus J. Littles, "Transforming an American Region: Recommendations for Rebuilding the U.S. Gulf Coast after the Storms" (New Brunswick, N.J.: Initiative for Regional and Community Transformation, 2006) (www.policy.rutgers.edu/IRCT/publications/Transformation%20HiRes.pdf).

3. Foundation for the Mid South, "Where Hope and History Rhyme: Reflections and Findings from the Mid South Commission to Build Philanthropy" (www.fndmidsouth.org/images/user_files/files/MSCBP_report.pdf).

4. Roxanne Alvarez and Veronique de Rugy, "Visible Hearts, Invisible Hands: The Economics of Charity" (Arlington, Va.: Mercatus Center, George Mason University, 2009) (http://localknowledge.mercatus.org/articles/the-economics-of-charity-a-nonprofit%e2%80%99s-bottom-line/trackback).

5. Historically, the key question has always been how those resources would be controlled at the ground level. Only recently have historians begun to break down the myth of Southern resistance to outside support or philanthropy. Even before the New Deal, Southern states did not necessarily resist outside philanthropy, as long as the interests of people in power controlled how those resources were dispersed. That remains true today; see Benjamin Alexander-Bloch, "Taffaro: Feds Usurping Authority," *Times-Picayune*, March 3, 2011 (www.nola.com/news/t-p/frontpage/index.ssf?/base/news-16/1299137454235030.xml&coll=1)

6. Foundation for the Mid South, "Where Hope and History Rhyme."

7. MDC Inc., "State of the South 2007: Philanthropy as the South's 'Passing Gear'" (2007) (www.mdcinc.org/knowledge/strategicphilanthropy.aspx).

8. U.S. Government Accountability Office, *Hurricanes Katrina and Rita: Provision of Charitable Assistance,* GAO-06-297T (2005).

9. New York Regional Association of Grantmakers, "Best Practices in Disaster Grantmaking: Lessons from the Gulf Coast" (2008) (www.philanthropynewyork.org/s_nyrag/bin.asp?CID=6685&DID=16026&DOC=FILE.PDF).

10. Ibid.

11. Alliance for Justice, "Power amidst Chaos: Foundation Support for Advocacy Related to Disasters" (2007) (www.afj.org/assets/resources/nap/monograph.pdf).

12. Foundation for the Mid South, "Where Hope and History Rhyme."

13. Foundation Center, "Snapshot of Philanthropy's Response to the Gulf Coast Hurricanes" (2006) (http://foundationcenter.org/gainknowledge/research/pdf/katrina_snap.pdf).

14. New York Regional Association of Grantmakers, "Best Practices in Disaster Grantmaking."

15. New York Regional Association of Grantmakers, "Donor's Guide to Gulf Coast Relief and Recovery" (2008) (www.philanthropynewyork.org/s_nyrag/bin.asp?CID=8547&DID=14800&DOC=FILE.PDF).

16. Ibid.

17. Littles, "Transforming an American Region."

18. Robert B. Olshansky and others, "Longer View: Planning for the Rebuilding of New Orleans," *Journal of the American Planning Association* 74, no. 3 (2008): 273–87.

19. Tom Burns, Sandra Jibrell, and Patricia Patrizi, "The Rockefeller Foundation's Rebuilding New Orleans Initiative," unpublished paper, OMG Center for Collaborative Learning, Philadelphia, 2008.

20. JPMorgan Chase, "Corporate Responsibility Report" (2007) (www.jpmorgan chase.com/corporate/Corporate-Responsibility/document/jpmc_corpresp_jpmc_ crr07.pdf).

21. Littles, "Transforming an American Region."

22. Alliance for Justice, "Power amidst Renewal: Foundation Support for Sustaining Advocacy after Disasters" (2010) (www.afj.org/for-nonprofits-foundations/resources-and-publications/free-resources/poweramidstrenewal.pdf).

23. New York Regional Association of Grantmakers, "Best Practices in Disaster Grantmaking."

24. Alliance for Justice, "Power amidst Chaos"; Mia White, personal interview, 2011.

25. Pablo Eisenberg, "After Katrina: What Foundations Should Do," *Chronicle of Philanthropy*, 2006 (http://philanthropy.com/article/After-Katrina-What/57869).

26. Alliance for Justice, "Power amidst Chaos."

27. Alliance for Justice, "Power amidst Renewal."

28. Equity and Inclusion Campaign, "Alabama Disaster Housing" (www.equityand inclusion.org/web/page/715/interior.html).

29. See Oxfam America, "Coastal Communities Criticize Slow Katrina Recovery Effort," news release, August 26, 2006 (www.oxfamamerica.org/press/pressreleases/coastal-communities-criticize-slow-katrina-recovery-effort/?searchterm=None).

30. Foundation for the Mid South, "Where Hope and History Rhyme."

31. Effective Communities Project, "Pathways to Progress on the Gulf Coast: The Necessity of Funding Networks" (2010) (www.effectivecommunities.com/pdfs/ECP_FundingVitalNetworks.pdf).

32. U.S. Government Accountability Office, *Hurricanes Katrina and Rita.*

Contributors

IVYE ALLEN
President, Foundation for the
    Mid South

ROLAND V. ANGLIN
Faculty Fellow and Executive Director
    of the Initiative for Regional and
    Community Transformation
Rutgers University

LANCE BUHL
Deputy Director, Center for
    Leadership and Public Values
Duke University

ANN CARPENTER
Research Associate
Federal Reserve Bank of Atlanta

ROBERT A. COLLINS
Dean of the College of Arts and
    Sciences, Professor of Urban
    Studies and Public Policy
Dillard University

MARK S. DAVIS
Senior Research Fellow and
    Director, Tulane Institute on
    Water Resources Law and Policy
Tulane Law School

BREONNE DEDECKER
Master's candidate in Sustainable
    International Development,
    Heller School of Social Policy
    and Management
Brandeis University

KAREN B. DESALVO
Professor of Medicine
Tulane University School of
    Medicine

KATHRYN A. FOSTER
Director, University at Buffalo
    Regional Institute
State University of New York

LINETTA GILBERT
Co-Leader
The Declaration Initiative

JAMES A. JOSEPH
Professor of the Practice of Public
    Policy; Director, U.S.-Southern
    Africa Center for Leadership
    and Public Values and Leader
    in Residence, Hart Leadership
    Program
Duke University

MUKESH KUMAR
Associate Professor, Department of
  Urban and Regional Planning
Jackson State University

LUCEIA LEDOUX
Vice President, Public Safety/
  Governmental Oversight Grants
Baptist Communities Ministries

SILAS LEE III
Ernest N. Morial Endowed Professor of
  Social Policy, Sociology Department
Xavier University of Louisiana

AMY LIU
Senior Fellow and Deputy Director,
  Metropolitan Policy Program
The Brookings Institution

DAVID A. MARCELLO
Executive Director, The Public Law
  Center
Tulane University

RICHARD L. MCCLINE
Professor and the James A. Joseph
  Endowed Chair in Small Business
Southern University, Baton Rouge

RICHARD M. MIZELLE JR.
Assistant Professor, Department of
  History
Florida State University

NANCY T. MONTOYA
Senior Regional Community and
  Economic Development Manager
Federal Reserve Bank of Atlanta

REILLY MORSE
Policy Director
Mississippi Center for Justice

ANDRE M. PERRY
Associate Dean, College of Education
  and Human Development
University of New Orleans

ALLISON PLYER
Deputy Director, Greater New Orleans
  Community Data Center
Nonprofit Knowledge Works

KALIMA ROSE
Senior Director
PolicyLink Center for Infrastructure
  Equity

JOHN L. RENNE
Early Research Professor of Planning
  and Urban Studies
University of New Orleans

MICHAEL SCHWAM-BAIRD
Researcher, Cowen Institute for Public
  Education Initiatives
Tulane University

NADIENE VAN DYKE
Director of Justice Innovation
New Orleans Police and Justice
  Foundation

JASMINE M. WADDELL
Visiting Lecturer, Sustainable
  International Development, Heller
  School for Social Policy and
  Management
Brandeis University

ALANDRA WASHINGTON
Program Director, Philanthropy and
  Volunteerism
W. K. Kellogg Foundation

FREDERICK WEIL
Associate Professor, Department of
  Sociology
Louisiana State University

LESLIE WILLIAMS
President
LeaderShift Consulting

JON WOOL
Director, New Orleans Office
Vera Institute of Justice

Index